Mother Love/Mother Hate

———————

Mother Love/Mother Hate

THE POWER OF MATERNAL AMBIVALENCE

ROZSIKA PARKER

BasicBooks
A Division of HarperCollins*Publishers*

First published in 1995 by Virago Press Ltd., London.

Library of Congress Cataloging-in-Publication Data
Parker, Rozsika
    Mother love/mother hate : the power of maternal ambivalence / Rozsika Parker.
      p.   cm.
    Includes bibliographical references and index.
    ISBN 0–465–08661–6
    1. Mothers—Psychology.   2. Motherhood—Psychological aspects.   3. Mother and child.   4. Love, Maternal.   5. Ambivalence.   I. Title.
HQ759.P285   1996
155.6'463—dc20   95–44317
                                                    CIP

96 97 98 99 ❖/HC 9 8 7 6 5 4 3 2 1

FOR JOEL AND LYDIA

Contents

Acknowledgments

In writing this book I have been sustained in different ways by the generous interest, thoughts and support of many people. I particularly want to thank Sally Alexander, Bobby Baker, Michèle Barratt, Christopher Bollas, Sheila Butterworth, Anthea Callen, Meredith Churchill, Alan Danks, Sally Dean, Rosalind Delmar, Briony Fer, Charlotte Lane, Juliet Newbigin, Michael-Ann Mullen, Janie Prince, Ann Scott, Sara Rance, Marsha Rowe, Stef Pixner, Jenny Thompson, Michelene Wandor, Ruth Windle, and Claire Zeitlin.

For reading the entire manuscript with great care and thought I am most grateful to Nina Farhi, Jane Haynes, Jenny Sharman, Cathy Urwin and Margot Waddell.

My thanks are especially due to my patients who have given me permission to write about their experiences of being mothers, and to all those other mothers who, also remaining anonymous, agreed to be interviewed for the book. Jo Foster earned my gratitude and admiration for her capacity to transform my indecipherable pages into impeccable text. I am grateful to my editor Ruthie Petrie for her astute comments and generous support.

Andrew Samuels accompanied the book at every stage and I am hugely indebted to him for his detailed criticisms, invaluable suggestions and (understandably) exasperated encouragement.

Above all, Joel and Lydia – thank you.

Acknowledgments are due to Chatto and Windus and Anne Tyler for permission to quote from her novel *Dinner at the Homesick Restaurant* (1982).

Preface

When a mother and a child recollect their relationship, two separate narratives emerge. Sometimes it is hard to believe that it is the same relationship, the same circumstances and the same emotional events that are being described. But sometimes there are two stories that are comfortably linked and clearly connected.

As a psychoanalytic psychotherapist I have tended to hear the child's 'side' from my patients, understanding her or him as a child, of whatever age. In this book I deliberately shift my focus to listen to the mother's side – her version of events. I use the somewhat provocative word 'side' quite deliberately because I want to highlight the conflictual aspect of the relationship. I shall suggest that conflicts generated by maternal ambivalence are potentially creative. Yet the personal and cultural pressures under which women mother often render us inordinately anxious and guilty, until all that is stimulated by conflict is shame, or an unmanageable sense of persecution.

I had children after completing my psychotherapy training. I lost count of the number of people who commented, 'It must be very difficult for you now, I'm glad I had my children in blissful ignorance.' Thinking about such double-edged remarks it struck me as significant that psychoanalytic theory and developmental psychology should have been seen by so many as offering a book of rules with appended warnings, rather than as revealing the power of the unconscious, emphasising how limited our control is over the impact we have on our children. So I explore the question of why psychoanalysis, which after all acknowledges precisely that motherhood is inevitably conflictual, can be understood as a potential source of reproach for mothers, rather than providing a possible release from the omnipotent burden of getting it right. The question of the influence of psychoanalytic thinking on social and cultural practices – such as parenting – is one that historians of ideas recognise as a thorny one. I think that a consensus exists that such influencing has certainly taken place, even if there is room for disagreement over the extent and the nuances involved. Moreover there is a two-way influencing to consider: the take-up of psychoanalytic ideas is due to the fact that they are as much the product of their specific time and place as they are a formative influence. The existence of this dialectic weakens the argument that because only a tiny minority of mothers have had direct contact with psychoanalysis, its influence on mothering has been negligible. My view is that psychoanalysis reflected in the work of writers like Bettelheim, Bowlby or Spock has touched the lives of an infinitely greater number of women than those who have been patients in analysis.

There can be no single answer to questions of mothering. In part this is because there is no one experience of mothering. We bring to it diverse histories and we mother in very different social, economic and ethnic contexts. Mothering has its own history, in fact. Thinking about mothering demands our holding in mind many complex interactions of inner and external reality. This I have tried to do. I have attempted, for instance, to show how cultural and public representations of good and bad mothering interact with the unique, personal, private, emotional meanings mothering has for a woman. Mothers both reproduce and resist assumptions of what it means to mother – but those assumptions cannot be escaped. Moreover, they tend to militate against the very acknowledgement of maternal ambivalence. Yet, in my view, a deeper understanding of the production, purpose and prohibition of maternal ambivalence can enable mothers (and others) to see that most mothers are neither as 'bad' as we fear, nor as 'good' as we desire.

In exploring ambivalence I have needed both to employ recent feminist theory and to reconsider established psychoanalytic theory from the point of the mother, rather than the child. And, as well as paying attention to mothers' private response to ambivalence I have looked at how public institutions mediate ambivalence. But first, Chapter 1 considers the basic issue – what is ambivalence?

I

What Is Ambivalence?

Maternal ambivalence is the experience shared variously by all mothers in which loving and hating feelings for their children exist side by side. In this book I suggest that much of the guilt with which mothers are familiar stems from difficulties in weathering the complicated and contradictory feelings provoked by maternal ambivalence. Our culture plays a part in producing the difficulties, virtually prohibiting the kind of full discussion and exploration that would reveal the hidden contribution to creative mothering that maternal ambivalence can make.

Sometimes mothers use other mothers as mirrors. Each mother scrutinises the other in pursuit of a reflection of her own mothering. They look for differences from their own style of mothering and they look for sameness. But above all they look for confirmation that they are getting it right, in the face of fears that they are getting it hopelessly wrong. To the outsider, especially to the child-free observer, exchanges between mothers seem to be carried out in a language of measurement and invidious comparison, but the desired outcome is not so much a victory as a search for deeply-needed reassurance.[1]

At the superficial level, such a search is for information by women who have on the whole grown up insulated from birth and child-care – as well as death – in a society with strong views on the upbringing of babies and children. Our culture permits flexibility in other activities that involve intimacy, some heterogeneity, some diversity of style, but hardly any at all when it comes to mothering. A sense of the rigidity imposed on mothering can paradoxically be gauged from the schism that opens up between different generations of mothers. Sometimes the changes in culturally sanctioned modes of mothering can happen very quickly. For instance, up to 1991 most babies were laid to sleep on their fronts, for safety reasons. Following the publication of research findings, babies are nowadays placed on their backs or sides for their own protection. Those of us who laid our babies on their stomachs can resort to defensive mockery or quake with retrospective guilt and anxiety. Children also absorb the imperative that there is only one way to be a good mother, and often police their own mother out of a real sense of anguish should she step out of the maternal right line. Yet alongside prescriptions on mothering there flourishes the assertion that 'mother knows best', with the implication that there can be no hard and fast rules for mothering which is an essentially instinctive, intuitive affair.[2]

How a mother feels about mothering – or the meanings it has for her – are heavily determined by such cultural representations of motherhood. These, I suggest, are becoming more static and idealised as the mobility of women's lives increases. Yet – and this is important – *they are not only imposed* on mothers. We all help to maintain them. Becoming a mother inevitably entails encountering dissonances and disjunctions between the lived experience of mothering and the sometimes contradictory yet usually prescriptive or normative ideals that mediate mothering.

Each chapter of the book explores ambivalence from the point of view of different maternal states, for example feelings evoked by the desire to love, by separation, by power, violence and, in the final chapter, by the gender of the child. And in each case I look at how mothers negotiate the interplay between psychic reality and external reality in the intensely demanding task of childcare. For example, in Chapter 2, I describe how some mothers transform the ideal of mother–child oneness into an at times utopian longing for mutuality and shared joy, while in Chapter 7 I explore the psychological conflict engendered by the experience of mothering between a woman's adult self and the infantile aspects of her personality, relating the conflict to the cultural representation of mothers either as icons of maturity, or as 'one of the children'.

I suggest that the ever-changing, contradictory prescriptions for 'perfect' motherhood are a manifestation of an underlying awareness of the 'imperfect' impulses in all mothers provoked by the conflicts engendered by maternal ambivalence – magnified by persecutory ideals. But, to return to mothers mirroring mothers, mothers both do and do not provide each other with comforting reflections and a place of safety in a society even more critical of mothers than they are of themselves. The role of mothers as containers for other mothers is increasingly utilised by organisations such as Newpin, a home-visiting and befriending project which started in south London with a drop-in centre. One mother attending Newpin described how she felt that the organisation had accepted her negative attitude towards her child and had tried to understand it, whereas professional helpers, primarily concerned with the child, had made her feel a worse and worse mother, destroying her already shaky self-esteem.[3]

As well as organised and funded groupings like Newpin or the national organisation Home Start, there are many informal groups of mothers arising, for example, out of mother and toddler clubs, or the work of the National Childbirth Trust. When interviewed, Jane describes a familiar state of affairs:

> I had very few friends with small children, and I was a long long way from my family – my mother and my sister. And I was lost. I was lost in these streets and this house. I remember walking up and down the streets feeling 'I am a person who walks up and down the streets with a pram and I have to cope with this'. But I lost myself. I really did. Slowly I found other mothers – particularly when Nicky started going to school. And to be part of a group – to share the experience with other people – transformed it for me. I so enjoy the humour and the strength of the mothers I meet.

Jane's defence against the anxieties of motherhood is a muscular humour which she successfully evokes in, and shares with, other mothers. But for many, the mirroring functions of other mothers are far from reassuring, in part because the mirrors provided are inevitably distorted by personal projections or, equally likely, elided with cultural expectations. Thus, while Jane found in other mothers a lifeline and a provision of an affirming sense of identity, Susan claims that it is amongst other mothers that she has felt most insecure, competitive and unhappy:

> I think my guilt as a mother gets stirred up by other parents, by what I feel they are doing for their children compared to what I am doing. I'm thinking of one woman I know. She takes her children to school every morning (she doesn't work).

> She takes them here, there and everywhere; to music, to ballet,
> to swimming. She always seems very calm and collected. She
> makes biscuits with them every weekend. And she never seems
> to be hassled by them . . . and I just think YUK!

Susan's projection of the perfect mother on to her acquaintance is
familiar but nevertheless revealing as to why women are seeking
reassurance. Susan's perfect mother has no negative feelings towards
her children, she is constantly loving, patient and available:
'she never seems to be hassled by them'. Susan both idealises and
denigrates this representation of love shorn of negativity, this
smooth surface unruffled by resentment or hostility. Yet her envy co-
exists with an awareness that something is missing in paradise – she
concludes 'and I just think YUK'. And, of course, there *is* something
missing in this representation of motherhood. Aggression is absent.
Moreover, something has gone missing in Susan, who projects her
own capacity for passionate love, care and attention on to the other
mother and finds herself depleted, hateful and hating.

Yet mothers do look to other mothers to find 'absolution' for
maternal emotions which the dominant cultural representations of
motherhood render unacceptable, and which mothers themselves
experience as both painful and unforgivable. I refer to the fleeting
(or not so fleeting) feelings of hatred for a child that can grip a
mother, the moment of recoil from a much-loved body, the desire
to abandon, to smash the untouched plate of food in a toddler's
face, to yank a child's arm while crossing the road, scrub too hard
with a facecloth, change the lock against an adolescent, or the
fantasy of hurling a howling baby out of the window.

Creative Conflict

As I said above, in my view the deepest roots of maternal guilt
feelings lie in the experience and handling of ambivalence – in the
way we both love and hate our children. Mothers will vary in the
extent to which they can tolerate and manage the conflict provoked
by loving and hating the same child. The mother of an adolescent
son summed up her feelings:

> I feel torn in two. I want to be a loving mother and to offer
> him a good home. Yet, at the same time, I just want him out
> of here – out of my home.

The novelist Fay Weldon commented, 'the greatest advantage of not having children must be that you can go on believing that you are a nice person: once you have children, you realise how wars start.'[4] As she indicates, children evoke such powerful positive and negative feelings that a mother is forced to recognise her 'nastiness' – her warlike side – as well as her capacity for love and peace-making. But note the tone Fay Weldon employs. Such painful truths can only be expressed through humour; it is only via irony and a light touch that ambivalence is rendered bearable. No one, from small children to mothers, from psychologists to politicians, finds it easy truly to accept that mothers can both hate and love their children.

The words 'hate' and 'love' are problematic. They carry a certainty and fixity which seems to be belied by the passionate mobility of feeling, on the one hand, and the passages of frank boredom which characterise motherhood. I searched for alternative words – experimenting, for example, with positive and negative feelings – but nothing captures the power of 'love' and 'hate'.

Love is, of course, an easier affect to acknowledge than hate; it is taken for granted in mothers. Love's absence is acknowledged to be a disaster. Hate, however, is frequently denied. Intellectually we may recognise that strong love is accompanied by hate, but emotionally it tends to be mentally dissociated or, in other ways, warded off. When hate outweighs love, even momentarily, it can become an easily identified affect. But for most mothers, most of the time, it is largely invisible – concealed, masked, contained – but never wiped out by love for the child. In my practice as a psychotherapist, if I interpret a mother's feelings of hatred towards her child, she more often than not will feel criticised or simply perplexed. Consciously she does not hate her child. And, indeed, both love and hate are rooted in the unconscious, but love has, so to speak, greater access to the light. Although not in all mothers; some for a myriad of reasons experience hatred as 'real' and love as 'pretence'. One mother said to me, 'All my life I've felt suspicious of love; only dislike feels tangible and true.'

Possibly it is the unacceptability of the element of hatred – the fear of hatred – that has led to the widespread misuse of the term 'ambivalence'. It is often employed to describe *mixed* feelings rather than the concept developed by psychoanalysis according to which quite contradictory impulses and emotions towards the same person co-exist. The positive and negative components sit side by side and remain in opposition.

The concept was elaborated by Melanie Klein, whose writing on ambivalence can be particularly helpful in thinking about maternal ambivalence. She emphasises that ambivalence is not a static condition: the polarity of love and hate remains constant, but the relationship between the two changes. Klein wrote of steps towards unification, towards mitigation of hatred by means of love, and thus to a general process of integration.[5] But although she believed in a process whereby the predominance of love over hate can become established, she concluded that 'full and permanent integration is never possible'.[6]

She observed, however, that 'in the course of normal development a relative balance between love and hate is attained, and the various aspects of objects are more unified'.[7] Nevertheless particular experiences – she instances mourning – can disturb the balance and intensify the conflict between love and hate, magnifying hate and hence provoking enormous guilt and anxiety, with the attendant defences against them. My suggestion is that the specific experiences of motherhood inevitably produce fluctuations in the intensity of feeling within ambivalence. Maternal ambivalence is not a static state but a dynamic experience of conflict with the fluctuations felt by a mother at different times in a child's development, and varying between different children. However ambivalence itself is emphatically not the problem; the issue is how a mother manages the guilt and anxiety ambivalence provokes. Hence I shall speak of manageable and unmanageable maternal ambivalence. Throughout the book I shall explore what provokes unmanageable ambivalence, how it evolves, and how it can resolve. But what of manageable ambivalence?

Klein considered that ambivalence had a positive part to play in mental life as a 'safeguard against hate'.[8] I want to go further and claim a specifically creative role for manageable maternal ambivalence. I suggest that it is in the very anguish of maternal ambivalence itself that a fruitfulness for mothers and children resides. Two therapists who led a group for mothers in Australia commented that every time the mothers in the group 'come into contact with guilt over deep ambivalent feelings . . . they begin to demonstrate, at least transiently, new initiatives and resourcefulness'.[9] They conclude that the impression gained from the mothers is of a sudden freedom in finding and using their own inner resources.

How are we to understand the increased capacity to think and act that these women achieved through the acknowledgement of ambivalence? Obviously the context was important. They were sharing their experiences in a supportive, empathic atmosphere. Mothers were mirroring mothers. However, I think there is more to it. Here, the psychoanalytic thinking of W. R. Bion provides an important key.

According to Bion, in addition to the conflict between love and hate, there is a crucial clash in the mind between knowledge or the desire to understand, and the aversion to knowing and understanding.[10] Where motherhood is concerned, I think the conflict between love and hate actually spurs mothers on to struggle to understand and know their baby. In other words, the suffering of ambivalence can promote thought – and the capacity to think about the baby and child is arguably the single most important aspect of mothering. Perhaps this becomes clearer if we invent a hypothetical mother who does not experience ambivalence but regards her child only with hostile feelings, or conversely only with untroubled love. In neither case will she find it necessary to dwell on her relationship with her child or to focus her feelings on her child's response to herself because she will not know what is missing. It is the troubling co-existence of love and hate that propels a mother into thinking about what goes on between herself and her child.

The psychoanalytic pioneer Sandor Ferenczi considered that it was the role of frustration in the production of ambivalence that led to expanded consciousness. His view has a particular pertinence for maternal ambivalence. He wrote:

> Things that always love us, i.e. that constantly satisfy all our needs, we do not notice as such, we simply reckon them as part of our subjective ego; things which are and always have been hostile to us, we simply deny; but to those things that do not yield unconditionally to our desires, which we love because they bring us satisfaction, and hate because they do not submit to us in everything, we attach special mental marks, memory-traces with the quality of objectivity, and we are glad when we find them again in reality, i.e., when we are able to love them once more.[11]

Mothers gain enormous satisfaction and receive gratifying devotion from their children. Yet, the children who love us are also the children who scream 'I hate you, Mummy' and, in Ferenczi's words, 'do not yield unconditionally to our desires'. Mothers expect – and are expected – to control children whose development as individuals demand that they 'do not submit to us in everything'. Motherhood is governed by frustration which, as Ferenczi argues, produces ambivalence which promotes consciousness, knowledge and a sense of reality in relation to self and child. But equally, the pain of ambivalence can lead to a desire not to know. As child psychotherapist Margot Waddell has written, 'It is the capacity to think about emotional experiences, to engage with them, suffer them, which promotes growth – a capacity constantly opposed by intolerance of frustration and of the pain of emotions.'[12] For some women, sometimes, the conflict evoked by motherhood becomes unthinkable. For example, unable to acknowledge the depth of hostile, complex feelings evoked by pregnancy, a woman carries her child physically but not psychologically. She simply does not 'know' she is pregnant. And even postnatally the child may be shut out of her mind to the extent that she neither feels nor fears being a bad mother, nor experiences emotional concern for the child.[13] In other words, ambivalence entirely denied, cannot provide a spur to thought.

Throughout the book I shall emphasise that maternal ambivalence creates a spectrum ranging from its creative to its destructive possibilities.

The Approach to Ambivalence

Unlike many clinicians who write on cultural themes, I illustrate my points with material gathered from interviews as well as from my clinical work as a psychotherapist. To protect the privacy of those who shared with me their response to mothering, I have kept details to a minimum and changed all names while hoping to maintain the meaning of their words. As the feminist academic Susan Rubin Suleiman puts it, 'Mothers don't write, they are written.'[14] Hence theorising motherhood seemed to demand the raw material of maternal voices. It is to generate such raw material that I decided to conduct interviews – they are neither scientific proof nor incontrovertible evidence. Rather they indicate and suggest diverse experiences and possible lines of exploration, with no claims to all-inclusivity being advanced. My intention is to find a format that could stress the position of mothers as autonomous, changing and developing subjects, rather than as their children's 'objects'.[15]

Personal experiences arise from the interplay of psychical and external forces. Maternal voices tell us that they bring to mothering their lives as black women, white women, women of different ethnicities and varying social classes and income brackets. They can be lesbian, heterosexual, single, married or divorced. They can become parents as a result of sexual intercourse, artificial insemination, *in vitro* fertilisation, adoption, co-habiting or step-parenting.[16] All these factors affect the meaning motherhood has for a woman. For example, Patricia Hill Collins, author of numerous works on African-American women, has pointed out the divergence between the experience of black mothers in African-American culture and the white perspective on motherhood:

> the assumption that mothering occurs within the confines of a private, nuclear family household where the mother has almost total responsibility for child-rearing is less applicable to black families. While the ideal of the cult of true womanhood has been held up to black women for emulation, racial oppression has denied black families sufficient resources to support private, nuclear family households. Second, strict sex-role segregation, with separate male and female spheres of influence within the family, has been less commonly found in African-American families than in white middle-class ones. Finally, the assumption that motherhood and economic dependency on men are linked and that to be a 'good' mother one must stay at home, making motherhood a full-time 'occupation', is similarly uncharacteristic of African-American families.[17]

At the same time, while acknowledging the significance of social class and 'race' on women's lives, Ann Phoenix, Anne Woollett and Eva Lloyd, in their writing on motherhood, emphasise that it is often assumed that working-class and black women constitute a unitary group when 'they are not homogenous or necessarily different from middle-class or white women in any essential ways'.[18] They point out that there is clearly a great deal of variability between women in the same 'race' or social class. They argue that the real danger is that prescriptions of mothering which designate mothers as either good and normal or bad and deviant gloss over *both* the different circumstances in which women mother *and* the commonalities that do exist between mothers.

A multitude of factors can determine women's experience of mothering, ranging from mundane issues of public transport to personal tragedy. Many cultures have structures and even ceremonies which acknowledge that the crucial moments of childbirth and motherhood constitute a juncture of such issues. But Western industrial cultures offer very few meaningful rituals, falling back on a questionable medicalisation of life and death. The individual mother is left to grapple with the fact that she is not only the source of life but also of potential death for her child.[19] By that I mean that she is responsible for keeping alive a child unable to fend for itself outside the womb. The absence of public structures of recognition means that a mother feels solely responsible for life and death when, of course, these matters do not lie in her total control. This kind of anxiety mobilised by motherhood can magnify the conflicts provoked by ambivalence, although women do respond differently to the fantasies engendered by this aspect of mothering. Some may enjoy a new sense of potency and agency but others, besieged by images of loss and disaster determined by their own social circumstances, states of mind, or possibly their child's physical condition, may be swamped by the depressive guilt I describe in Chapters 3 and 8.

Consideration of maternal ambivalence raises the related issue of paternal ambivalence. I thought about enlarging my canvas to include fathers who, after all, do also experience ambivalent feelings towards their children. Moreover, I did not want to appear to condone a limited view of the potential importance of the father, relegating him to the role of one who intervenes in, or breaks up, the primary relationship of mother and child. However, eventually I decided to focus on maternal experiences. Although we speak of parenting, the experience of being a father and being a mother are significantly different. Fathers need books unto themselves, and there is a growing literature on fathers. One further reason for restricting my scope to mothers is that even now being a parent is a less embracing definition for a man than it is for a woman. To know that a man is a father is generally less of an indication of how he lives his life than it is for a mother.[20] For example, for women, conflicts concerning motherhood, often expressed as the tension between independence and dependence, between self-assertion and self-abnegation, and between love and hate, can be a central reason for seeking therapy. I do not think the same is yet true for men in relation to fatherhood.

Even though I am not dealing directly with paternal ambivalence, fathers figure because a woman's relation to her partner, whether male or female, whether the biological or the social and emotional parent of her child, whether absent or present, is of critical importance in shaping a mother's experience of ambivalence.

Quite apart from whether or not a partner shares in the practical work of childcare or psychological responsibility for the children, the attitude a partner maintains towards a woman's mothering powerfully affects her. In her study of mothers in London with preschool children, the sociologist Mary Georgina Boulton discovered that a husband's view of her work as a mother was a central component in the meaning mothering had for a woman. This was much the same for working-class and middle-class women.[21]

The mothers in the study reported that if their husbands recognised the difficulties inherent in childcare and believed that frustration and irritation were legitimate responses, they found their own negative feelings easier to accept. By contrast, an intolerant partner's belief that childcare ought to be naturally enjoyable made maternal ambivalence more difficult to live with. Boulton comments, 'Rather than facing and coming to terms with her negative feelings she was therefore more likely to feel guilty about them and to try and repress them.'[22]

What a mother senses as her partner's denigration may originate in her own self-blame projected on to the partner. But sometimes it is the partner's own response to parenthood and partnership that is evoking enormous bitterness in a mother. However, guilt and fear arising from her sense of inadequacy as a mother can stop her directing her anger towards her critical partner. She fears after all that he or she may be right and that she is indeed a bad mother. Then she may turn on the baby. One mother I interviewed described how she passed blame on 'down the line':

> I remember sitting on the stairs with Billy when he was a baby and wouldn't sleep. I knew that Stan blamed me. I knew he was furious and thinking, 'this child is awake at night because of *you*'. I felt the weight of his blame and that doubled my

desperation for Billy to sleep. I sort of passed the blame down the line and had a really strong impulse to throw him down the stairs.

The arrival of a baby so often provides a couple not with the desired cement of a shared concern but with a catalogue of grievances. The status quo between them is violently shaken and old wounds are opened, leaving one or both partners feeling aggrieved, unsupported, isolated or overburdened. In such circumstances, the element of hatred in a mother's feelings towards her baby can become huge, almost drowning out love.

Mothers without a partner do not suffer from this dynamic. Rather they fear that sole responsibility for childcare might magnify their negative response to the baby. A pregnant single mother said to me, 'I'm really afraid that, alone with the baby at night, without anyone to hand the baby to when she screams, and screams, I'll simply lose control – go crazy.'

After her daughter was born the mother expressed surprise at how well she coped. She told me that there were enormous advantages to being in a situation where there was no fighting over whose turn it was to get up when the baby cried at night, and concluded, 'She and I just have to manage together.'

A Double-Edged Role

Throughout the book I address the double-edged role of psychoanalysis in relation to maternal ambivalence. Women analysts and psychotherapists both in the past and today – most recently Dinora Pines and Joan Raphael-Leff – have produced immensely valuable work on motherhood and on the ubiquity of maternal ambivalence.[23] But where psychoanalysis in general is concerned the clinical focus has more usually been on its negative outcome for the child, rather than on its contribution to maternal thinking.

The myth of Oedipus is not constructed around his mother Jocasta's feelings when her baby son's foot was pierced and he was exposed to the elements on a mountainside. In my view, feminists have rightly criticised psychoanalysis for looking at life from the point of view of the child to the detriment of our understanding of maternal development. For example, Jane Flax has noted that, even within psychoanalytic approaches centring on the mother–baby relationship, such as object relations theory (see Chapter 5), the extent to which any mother's processes are unique and internal to her is largely ignored.[24] Instead, mother and child are presented in a misleadingly symmetrical developmental process. In fact, as she points out, there are developmental processes specific to both mother and child as well as the mutuality and interaction on which contemporary psychoanalysis has focused. The mother has her own processes of separation, union and reciprocity just as the child does – but the psychological meanings of these moments are particular to her. Of course within developmental psychology mothers are minutely observed and described, but generally in their role as origin and environment in a theory of childhood.

It is in this context that psychoanalysis as a discipline has often been accused of mother-blaming. Paula J. Caplan and Ian Hall-McCorquodale studied 125 articles in major clinical journals for 1970, 1976 and 1982 in which etiology and treatment of 72 different forms of psychopathology were discussed.[25] They found that where any causes for pathology were mentioned, almost invariably mothers were it. Not only does psychoanalytic theory militate against mothers getting a 'fair hearing', but clinical practice leads to an understandable tendency to form an allegiance with the child in the patient against the patient's mother. Monique Plaza, a French psychoanalyst, described how she experienced a split between her personal sympathy with the lot of twentieth-century mothers and her professional work 'accompanying children in difficulty'.[26]

She writes, 'In my psychoanalytic practice with children, I am confronted with the Mother, a violent and painful confrontation [resulting in] a feeling of impotent solidarity which makes my writing difficult, hesitant, and full of doubts'.[27] She is confronted with both the mother in the narratives of her patients and the mother in psychoanalytic theory, delineated as overprotecting, rejecting, smothering and depriving. She concludes that mothers truly are victims of circumstances – historically, mothering has become constructed and re-constructed so that it cannot be other than an intolerably difficult role. Meanwhile psychoanalytic theory and practice has tended to become deeply implicated in what Plaza calls the 'patriarchal regulation of families'. I agree with Plaza that across the heterogeneous schools of psychoanalysis there is a homogenising tendency to reproduce normative and oppressive representations of motherhood. Nevertheless, psychoanalysis does offer an invaluable tool for building a deeper understanding of the subjective experience of mothering and must be credited with having opened up the initial recognition of the ubiquity and strength of maternal ambivalence – only to close the door on an extended exploration of it. Accordingly, I have tried to unpick the idealisation and denigration of motherhood[28] within psychoanalysis itself and to demonstrate how psychoanalytic theory can in fact be used to illuminate *constructively* the experience of motherhood.

Marianne Hirsh in her work on narrative, psychoanalysis and feminism, has asked: 'Is it possible to tell the untold tale of maternal participation in the psychoanalytic narrative, staying within psycho-analytic terminology?'[29] I think we have no alternative.

In a deliberate attempt to compensate for the domination of the infant's perspective in psychoanalytical writing (that purports to focus on the mother and infant), I concentrate on the mother's perspective – and specifically on maternal ambivalence as a central dynamic. Because psychoanalysis has usually viewed the mother from the child's position, whether current or recollected, concrete or symbolic, maternal ambivalence is primarily read from the point of view of the dangers and advantages of it to the child. Even D. W. Winnicott's 'Hate in the Countertransference' (perhaps the best-known text on maternal ambivalence) dwells primarily on the developmental importance *for the baby* of maternal ambivalence and says little on the role of ambivalence in what I want to call maternal development.[30] He sees maternal hatred as facilitating a baby's capacity for hatred; as for the mother, we are told that without the ability to hate appropriately she is constrained to fall back on masochism. I argue that maternal ambivalence, despite – even because of – all the distress it can engender in mothers, may have a transformative and positive impact on the mother and, hence, on the work she has to do.

Ambivalence in Psychoanalytic Theory

In *The Interpretation of Dreams*, published in 1900, Freud recog-nised that to dream of the death of a loved person signified an unconscious death wish towards that person.[31] The co-existence of love and hate – evident in dream life – was in Freud's view an archaic feature of mental life originating in early infancy.

He elaborated his understanding in 1909 in 'A Case of Obsessional

Neurosis', where he wrote that 'in every neurosis we come upon the same suppressed instincts behind the symptoms . . . hatred kept suppressed in the unconscious by love'.[32] Shortly afterwards he adopted the specific term 'ambivalence' which had originally been employed by the Swiss psychiatrist Eugene Bleuler in 1910.

By 1915, in 'Instincts and Their Vicissitudes' Freud had moved on to explore the genesis of love and hate and concluded that the experience of hate preceded love developmentally, having its origins in the instincts of self-preservation, while love originated in the sexual instincts.[33] In his formulation concerning the conflict between the life and death instincts he placed love among the life instincts and incorporated hate in the service of the death instincts.

Although ambivalence became increasingly significant in Freud's thinking – Oedipal conflict was conceived as a conflict of ambivalence – he displays the ambivalence towards ambivalence which I suggest still colours our culture's evaluation of maternal ambivalence. In 1915 he wrote elsewhere of the creative potential of ambivalence, observing that

> it is indeed foreign to our intelligence as well as to our feelings
> to couple love and hate; but Nature, by making use of this pair
> of opposites, contrives to keep love ever vigilant and fresh,
> so as to guard against the hate which lurks behind it. It might
> be said that we owe the fairest flowering of our love to the
> reaction against the hostile impulse which we sense within us.[34]

Two years later he focused on the negative outcome of ambivalence. In the paper 'Mourning and Melancholia' he suggested that the conflict of ambivalence 'gives a pathological cast to mourning, and forces it to express itself in the form of self-reproaches, to the effect that the mourner himself is to blame for the loss of the loved object, i.e. that he has willed it.'[35] Thus, the aspect of hatred in ambivalence towards a loved one is turned round upon the self and instigates self-torment. Where mothers are concerned, I think the process by which ambivalence is expressed in self-reproach and depression is facilitated by the desire to protect their children against hostility, and the wish to believe in their children's unequivocal lovableness.

Despite Freud's passionate acknowledgement of the inevitability and positive purpose of ambivalence in 1915, by 1931 his negative conviction was that it constituted an 'archaic inheritance' to be grown out of. Then he wrote:

> Normal adults do undoubtedly succeed in separating those two attitudes from each other, and do not find themselves obliged to hate their love-objects and to love their enemy as well as hate him. But this seems to be the result of later developments. In the first phases of erotic life, ambivalence is evidently the rule.[36]

Seventeen years later the psychoanalyst John Bowlby questioned this later view of Freud's on ambivalence. In Bowlby's opinion ambivalence was inherently natural and unavoidable ('all animals are constantly beset by impulses which are incompatible').[37] His concern is with the 'regulation' of ambivalence *in children* through appropriate parental care. A constant maternal presence, he believed, protected against too powerful a development of ambivalence (see Chapter 5).

For Melanie Klein the notion of ambivalence became central. Within her developmental framework, the baby's capacity to experience ambivalence towards the mother and manage the attendant anxiety is deemed an 'achievement'. I will give a brief summary of Melanie Klein's ideas so as to orientate readers not familiar with her thinking. In the second quarter of the child's first year it begins to experience the mother as a whole person, in contrast to the previous state in which the mother is phantasised as split into part objects, specifically into a persecuting and an ideal maternal image.[38] Such splitting is due to the infant's inability to acknowledge that the parent it loves for gratifying it is the same entity as the parent it hates for frustrating it. This is a mode of organising experience that helps to separate the endangering and the nurturing aspects of the mother, and of life itself. Klein emphasised that the hating self and its relation to a hateful or hated and therefore hating mother (or object, in Klein's terms) is split off from the loving self and its relation to a loved and therefore loving object. Thus splitting safeguards the infant's need to love *and* its need to hate, and it works well to allay any anxiety that the mother who cares for it might be harmed. In its mind she is kept separate from the bad mother who fails to smooth its path. Klein termed this state of mind the paranoid schizoid 'position', rather than phase or stage to emphasise that, though prominent in infantile dynamics, the paranoid-schizoid position will also exist in adult life.

According to Klein, with growing integration, the infant begins to experience the mother differently – now as a whole object who can safely be loved as a whole person. This second mode she termed the depressive position because it is the essence of depression to have anxious feelings about damaging someone or something you love. It involves the gradual recognition of the fact that the loved and hated mother are one and the same. The quality of anxiety associated with the paranoid-schizoid position and the depressive position is significantly different. With the former, anxiety is experienced on behalf of the self; in the latter anxiety is felt for the other. For with the dawning of ambivalence, the (m)other is seen as a loved person who might potentially be lost and driven away by hatred. Though reparation can be attempted, harm is nevertheless felt to have been done. Therefore, with the depressive position comes a sense of responsibility, an awareness of there having been a relational history, a differentiation of self from others, and a capacity for symbol formation, in that concrete modes of understanding are superseded by a 'psychological capacity'. But equally associated with the achievement of the recognition of ambivalence are loss, sorrow and separation.

Following this schematic summary of Klein's thinking, I want to ask what would happen if we were to reverse this schema, placing the mother as having to negotiate entry into a maternal depressive position? Then we can see that the mother's achievement of ambivalence – the awareness of her co-existing love and hate for the baby – can promote a sense of concern and responsibility towards, and differentiation of self from, the baby. Maternal ambivalence signifies the mother's capacity to know herself and to tolerate traits in herself she may consider less than admirable – and to hold a more complete image of her baby. Accordingly, idealisation and/or denigration of self and, by extension, her baby, diminish. But the sense of loss and sorrow that accompanies maternal ambivalence cannot be avoided. Acknowledging that she hates where she loves is acutely painful for a mother. The parallel is with the loss Klein's baby undergoes when it gives up the image of the all-perfect, all-loving mother.

In 'Love, Guilt and Reparation' Melanie Klein elaborated her theory of ambivalence and did relate it to the experience of adult love relationships, friendships, being a father, and being a mother.[39] She described how the urge to put right loved people who in phantasy have been harmed or destroyed becomes a central element in adult love. Because the conflict between love and hate is lifelong, reparation plays a crucial part in the experience of being a parent:

> Our grievances against our parents for having frustrated us, together with the feelings of hate and revenge to which these have given rise in us, and again, the feelings of guilt and despair arising out of this hate and revenge because we have injured the parents whom at the same time we loved – all these, in phantasy, we may undo in retrospect . . . by playing at the same time the parts of loving parents and loving children.[40]

However, what this quote makes plain is that in Klein's view maternal ambivalence signifies a re-experiencing of feelings a woman held in relation to her own mother during childhood. Thus, for example, the death wishes she harboured unconsciously towards her mother are now experienced in relation to the child who stands symbolically for her own mother. And, when she makes reparation to her children, it is, from a psychoanalytic point of view, her own mother who is the true recipient of her reparative impulse.

In other words Klein has specifically situated maternal reparation primarily as a replayed form of infantile process. The mother's intense relationship with her children mobilises her infantile hatred and her infantile wish to care and repair. A baby girl's 'intense desire to possess children'[41] is what motivates an adult woman's behaviour. Although Klein's infant may be intended as a metaphorical infant, something quite specific in adult maternal love and hate may have been lost. Continuing to rework Klein's theses with a mother's eye as a contribution to the evolving body of work on 'mother as subject', some interesting issues emerge. It becomes apparent that we need to take a fresh look at maternal ambivalence, one that teases out, explores and discusses differences and similarities between adult and infantile modes of ambivalence. Certainly the central importance of ambivalence for infant and adult cannot be overestimated. The development of feelings of responsibility and concern for the other is intricately linked with and even stimulated by hatred and harming impulses. But the ways in which such feelings unfold in a small baby and an adult woman may not be identical. If we do not take care to make these careful discriminations, all kinds of confusions can follow.

A far more extreme example of a reading of maternal ambivalence that fails to differentiate its possible origin in infantile development from the lived experience of mothers can be found in the work of the psychoanalyst Joseph Rheingold. He elaborated his views on maternal hatred in his book *The Fear of Being a Woman: A Theory of Maternal Destructiveness.*[42] He claimed that the acquisition of feminine identity is essentially terrifying for female babies. Later in life, such identity is sealed by becoming a mother. Thus a woman's infantile desire is at all costs to destroy her baby, thereby saving herself from motherhood/femininity. He writes that 'Most mothers do not murder or totally reject their children, but death pervades the relationship between mother and child.'[43]

The inevitable and damaging outcome of this kind of thinking is the pathologising of maternal ambivalence, rendering it unavailable for constructive scrutiny. Amongst contemporary psychoanalysts and psychotherapists there are still those who view ambivalence as a 'risk factor'[44] and as a failure to achieve a 'fully maternal personality',[45] to use Klein's term.

Making Passions Circulate

Perhaps more than any other group, it is mothers who need to 'achieve' ambivalence in relation to their children, who need to be able to love and hate the baby at the same time, if they are to move beyond what psychoanalyst Joan Raphael-Leff has termed 'primary maternal persecution'.[46] A mother I interviewed said,

> I can remember hurling the baby down on the pillows once, and just screaming, and not caring. I wanted to kill him really. I think it was to do with being so tormented, worried, and guilty. You know, the anxiety and guilt at feeling I was getting it all wrong, and that I was bad and useless. I just wanted to get away from the situation. I felt unable to tolerate it. I hated the baby for constantly being there.

In the pain of these words of this interviewee – Frances – we can see the paradoxical face of maternal ambivalence in an adult woman. On the one hand, the guilt evoked by ambivalence is at the heart of her distress and, on the other hand, it is precisely the co-existence of love and hate for the baby which protected the baby from her raging despair, and finally forced her to search for solutions.

Similarly, Selma, the mother of a four-month-old boy, described the unexpected outcome of a sudden uprush of unmanageable ambivalence:

> Last week when he wouldn't stop crying, I shook him, which I know is a really bad thing to do. Afterwards I thought about it, and found myself admitting, really for the first time, the full weight of his dependency on me – acknowledging that the baby is entirely dependent on me for twenty-four hours a day – and what a huge drain that is. The funny thing is that since then his crying has not got to me in the same way.

The shock of her encounter with unmanageable ambivalence opened Selma's eyes to the reality of maternal responsibility. Once she was able to acknowledge the 'full weight' of the baby and to allow herself to feel burdened, she no longer needed to save herself from his distress. She was able to think about it.

The French philosopher and psychoanalyst Julia Kristeva has observed that motherhood makes passions circulate.[47] I would say that it is ambivalence, in particular, that makes passions circulate, as well as firming boundaries, forcing reflection, provoking both separation and unification, and thus providing a spur to individuation for both mother and child.

Writing on motherhood and politics, Sara Ruddick commented that 'a single typical day can encompass fury, infatuation, boredom, and simple dislike'.[48] She names the affect that overarches these states of mind, 'preservative love'. I suggest that the fuel for such love is found in maternal ambivalence.

However, the guilt stirred by the recognition of ambivalence can become overwhelming, immobilising maternal passions rather than provoking their circulation. Then a mother regresses to a schizoid state, making an over-rigid split between baby and self. She experiences herself as the good, persecuted mother while the baby is seen as primarily bad, utterly persecuting and the justifiable object of hatred. Now, of course, there are many reasons why guilt works to split love and hate so far apart that love ceases to mitigate hate, but a primary cause is our culture's ambivalence towards maternal ambivalence – a theme which echoes throughout the book. For parents and non-parents alike, ambivalence about ambivalence is based on the terror that hate will always destroy love and lead to isolation and abandonment. Our culture defends itself against the recognition of ambivalence originating in the mother by denigrating or idealising her. A denigrated mother is simply hateful and has no love for the child to lose. An idealised mother is hate-free, constant and unreal.

In sum, mothers experience their maternal ambivalence across a spectrum, ranging from the tolerable and constructive to the intolerable and destructive. Society's wariness of maternal ambivalence, fuelled perhaps by infantile fears of loss, defended against by the idealisation or denigration of mothers, provides a context which inflates maternal guilt, rendering ambivalence at times unmanageable.

Introducing her biographical account of mothering her son in his first years, Jane Lazarre suggests that what has been called 'neurotic' in the woman and 'pathogenic' (i.e. causing illness) for the child is 'on the contrary a normal part of the experience of being a mother'.[49] She comes to the conclusion that 'the only thing which seems to be eternal and natural in motherhood is ambivalence'.[50]

She is making an important point and one I agree with. However, the taboo on maternal ambivalence and the anxiety it arouses are still evident, revealed in her language. She emphasises that ambivalence is *normal, natural* and *eternal*. I think, however, that ambivalence is hugely variable within families as well as being historically specific in its form and expression. For example, at a certain period in her life, a woman with two children may experience acute conflict in relation to one of the children, with powerful hate only just balanced by passionate love, while harbouring more easily manageable feelings for the other. This state of affairs may reverse at another point in their lives. Equally, at different historical moments, the social conditions of mothering can work to render maternal ambivalence manageable or unmanageable. I argue that the conditions of late twentieth-century mothering do significantly augment and intensify the unbearable aspects of ambivalence.

A taboo on maternal ambivalence inflects both cultural representations of the mother and the social arrangements of motherhood. Elsewhere I have distinguished between the *construction* of femininity, the feminine *ideal* and the feminine *stereotype*.[51] Definitions of femininity as a lived identity for women have, thanks to feminism, gained a certain flexibility over the past few decades, and we can observe that femininity is, at any one moment, both embraced and resisted. But the feminine ideal (by this I mean a historically changing concept of what a woman *should* be) in relation to motherhood has remained curiously static. In fact, the faster women's lives change, the more ossified and stereotyped become dominant representations of ideal motherhood. Despite changing beliefs about babies' capacities and thus childcare priorities, the representation of ideal motherhood is still almost exclusively made up of self-abnegation, unstinting love, intuitive knowledge of nurturance and unalloyed pleasure in children. In the following chapter I explore how the longing for this mother shapes women's experience of mothering.

2

The Fantasy of Oneness

For a long time I didn't feel I wanted to have children. I'd had a very bad relationship with my mother, and I felt I would be bound to repeat it. And then I had a dream in which I was in a room, a comfortable room with a fire and books, and the rain was lashing outside. I had a baby and the two of us were peacefully and comfortably together in this beautiful, warm place. And that was the first time I ever had an actual positive image of motherhood. It stayed with me and I looked forward to being able to create that sort of a relationship with a child.

For Shelley this dream signified both the recognition of her own capacity for love and intimacy and the attainment of the protective nurturance she felt she had lacked from her mother. Shortly after having the dream she became pregnant and now has three children. Rather than pursue the meanings of the dream for Shelley, as one would in therapy or analysis, I want to look at the familiar fantasies of motherhood contained within it. Most obviously there is a woman's desire that motherhood will heal the shortcomings of her own childhood. At a conscious level this means that she will not repeat her own mother's 'mistakes' with her child, who stands in for her baby self. The dream, however, illustrates the workings of this basic wish at a deeper level. The overwhelming feeling is that motherhood means *shared* warmth – a fire burns in the grate. Fear, discomfort, cold and conflict are locked outside to take the lashing of the rain. Mother and baby *together* enjoy comfort, peace and beauty in the shared space of a book-lined room. The mother regains her mother's womb, but it is a better womb in so far as infantile pleasure unites with adult knowledge, power and the ability to love and care for a baby. The welcome fantasy of mother-hood invokes a dual identification – with the mother who cares *and* with the baby who is cared for, with the container *and* with the contained. Here lie the delights and the dangers of mother love. Shelley could only envisage becoming a mother once her infantile self felt sufficiently nurtured. Internally, feeling mothered and her capacity to mother fed one another. In the external world mothers long to achieve a state of affairs where both themselves and their children feel simultaneously 'well fed and satisfied'. Ideal moments of motherhood escape the everyday conflict of wills and the degree of self-denial which inevitably characterises parenting. Mothers yearn for conflict-free times of warmth, love and ease. The inevit-ability of maternal ambivalence intensifies the desire, indeed almost creates it. For the negative and positive aspects of motherhood are determined and defined by their opposite and shaped by individual subjectivity: in Shelley's case, for example, her utopian dream of motherhood rested upon her sense of having had a nightmarish relationship with her own mother.

Equally important in shaping a woman's desires and fantasies in relation to being a mother are its dominant cultural representations. Jessica Benjamin has suggested that, in reaction to recent historical changes in modes of mothering, Western culture is under the sway of a sentimental idealisation of motherhood: the ideal mother is 'an all-giving, self contained haven'.[1] Her dominance impedes change in relation to the provision of better day care, medical care, maternity leave and flexible work times, which are all so necessary for the actual conditions of mothering – and unnecessary for the ever-present, omnicompetent ideal.

In this chapter I shall explore the fundamental characteristic of the maternal ideal, noting the tension between this ideal and women's descriptions of ideal moments in the lived experience of mothering. Although the maternal ideal inevitably shapes women's view of what does constitute ideal *moments* in their experience of mother-hood, there is a significant difference between the two. The culture's maternal ideal is founded on a representation of the unity of mother and child, while the moments mothers themselves define as ideal are founded on mutuality. The tension between the two can render women's pleasure in mothering somewhat suspect in their own eyes. For the maternal ideal suggests that mother love means *oneness*, while what mothers long for are loving moments of *at oneness*.

What the cultural image of the maternal ideal and the ideal maternal experience (representations of ideal moments) share is a desire to banish ambivalence, maintaining love alone.

'More to Love'

Ask a mother what she anticipated with greatest pleasure in having a baby and many will echo Margaret's sentiments: 'I suppose I just wanted something to love, some small creature to expand my love into.' Another interviewee, Molly, felt that that was exactly what she had achieved when her daughter was born:

> I did not anticipate the intensity of the feeling; the enormity of the experience. I was overwhelmed by love. I had never been loved like that. She was ecstatic when I came into the room and miserable when I went away. It wasn't that I became more loving – it was that there was more to love.

Simone de Beauvoir in her brilliant, but jaundiced, writing on motherhood would consider that such a comment reveals mother love to be a compensation for all that heterosexual love fails to provide for women: 'The mother finds in her infant – as does the lover in his beloved – a carnal plenitude, and this not in surrender but in domination; she obtains in her child what man seeks in woman: an other, combining nature and mind, who is to be both prey and double.'[2] It is the intensity of love itself that can render the rush of ambivalence so surprising, so painful and seemingly so dangerous. De Beauvoir's 'carnal plenitude' is imaged by mothers in myriad ways, from a desire to gobble up the child to feelings of passionate protectiveness: 'If she steps off the pavement for a second, I go bananas.' Possibly this particular mother's panic does conceal an unconscious wish to push the child off the pavement but, true to the dynamics of ambivalence, the imagined loss of the child puts the mother in touch with the full force of her desire and love for the child.

Freud considered parental love to be essentially narcissistic. He wrote of mothers that, 'In the child which they bear, a part of their own body confronts them like an extraneous object to which, starting out from their narcissism, they can give complete object-love.'[3] And of parents he commented that, 'Parental love, which is so moving and at bottom so childish, is nothing but the parents' narcissism born again.'⁴ The baby exists to fulfil the parental wishes and dreams, receiving all the narcissistic supplies the parents wanted for themselves. Freud highlighted the combination of infantile wishes and adult desires that play into motherhood. However, since the publication of his paper on 'Narcissism' in 1914 there has been an intellectual revolution in psychoanalysis. The judgmental contrast between the self-love of narcissism and object love has given way to the acknowledgement that the two must co-exist – though often in tension.⁵ Behind Freud's remark on parenthood lies a view of narcissism as a primitive state which, ideally, became transformed into libidinal relations with others. Narcissism is nowadays seen by many rather as a necessary concomitant of personality manifesting in healthy self-esteem.*

Some contemporary psychoanalytic theorists understand maternal narcissism as making a contribution to infantile development. A mother derives pleasure from loving her baby. She loves the baby for her own sake. This love derives not from the baby's needs and projections, but from her desire. However, it provides the baby with experiences of being 'wanted rather than catered for'.⁶

At the same time motherhood makes for a particular tension between self-love and object love. For the child which was once part of the mother's body is indubitably other and yet still regarded as the mother's personal responsibility both socially and psycho-logically. And to the extent that experiencing the pleasure of mother love enhances a woman's sense of self-worth, suffering maternal hate undermines it.

Gina describes how she feels when she sees her own 'flaws' reflected in her daughter:

> Maggie has my figure. She's pear shaped. And although I'm ashamed to admit this, I really can't stand it. My impulse is to urge her to dress like I do – in such a way as to disguise her shape. I hate myself for minding. On the other hand I can see that she is a more courageous person than I am – with a devil-may-care attitude – and I'm very proud of that.

Thus a mother's self-esteem is locked into the feelings she has for her child. In so far as the child is experienced as loved and 'good',

---

* This does not require us to overlook narcissistic disturbance in which a profound lack of self-esteem produces a split between grandiose, inflated conceptions of self and torturing self-doubt.

motherhood can enhance a woman in her own eyes, but given that motherhood inevitably incurs a mother's anger, irritation, disapproval and antagonism, motherhood can equally constitute a serious depletion of healthy narcissism. Some mothers react by omnipotently trying to control the child and change it; others respond by trying to achieve impossible levels of self-control; many veer between the two positions.

One moment when an experience of maternal hate causes the self-esteem engendered by mother love to change into anguished self-doubt often occurs when a child reaches adolescence. Then conflicts provoked by ambivalence, intensified by the complexities of the separation process, can produce a peculiarly painful type of hatred for the child and a resultant self-denigration.

For example, Sylvia sought therapy with me because she became extremely depressed in the face of her older daughter's adolescent disruptiveness. She experienced herself as entirely immobilised as Sarah, aged fifteen, fought for independence on the one hand, and on the other manifested a reproachful dependence.

All her life Sylvia had maintained a pattern of loving others 'despite' their behaviour towards her. She loved her father despite feeling deeply let down by him. She loved her brother despite his violence. She told me, 'I have a need to love. It's inside me. I have had it all my life.' Sarah, however, was kicking through her defence. In tears, Sylvia exclaimed, 'I never expected to have a child who would fight my love.' I think that to a lesser or greater extent the hope that many women carry with them into motherhood is that at last their love will be entirely welcome and put to good use.

The psychoanalyst W. R. Fairbairn considered that aggression, rather than arising spontaneously as an innate factor, is a reaction to the 'frustration of the primary motivational aim – the striving for contact with objects'.[7] Of course Fairbairn was referring to infants; but once again we can turn his observation round and view a mother's love for her child as the primary motivational aim, and maternal aggression as a reaction to its frustration.

The need to love and the fear of its frustration had been a lifelong dynamic for Sylvia. She commented, 'I could only tell my mother I loved her when her back was turned.' Realigning psychoanalytic theory, so that adult maternal psychology is illuminated, we can see it was fear that her love would be frustrated that was at work in Sylvia. Defending against the phantasised consequences of her own

aggression towards her children, she was forced to maintain an
ideal of unconditional love and rational care for her one son and
three daughters. For years she had denied any negative feelings for
her family, for in her mind hatred was twinned with abandonment.
Either she loved and stayed, or she hated and lived out a myth of
abandonment and abandoning. Looking back at Sarah's childhood
she said, 'I could never really admit how difficult I found her in case
someone took her away from me.'

Encouraged to acknowledge ambivalence towards the adolescent
child, Sylvia felt both frightened and humiliated. Initially she
experienced me as a mocking figure who seemed to crow as she
and Sarah ricocheted from one crisis to another. She attempted to
bind the wounds by frequently describing her daughter's beauty
to me, as if our mutual contemplation of the girl's loveliness would
obliterate the bad feelings she assumed existed between us.

Very slowly she began to use me as someone to whom she could
at last safely acknowledge hostility towards her daughter. Initially,
the acknowledgement had a defensive and self-justifying element.
She was the good, abused mother and Sarah was the worthless
daughter. The characteristic split in narcissistic disturbance between
inflated self-worth and low self-esteem became constellated between
Sarah and herself. After Sarah had run away from home, Sylvia said
to me: 'I'm thoroughly glad she's gone. I wish she would leave, in
fact I wish she would live anywhere except in my house, creating
chaos and upsetting the little ones.' Some time later, however, once
Sarah had returned, she said with a renewed sense of humiliation,
'I've realised why we have rows whenever Sarah goes out. I just don't
want her to leave. I don't want her to go out. I miss her.'

When she was able more fully to acknowledge maternal ambivalence, Sylvia likened herself to a caged bird who had fallen off its
perch. It had been an enormous strain sitting chirping and singing
loyally and lovingly. On the other hand, something had undoubtedly
been lost whilst gaining the freedom to 'fall silent' and admit to
maternal hate as well as maternal love. Another mother expressed
the sense of shame and bewilderment produced by ambivalence:
'How can I have such hostile thoughts about them when they are
so little – and mine?'

Sylvia's depression at the onset of her daughter's adolescence is
explicable in terms of her personal pattern – the particular meanings that love and hate carried for her. However, the intensity of

humiliation and fear of loss occasioned by her dawning awareness of ambivalence need to be placed in a wider cultural context. The particular representation of motherhood which, above, I term the 'maternal ideal' functions to deny maternal ambivalence at the level of the social – and ends up making maternal ambivalence feel unmanageable to women by rendering them guilty for failing to achieve the ideal.

Mrs Ramsay Re-considered

The guilt-inducing effect of the inability to live up to the maternal ideal is all too familiar. Indeed, the madonna image of maternity has become a cliché. But, though we may mock it, demystify it, reframe it, turn our backs on it, deconstruct it, we cannot dismiss it. It is too deeply embedded in our psychocultural life to be eradicated. I shall try to unpick the maternal ideal to discover the threads that weave it together and permit it to retain its shape, but first I want to explore the way its maintenance within the individual *and* within society functions as a defence against the acceptance of the very existence of maternal ambivalence.

Virginia Woolf's novel *To the Lighthouse*[8] provides a case history of the workings of the maternal ideal in the attitudes of her characters towards the mother figure, Mrs Ramsay. In their various musings on Mrs Ramsay, we can perceive from differing angles how the maternal ideal functions in a psychologically regressive manner. We can also perceive the pervasive and unexpected cultural strength of the maternal ideal that has inflected critical readings of this much-discussed text. The majority of critics consider this to be primarily a book about *daughterly* ambivalence, failing almost completely to grasp the extent of Mrs Ramsay's maternal ambivalence, and, hence, her discomfort with the maternal ideal.

Virginia Woolf was familiar with the work of Sigmund Freud. Throughout the 1920s her narratives focused increasingly on the early mother–child relationship, indicating her knowledge also of the ideas of Melanie Klein. She said of *To the Lighthouse* that 'when it was written, I ceased to be obsessed by my mother'.[9] She even likened the experience of writing the book to psychoanalysis in that it 'expressed some very long felt and deeply felt emotion. And in expressing it I explained it and then laid it to rest.'[10] Not only does the book go some way to expressing and explaining her ambivalence as a daughter towards her mother, but, at an altogether less worked out and conscious level, she was able to envisage something that we could call maternal ambivalence.

The novel has been described as a presentation of a series of oppositions: mother and father, life and death, light and darkness, affirmation and destruction, enclosure and separation.[11] One crucial opposition in the book concerns the idealisation and denigration of the mother. Mrs Ramsay, fifty years old and the mother of eight, is the object of idealisation as a mother and, inevitably, denigration of her will follow. This is displayed obliquely in Charles Tansley's feelings for Mrs Ramsay. He is a young man staying with the family during their seaside holiday. Walking one day with Mrs Ramsay he suddenly perceives her as a domestic madonna:

> it was this: she was the most beautiful person he had ever seen.
>
> With stars in her eyes and veils in her hair, with cyclamen and wild violets – what nonsense was he thinking? She was fifty at least; she had eight children. Stepping through fields of flowers and taking to her breast buds that had broken and lambs that had fallen; with the stars in her eyes and the wind in her hair – He took her bag.[12]

Tansley's image is of a Pre-Raphaelite madonna. It links motherhood with nature – protective and benevolent, delicate and eternal. Mrs Ramsay is a goddess in whose service Tansley becomes good and effective in his own eyes. 'He took her bag.' The image could be of a little boy helping Mummy. Proximity to the maternal ideal renders him powerful but somehow pathetic. And, with the recognition that he cannot perfectly please her, comes the desire to denigrate Mrs Ramsay, to turn his back contemptuously upon her: 'They did talk nonsense, he thought, the Ramsays; and he pounced on this fresh instance with joy . . .'[13] The fantasy of the maternal ideal thus dispenses feelings of inadequacy right across the board from guilt-ridden mother to the child in the adult man or woman who comes to believe they have accorded too much power to the mother.

The fantasy which fuels the maternal ideal is evident in the relationship of the painter Lily Briscoe to Mrs Ramsay:

> Sitting on the floor with her arms round Mrs Ramsay's knees, close as she could get, smiling to think that Mrs Ramsay would

never know the reason for that pressure, she imagined how in the chambers of the mind and heart of the woman who was physically touching her, were stood, like the treasures of tombs of kings, tablets bearing sacred inscriptions, which if one could spell them out would teach one everything . . . Could loving, as people called it, make her and Mrs Ramsay one? For it was not knowledge but unity that she desired, not inscriptions on tablets, nothing that could be written in any language known to men, but intimacy itself which is knowledge, she had thought, leaning her head on Mrs Ramsay's knee. Nothing happened. Nothing! Nothing! as she leant her head against Mrs Ramsay's knee. And yet she knew knowledge and wisdom were stored in Mrs Ramsay's heart.[14]

The archaic imagery, the longing for unity, the pre-verbal condition, all indicate that Virginia Woolf is painting a picture of the desire to regain or return to the pre-Oedipal mother–child relationship, as represented in the psychoanalytic texts with which she was familiar. Lily Briscoe desires to achieve a state of merger with Mrs Ramsay. She asks, 'What device for becoming, like waters poured into one jar, inextricably the same, one with the object one adored'.[15]

The image of waters poured into one jar beautifully evokes the emotions entailed in the desire for oneness which Virginia Woolf conveys through Lily Briscoe's reflections as she presses close to Mrs Ramsay. It is, however, a complex image. The fundamental equation between separation and castration means that strength – here imaged as knowledge – lies in symbiosis with the mother.[16] Equally in the longing for oneness, we discover a desire for the satisfaction of the incestuous wishes of the Oedipal child; while at another level the waters poured into one jar associates the mother with oblivion, obliteration and finally death. Jung described the undertow exerted by the initial pre-Oedipal attachment to the mother in terms of 'a deadly longing for the depths within, for drowning in [the child's] own source, for becoming absorbed into the mother, [the child's] life is a constant struggle with death, a violent and transient delivery from the always lurking night'.[17]

Thus, a depth psychological reading of early mother–child attachment positions the mother as the source of bliss and of destruction. And adult longings for and fantasies directed towards a state of unity with another are not only likened to but considered to replicate the mother–child symbiosis. I am thinking here of states of unity reached in meditation, in romantic and sexual passion, in religious experience or in the analytic relationship of transference and countertransference. Whatever the precise context, the states of merger are equated with mother–child symbiosis.

Fantasies of union with mother as the source of bliss and plenitude lead inexorably to fantasies of the denying, frustrating, insufficient mother. Kaja Silverman, an American writer on film and semiotics, well summarises the sadness associated with the swing or movement, observing that it functions 'as a bridge between two radically disjunctive moments – an infantile moment, which occurs prior to the inception of subjectivity, and is consequently "too early" with respect to meaning and desire, and a subsequent moment, firmly rooted within both meaning and desire, but consequently "too late" for fulfilment'.[18] Thus, though Lily Briscoe welds herself to Mrs Ramsay, 'Nothing happened. Nothing! Nothing!', even though she is convinced that Mrs Ramsay possesses all she desires.

As I have said, *To the Lighthouse* is usually recognised as an account of daughterly ambivalence. Literary theorist Elizabeth Abel, for example, writes that 'ambivalence towards Mrs Ramsay pervades Lily's experience; she is buffeted by opposing impulses towards merger and autonomy',[19] and Marianne Hirsh[20] describes the novel as remaining the narrative of the daughter. Historically, this view has substance. Virginia Woolf was a daughter not a mother, and a daughter deeply conscious of daughterly ambivalence. 'It was only the other day when I read Freud for the first time,' she wrote, 'that I discovered that this violently disturbing conflict between love and hate is a common feeling; and is called ambivalence.'[21] In *To the Lighthouse*, she transcends the limits of her experience and conveys not only daughterly, but also maternal ambivalence. Possibly it was a way in which she was able to explore and reflect on her own mother's ambivalence towards her. It is a measure of the strength of our culture's denial of maternal ambivalence that this only rarely receives critical attention. The majority of readers, blinkered by the force of the maternal ideal, with attendant longings for a totally beneficent mother, overlook Mrs Ramsay's ambivalence.

Mrs Ramsay is herself both drawn to and deeply discomfited by the maternal ideal. It leads her to doubt her own positive impulses:

For her own satisfaction was it that she wished so instinctively to help, to give, that people might say of her, 'O Mrs Ramsay! dear Mrs Ramsay . . . Mrs Ramsay of course!' and need her and send for her and admire her.[22]

Feeling within herself the immense pull of the maternal ideal, and within those surrounding her, she grows suspicious of her own altruism. In a culture which defends against an awareness of maternal ambivalence by means of the myth of the maternal ideal, it is all too easy for a mother like Mrs Ramsay to disbelieve her own good impulses. A guilty awareness of forbidden negative impulses casts doubt on the validity or even the reality of good impulses.

Mrs Ramsay is also aware that the maternal ideal with its accompanying image of maternal omnipotence is simultaneously an emblem of impotence and entrapment. The all-powerful mother quickly becomes the too-powerful mother. Mrs Ramsay reflects defiantly that

she would have liked always to have had a baby. She was happiest carrying one in her arms. Then people might say she was tyrannical, domineering, masterful, if they chose; she did not mind.[23]

This desire always to have a baby in her arms, as the source (and maybe excuse for a potency that already exists yet is prohibited by the culture) does not rule out a desire to get away from her children – to be alone:

and it was a relief when they went to bed. For now she need not think about anybody. She could be herself, by herself. And that was what she often felt the need of – to think; well not even to think. To be silent; to be alone.[24]

Mrs Ramsay's relief when they go to bed; the lifting of the constricting anxious sense of responsibility, the re-establishing of her boundaries and the regaining of a coherent sense of identity, are feelings most mothers would recognise or confess to. Negative emotions in relation to children can be a means of self-preservation for parents. For Mrs Ramsay, there's relief when they go to sleep, there's relief when they go out – and there's enormous relief when they come safely in again.

For a mother, ambivalence spells the dissolution of her particular version of the maternal ideal – a letting go of fantasies of omnipotence and perfectibility, with all the guilt they entail. And ambivalence forces the abandonment of the representation of mother and child as a united, mutually fulfilled and fulfilling couple. Mrs Ramsay recognises, with a depression she terms 'pessimism', that she can never fulfil her children's desires, never be enough, never be accepted by them for the limited being she knows herself to be. So, for example, reflecting on her daughter Rose, she perceives in her

> some buried, some quite speechless feeling that one had for one's mother at Rose's age. Like all feelings for oneself, Mrs Ramsay thought it made one sad. It was so inadequate what one could give in return; and what Rose felt was quite out of proportion to anything she actually was.[25]

Here Mrs Ramsay sees and is saddened by the discrepancy between the maternal ideal and external reality. Yet, as I mentioned above, most readings of the novel focus on daughterly ambivalence, and readers remember Mrs Ramsay with nostalgic longing, idealising and denigrating her in the process. For example, Jennifer Uglow, writing in the anthology *Balancing Acts: On Being a Mother*, takes Mrs Ramsay as the representative of an ideal which contrasted starkly with her personal experience of motherhood. She owns that for years she longed to be like Mrs Ramsay, 'to sit at the head of a table haloed in lamplight, dispensing *boeuf en daube* to an adoring tribe'.[26] The mother of four children, she promised herself after each birth that next time she would take time off and sit like Mrs Ramsay, 'surrounded by my infants knitting and offering consoling wisdom'. She concludes, 'It never happened of course. Mrs Ramsay remains a seductive image precisely because hers is the kind of maternal role the working mother has to learn to sacrifice'.[27]

Not only mothers in paid employment but all mothers have to negotiate their lived experience of motherhood with the maternal ideal. It is an indication of the oppressive effect of the ideal that we start to believe that some mother somewhere is managing to achieve it: a mother who is not in paid employment, a mother with more money, a mother with fewer children, a mother with a more supportive partner, a mother from another ethnic background etc.

The precise strength and content of this self-persecuting fantasy varies with each individual, but we can see its grip in the insistent fashion with which it mediates readings of *To the Lighthouse*, quite obliterating Mrs Ramsay's own internal struggle. Her 'case history' reveals that at the heart of the maternal ideal lies a fantasy of union. Julia Kristeva comments that the fantasy of the omnipotent, beneficent mother involves less an idealisation of mother than the idealisation of the *relationship* that binds us to her. Here she claims that our culture is in the sway of an 'idealisation of primary narcissism',[28] which she sees as characterising the archaic mother–child relationship. What is being idealised is a relationship of unproblematic unity.

The mother–child relationship not only signifies states of merger but is also seen as the *source* of such states. For example, the psychoanalytic writer Erik Erikson characterises religion as gratifying 'the simple and fervent wish for a hallucinatory sense of unity with the maternal matrix'.[29] Similarly the American psychoanalyst Ethel Person considers that the dynamics of romantic love involve a longing for infantile bliss and plenitude within the mother–child fusion.

> In love, the lover regains his lost omnipotence, takes total possession of the beloved and achieves Oedipal victory. In achieving a union with the beloved, he undoes the defects, losses, and humiliations of the past. In doing so, he identifies with the victorious rivals of his childhood and assuages his wounded narcissism.[30]

Person qualifies her psychoanalytic narrative of regression with her view that adult love signifies not only an infantile mingling of self and other but also an expansion of the grown-up self. However, this qualifier still represents rather a minority view.

When Kristeva claims that we are in the grip of an idealisation of the state of primary narcissism, she is referring to Freud's by now controversial description of the very early mother–child relationship. In fact, Freud provided two accounts of so-called primary unity with the mother, one involving a 'self sufficient' and psychologically isolated infant and the other suggestive of a blissful state of union. This gave rise to two opposing ways of thinking about infantile experiences. On the one hand, infant as *self-contained isolate* and, on the other, *infant and mother as undifferentiated from each other* (at least in the infant's experiencing of it) but within a state of affectionate relation. The psychoanalyst Michael Balint's theory of the existence of 'primary love' in the early stages of life exemplifies the latter position. In this view there is a certain quality of relationship between the two persons but this proceeds without the clear-cut distinction between self and other that we expect to see, or assume to exist, in adult relationships. Mother and child interpenetrate in a conflict-free harmonious mix-up [31] The idealisation of a symbiotic, conflict-free connection is described exclusively from the child's position in that the mother is either gratifying or frustrating, rejecting or facilitating. Hence, an impression exists that mothers lack subjecthood; they are just the child's object.

However, the very existence of infantile fusion states is increasingly being questioned. Infant observation suggests that depictions of this state, whether as object relations formulation or as Jacques Lacan's psychoanalytic positioning of mother–infant fusion within the Imaginary, are retrospective fantasies on the part of adults. It would follow that states of fusion entered into by adults do not necessarily contain traces of infantile experiences. As psychoanalyst and writer Juliet Mitchell, reviewing Kristeva's work in the *International Journal of Psychoanalysis*, has pointed out, that which we long to unite with is deemed maternal 'only once it is looked at backwards from within the already constituted society, from a post-oedipal psychic world that has by this stage given meaning to masculine and feminine'.[32]

The expectation that the mother–child relationship will achieve and satisfy a woman's longing for union is thus embedded deeply in our culture. It is a belief system that outlaws ambivalence, rendering it a source of shameful guilt. Take the following familiar example. Immediately after giving birth, most women expect to experience a joyful sense of love and oneness with their baby: some do but many don't and warnings that it may not happen tend to fall on deaf ears. For women carry babies for nine months within a culture which represents the postnatal mother–child social relationship as if it replicated the intrauterine state of antenatal union. The nineteenth-century tradition of presenting a new mother with a pincushion bearing pins arranged to spell out the words 'Welcome Little Stranger' was in many ways a more appropriate representation of the state of affairs.

'Mommy and I are one'

I have used Mrs Ramsay to illustrate the way the maternal ideal works, the manner in which it magnifies ambivalence, and the power of the ideal evident even in critical readers' remembrance of her.

As discussed above, the ideal both feeds into and is fed by social conditions of mothering that have developed since the nineteenth century. Successful, correct mothering is equated with primary responsibility for a child sustained in relative isolation within the nuclear family, and social and institutional structures are mobilised to maintain it. This organisation of mothering leans heavily on a maternal ideal based on the representation of mother and child as a fused unit.

It would be simplistic to suggest that the ideal is somehow imposed on women. In the very early months of infancy mothers, and perhaps babies too, often experience a profound and sustaining sense of oneness. As a mother said to me, 'After he was born I had the fantasy that the hospital bed was an island containing and cradling us away from the rest of the world.' My concern is that the fantasies of individual mothers have, as it were, expanded to produce a particular cultural expectation of the mothering experience. We can see this in the way the ideal has determined a quite specific and selective take-up of psychoanalytic ideas in relation to recent notions of what constitutes satisfactory childcare.

Clinical experience with adult patients in psychoanalysis has indirectly reinforced the hold of the maternal ideal on attitudes towards the mother–child relationship. The analyst's provision of a 'holding environment' together with an empathic responsiveness activates unconscious fantasies and desires, one of which is the fantasy of achieving oneness with the analyst. Although this can often be a negative fantasy of engulfment as opposed to a blissful or fulfilling fantasy, this is not my main interest here. The general problem is the way in which the analytical relationship is uncritic-ally assumed to replicate the mother–child relationship. It is considered that when the patient regresses in the course of treatment, it is to the level of a child merged with and dependent on its mother. Images or feelings of union with the analyst are undoubtedly experienced in psychoanalysis and analytic therapy. But what can be beneficial for individuals within the consulting room may have gone sour when transposed on to evolving notions of what constitutes good childcare. I shall return to this issue in Chapter 7, but here I want to pursue further the links between psychoanalysis, the maternal ideal and childcare.

I will begin by describing a set of experiments conducted in 1975 which inadvertently transmuted an aspect of ordinary analytic practice with adults into a supposedly scientific measurement of what constitutes good mothering in a modern society.

In their book *The Search for Oneness* clinicians and researchers Silverman, Lachmann and Milich give details of experiments in which subjects are provided with the subliminal message 'Mommy and I are one'.[33] The findings were that to receive this message had an ameliorative impact on a wide variety of psychological conditions, ranging from nicotine addiction to schizophrenia.

It is possible to feel moralising, derisive or both towards such experiments, but nevertheless they provide fertile breeding grounds for cultural attitudes which can only promote maternal guilt. Consider the following quotation from *The Search for Oneness*:

> In keeping with the findings of Kaplan and Bronstein, Kaye found that 'Mommy and I are one' decreased pathology, whereas 'Daddy and I are one' did not, again suggesting the special properties of the former stimulus. But the third oneness stimulus *did* produce an ameliorative effect. 'My girl and I are one' lowered pathology, and to Kaye's surprise, to a degree that was greater than that produced by the 'Mommy and I are one' stimulus.[34]

It is not at all surprising within a culture wedded to the maternal ideal to find that oneness fantasies extending to situations other than the mother–child relationship are automatically returned to mother. Thus that 'My girl' had a more positive stimulus than 'Mommy' was taken to mean that 'the words *My girl* refer to a more positive *good mother* image than the word *Mommy*'.[35] In other words, if the *Mommy* stimulus does not evoke in the subject of the experiment blissful unity and plenitude with its ameliorative effect, they must have experienced something wrong with mother. And indeed we are informed elsewhere in the book that this has to do with her 'failure to provide an adequate climate within which the necessary symbiosis can be established and maintained in the early months of the infant's development'.[36]

The experiment was said to be informed by experiences within the consulting room in conjunction with the object relations theory of infantile development, and was intended to reinforce specific tendencies within psychotherapy. That this kind of work leads to the production of a moral imperative for mothers was clearly incidental to the experimenters, though the fact that this is what happens provides support for my thesis.

Childcare manuals, on the other hand, are concerned to influence maternal behaviour directly. In Bruno Bettelheim's *A Good Enough Parent* we can see a similar transplantation of psychoanalytic consulting-room values, but this time into the home, where mothers are urged to replicate the reflective, containing environment of the consulting room.[37]

A Good Enough Parent popularised Bettelheim's version of D. W. Winnicott's ideas. He emphasises the unique character of each parent–child relationship, and urges parents to rely upon and trust their own feelings. He suggests that the key to good enough childcare is empathy, stimulated by a parent's capacity to recall their own childhood emotions and experiences. Bettelheim fully acknowledges parental ambivalence, and recognises how conflict can obscure love and magnify hate for a child. But, rather than considering the potentially creative aspect of conflicts generated by ambivalence, Bettelheim's primary aim is to defuse parental negativity and hostility. He offers the following solution:

> Our memories of our own childhood will make us patient and understanding; and as we realise that despite our child's obstinacy he suffers now as we suffered then, our love for our child, in whom we recognise so much of our old selves, will, all on its own, return.[38]

Of course, the techniques Bettelheim offers for defusing parental rage might well work, and the very offering of such strategies points to the ubiquity of anger and hatred in parenting. But the whole tenor of the writing militates against the conscious acknowledgement of ambivalence and is infused with an unconscious acceptance of the maternal ideal. It may be that such texts display a profound longing for oneness on the part of the writers. In *Dialogues with Mothers* (1962), for example, Bettelheim confronts a mother who admits to the need for some time for herself.

> There is certainly nothing wrong in wanting something for yourself. My suggestion is that you start out by thinking, 'I

need some rest; if I can now get her to take her nap, we can
both have our rest and then we'll both be better off.'[39]

Faced with maternal desire in conflict with the demands of the
child, Bettelheim pays lip service to the parent's needs but consigns
the mother–infant couple to a conflict-free oneness, banishing
the spectre of ambivalence by suggesting both sets of needs can
be met. This maintains the mother as the child's object with little
existence of her own. She has no life apart from the child; she
has no imperatives outside the child's desire for her. Ironically,
a perspective infused with an unacknowledged maternal ideal
effectively increases mother–child tensions, as any mother of a
young baby can testify who has attempted the longed-for solution
of the simultaneous nap.

Moments of harmony and unity do of course occur within the
mother–child relationship. Moments of unity take on their intensity
precisely because of the co-existence with moments of disunity.
Sometimes, the two states can become split between two children
within the same family. For example, a patient of mine, a first
sibling herself, described how when her oldest son was born she felt
he lay in her arms and looked at her with total love. The harmony
between the two persisted. When her second son was born, her
husband placed the baby in her arms and she experienced the baby
giving her a look which seemed to say, 'Is this the best you can do?'
Her distress at her relationship with her second son was a primary
reason for seeking therapy, but for a long time her guilt prevented
her from thinking about the intra-psychic, familial and social
reasons for the discrepancy in her feelings for the two boys.

What do mothers want?

There is a curious contradiction at the heart of the maternal ideal.
While harmony, unity and the attainment of ever greater emotional
closeness through the employment of empathy are held up as the
goal of mothering, the pursuit of a sense of oneness is simultaneously
considered to be a symptom of maternal inability to separate.
Oneness is itself both idealised and denigrated in our culture: women
pursue mothering in a culture which warns against the Scylla of
overprotection on the one side and a Charybdis of rejection on
the other (see Chapter 4 for further discussion of this). Mothers are

expected to function as their small children's sole life-support system and then to drop them off unproblematically at school or the play-group door.

So how do mothers negotiate these cultural contradictions in conjunction with their own fantasies and desires in relation to motherhood? The ideal drawn from the fantasised fusion of the early mother–child couple leaves none of us untouched. It can cast a sort of sadness over motherhood – a constant state of mild regret that a delightful oneness seems always out of reach. The precise effect of the maternal ideal on the individual mother is, however, significantly shaped by social, economic and ethnic factors. Thus, for example, Patricia Hill Collins describes how it impacts on some black mothers and daughters in the United States:

> For far too many black mothers, the demands of providing for children are so demanding that affection must often wait until the basic needs of physical survival are satisfied. Black daughters raised by mothers grappling with hostile environments have to confront their feelings about the difference between the idealized versions of maternal love extant in popular culture and the strict, assertive mothers so central to their lives.[40]

She concludes that for these daughters adulthood means understanding that offering physical protection is an act of love.

Writer and journalist Rosalind Coward explores the working of the maternal ideal in a very different constituency – British middle-class mothers.[41] She considers that a new maternal ideal has arisen out of increased affluence and leisure opportunities for children in conjunction with loss of confidence in state provision and the new coercive ideals of childcare. She suggests that the middle-class maternal ideal today centres on the capacity to pour endless energy into the provision of creative activity for children. She describes middle-class mothers becoming taxi drivers, managers, teachers and therapists as they orchestrate their children in an endless round of birthday parties, French clubs, pottery classes and swimming lessons, in their struggle to attain the ideal. She comments that, despite exhaustive effort on behalf of their children, mothers berate themselves for failing to live up to the ideal, for it is founded on the belief that the really good mother is someone who 'enjoys mothering so much that her enjoyment would override all the stresses and strains of family life'.[42] These overstretched, guilt-filled mothers were patently not enjoying motherhood.

Coward questions how this state of affairs has come about; why women confess to finding paid employment a blessed escape from the insistent and draining demands of home life. She concludes that women are colluding: 'Instead of challenging how psychological and educational responsibility has been passed onto them, women have taken it all on board as their absolute responsibility.'[43]

In my view, however, the hectic round of extracurricular activities pursued by middle-class mothers does not constitute a new ideal, but is an attempt to achieve the old ideal of a sense of total devotion to and unity with their children untroubled by ambivalence. In other words, I think the tendencies Coward describes could be considered as manic defences against ambivalence – defences which, as we know, fail dismally. Far from uniting mothers and children, such behaviour makes for resentful mothers and recalcitrant children. As Coward herself puts it, 'Most believed that if they could become like this good mother, their lives would change from bad-tempered survival to idyllic peace.'[44] Ironically, if we explore the hyper-active lifestyle of these middle-class mothers from the standpoint of an evasion of maternal ambivalence, we see, in fact, a pursuit of conscience-soothing peace.

Silly Old Mum

The denial of ambivalence, as I have indicated, is not imposed on mothers by a fearful and punitive society. It lives in all of us.

Take, for example, the contents of a popular women's magazine, available at checkout points in supermarkets – *Family Circle*: the February 1991 issue can be taken as typical. The features are written by women, targeted at mothers, and devoted to enabling readers to rid themselves of distressing hostile impulses and to cultivate their reassuring good impulses.

There are three major categories of features: the instructive, the anguished confessional and the humorous confessional. An article by Michele Elliott, director of Kidscape, called 'The Ten Worst (and Best) Things You Can Say to Your Child' exemplifies the instructive genre. Top of the worst things you can say to your child is, 'You're so stupid.' Top of the best things is 'You've always been a plus in my life'.[45] The anguished confessional is provided by a distressing account of a mother who acted out her hostility towards her child. It is headed, 'You can damage your child in so many ways – I feared I would harm mine'.[46] The article functions as a moral or cautionary tale, yet is contained and distanced by emphasis on the immense stress suffered at the time by the abusing mother, and it is rendered bearable by the provision of a happy ending. The mother found help with Newpin, the self-help organisation which provides 'a lifeline to young mothers who feel lonely and desperate'. Similar organisations are listed, for example Home Start and Parentline – a tacit acknowledgement that the personal history was not quite so personal to the author as the presentation would have us believe.

Both categories of features do actually provide a means of acknowledging ambivalence even while refusing it. This is particularly true of the third category, which I have called the humorous confessional. It is represented in this issue by Davina Lloyd's article 'School for Scandal!', which describes a parent's response to her child's unwillingness to go to school:

> M. and I walked slowly hand in hand to First School gates round the corner. I observed that, although I have dressed for work, I haven't brushed my hair and am still wearing my slippers. Then we make peace. I retract the threats I made in the heat of the morning contretemps. I promise that I will not really send her to boarding school, tell the headmistress or put her up for adoption . . .[47]

The self-mocking confessional defuses the threatening representation of maternal rage. The reader can laugh indulgently – and with relieved recognition. The humorous confessional is becoming increasingly popular as a means of airing parental feelings. It is perhaps at its most successful in the *Guardian* newspaper's 'Bad Housekeeping' by Dulcie Domum. Dulcie is forever enraged, embattled, embarrassed by and wounded by her children. The articles are witty, entertaining and taboo-breaking. Ambivalence is acknowledged but reassuringly softened so that the Bad Mother becomes simply 'Silly Old Mum'.

Silly Old Mum does not disturb the maternal ideal, she is more hopeless than hateful or hate full. She is a feminine stereotype; a way of categorising everything women are and everything we do as entirely, essentially and eternally feminine, denying differences between women according to economic and social position, geographical and historical place, and specific psychic reality. And it is, of course, this kind of homogenisation which renders women so uncertain of their different ways of being a mother.

Living Happily Ever After

The maternal ideal I have been discussing is oneness, but the ideal that mothers themselves seek, as I said above, seems to be less concerned with unity than with the experience of mutuality. Even breastfeeding, which is held up as an icon of oneness, to many mothers means instead a sense of mutual satisfaction. The moments of loving pleasure with their children which mothers describe are often founded upon this sense of shared engagement in a mundane *activity* rather than intense involvement with one another, as Mary told me:

> There are a couple of afternoons a week when I am able to pick up the children from school, and all these fantasies of how good a mother I would be if only I had time and space get stuffed into those two afternoons. And yet we very often end up watching television – which is what I am always furious with the childminder for doing when she picks them up from school. But there was one afternoon when it all did go smoothly. It was one in a million. We actually came home and made scones together. It was terribly nice; we made a fire and sat eating scones and drinking tea in front of the fire. Letty turned to me and said, 'We're living happily ever after!' and, of course, she was right – it was the stuff of fairy tales.

Mary has three daughters under ten years old. For her, watching television signifies her failure as a mother because of the disengagement from her children she considers it creates. Susan, on the other hand, with a son and daughter also under ten years, experiences with the television the same ingredient Mary valued in scone-making – a shared focus away from the intensity generated by the mother–child relationship:

> What I really enjoy is the time after they get back from school, I make tea for us and we eat it cuddled on the sofa watching TV.

For both Mary and Susan one pleasure of motherhood involves a beneficent regression to childhood – to an idealised childhood of warmth, good food and conflict-free cuddles. Fleur offers another version of the same experience:

> I like having baths with Tom. We have baths together and play with his ships. I like it because it is contained. You don't have to stay in the bath for three hours! And we *both* enjoy bathing.

As in Shelley's dream of books, baby and burning fire with which this chapter began, mothers and children are together, mutually nurtured and comfortable. Hostility is locked out of the room and the mother's child and the child in the mother are equally satisfied. I think it is here that we can see the cultural ideal of unproblematic unity impacting on mothers' experience, but transformed and converted from a longing for unity into a longing for mutuality. This becomes clearer if we take an example from the mother of an adolescent. The humorous account by a mother of life with 'Treasure', her adolescent daughter, also published in the *Guardian*, captures a longed-for moment of mutuality:

> Treasure and I have a pleasant morning shopping, her favourite pastime. We go wild in Marks and Spencer and Rymans, replenishing our supply of knickers and tights, pens and cartridges. Even Treasure is staggered at the cost, 'Let's get out of here,' she says hoarsely, 'before we see anything else.' A harmonious morning.[48]

I think what we see in these narratives of maternal pleasure is a sense of relief that ambivalence can be kept in abeyance in situations which satisfy both mother and child; situations which could be deemed 'selfish' if viewed solely through the lens of the maternal ideal with its denial of independent adult maternal desire.

The maternal ideal constructed around a mythic portrait of a relationship of unity offers very little space for a partner's presence in relation to the child. The partner or paternal role is basically reduced to one of protecting the child from the negative consequences of the ideal – from the engulfment which is bound to function as the other side of the coin to blissful fusion. But once again we can see how mothers adapt, translate and negotiate the ideal into a maternal ideal experience – an experience of mutuality. Naomi's version of maternal pleasure in mutuality demands that the children's father be present and equally satisfied. She describes a 'good day' as follows:

> I think my standards are getting lower. I'm not expecting a whole day or afternoon to be good. I accept that there are going to be grizzles, demands, scenes and tantrums, but if they are at a minimum rather than a maximum, then that is a good day. There was a visit to a museum we all enjoyed. The children were happy and the adults were happy. Everybody's needs were addressed. And there was the pleasure in the four of us being together.

Naomi emphasises that it was not simply that she experienced a moment of shared satisfaction with her two children – but also with their father. For women like Naomi childbearing and childcare are crucially concerned with partnership – partnership of a kind at odds with the maternal ideal. Sandra describes her pre-conceptual fantasies of shared parenting:

> It wasn't until I fell in love with Barry that I actually began to want a child. And even then it wasn't exactly a child I desired. Rather I wanted Barry and I to love the same thing. I imagined us standing with our arms around one another, gazing down into a cot.

The image of the child as a shared creative project is rooted deeply in the unconscious and some would argue is a prerequisite for identifying with being a loving parent. However, the maternal ideal in conjunction with the sexual division of labour designated by Western culture is profoundly at odds with parenthood as partnership. In reality a mother more often than not finds herself alone beside the cot, whatever her pre-natal fantasies. And even those parents who do struggle to maintain a partnership in relation to childcare find they 'lose' one another. A lesbian parent observed,

> Before the children we used to do things together and go places together. Now at weekends we more often than not operate a shift system to look after the children and give each other a break. We rarely meet!

Thus an unobtainable parental ideal tends to magnify ambivalence in much the same way as the maternal ideal. Nevertheless, bearing in mind Naomi's description of her 'good' day at the museum, it is clear that moments of shared delight in children undoubtedly help to keep ambivalence manageable.

In sum, both the culture's maternal ideal and those moments designated by mothers themselves as ideal defend against ambivalence and both, paradoxically, promote ambivalence. The same desire for an escape from ambivalence is contained in the lover in pursuit of sexual and romantic passion, in the spiritual search for mystical oneness with God or the universe and in the search for oneness in the patient in psychoanalysis. That the mother and child relationship is taken as foundation and representation of such oneness lends a particular poignancy and pain to a mother's necessary confrontation with ambivalence. Adrienne Rich succinctly summarises the distress:

> My children cause me the most exquisite suffering of which I have any experience. It is the suffering of ambivalence: the murderous alternation between bitter resentment and raw-edged nerves and blissful gratification.[49]

The experience of ambivalence can undermine a mother's hope and expectation that here at last is someone to love unreservedly and wholeheartedly. Ambivalence (or so she assumes) denies her the chance to heal her own childhood disappointments, or to regain her childhood delights. Even to acknowledge ambivalence can be narcissistically wounding for some mothers, widening the gap between the ego and the ego ideal. The latter constitutes an ideal conception of selfhood on which the ego seeks to pattern itself. The ego ideal is originally formed in infancy through the internalisation of the inspiring aspects of the parental function. In adult life, therefore, experiencing oneself as a good parent can be immensely restorative, while to feel a bad parent seriously diminishes the sense of self.

The individual mother's ego ideal, in conjunction with our society's image of the maternal ideal, represents ambivalence as some sort of failure to love. As Freud commented, 'the realisation of . . . one's own inability to love . . . has an exceedingly lowering effect upon self regard'.[50] Now ambivalence is emphatically *not* synonymous with the inability to love, but in a society wedded to the maternal ideal, it can seem that way to women.

Although clearly related and superficially alike in how they position ambivalence, the cultural maternal ideal I have been describing, and the lived experience mothers describe as approximating an ideal for them, are significantly *different*. The cultural ideal insists that the mother's gratification springs from gratifying the child. The mother's desires are subsumed in the child's. The ideal moments mothers themselves describe sometimes look superficially like a living out of this 'oneness' but in fact the mother's needs for sustenance and pleasure are met not in a state of fusion with the child but through a shared gratification, often of a quite mundane nature, such as experiencing shopping and cooking together. In these moments of shared pleasure neither mother nor child experiences the other as the source of either plenitude or deprivation.

Julia Kristeva argues that mothers' experience is always mediated by structures of representation which produce a specific, circumscribed image of motherhood. I am suggesting that with their images of ideal moments mothers can discover a way of negotiating – if not subverting – the constrictions of the maternal ideal.[51]

3

The Unacceptable Face of Ambivalence

Not loving your child must be one of the hardest emotions to talk about. Almost from the moment their son was born, Hilary, 35, and Hugh, 36, were horrified to discover how they felt about him. They tell of the pain involved in admitting that they resent their baby.[1]

The melodramatic introduction to a feature in the woman's magazine *Marie Claire* led not to an account of maternal hatred but rather to one of maternal ambivalence in which Hilary somewhat bleakly and bravely acknowledges negative feelings towards her son, yet can simultaneously own that, 'I like to watch him playing and find it rewarding when he smiles and greets me when I come in.'

The presentation of the magazine feature as a story of parental hatred rather than as a narrative of ambivalence is, at one level, a response to the exigencies of journalism – the need to excite and entice readers. But equally it illustrates, at both a cultural and an individual level, profound difficulties in acknowledging and speaking ambivalence. In this chapter I shall explore first the cultural manifestation of the inhibition placed on facing ambivalence, and then look at the experience of mothers themselves, in an attempt to gain a deeper understanding of the dynamics of the unacceptable face of ambivalence.

Ambivalence is emotionally difficult to believe in even if, intellectually, many people recognise its inevitability. Accepting that hatred, resentment and hostility are unavoidable components of the full range of feelings for a child throws doubt, as I've said, on the reality of a mother's capacity for love in both her own and others' eyes. To return to *Marie Claire*'s Hugh and Hilary: the magazine was deluged with letters in response to the feature 'offering both criticism and support'. Hugh and Hilary were asked to comment on readers' reactions. Their replies suggest that the process of providing material for this feature and reading the correspondence it generated enabled them to think the unthinkable.

> *Hilary*: I was terribly apprehensive both before and after the interview, I thought that once I had finally voiced my feelings out loud they would seem so awful I would simply not be able to function as Toby's mother any more. But, in fact, when I finally read the article, I found I didn't sound as bad as I thought I would. Hugh and I spent a whole day analysing our views – which was good for us I think. When we started receiving letters of support, I really felt justified in having spoken out. If what we have done makes only one other guilty parent feel better, it has been worth all the anxiety.

> *Hugh*: I felt a tremendous sense of relief about having brought my feelings out into the open at long last. But later I did worry about how it would feel to see it all in print . . . I fully expected that a lot of people, particularly women, would be outraged by it and think we were monsters. So I was surprised and touched that so many of the letters we received were sympathetic. It made me feel a lot better about the whole thing. It's also interesting that in the time that has elapsed since the interview, I have noticed I am now far happier and more relaxed in Toby's company than ever before.

Hugh and Hilary's testaments indicate the immense cultural pressure they must have experienced against acknowledging negative feelings towards their son. The response their 'confessional' received rendered their ambivalence manageable and, it would seem, potentially a creative force in their lives as parents.

Did They or Didn't They?

Resistance to thinking about ambivalence runs like a subterranean fault through a number of disciplines. Within the historiography of motherhood this has produced a split between those who consider mother love to have been a constant in Western cultures over long stretches of time and those who believe it to be a recent (and man-made) arrival. In her polemical work, *The Myth of Motherhood*,[2] Elizabeth Badinter takes the latter position. She traces a history of motherhood in France over the last four centuries which maps great variations in behaviour, and in the quality of love felt and expressed, as well as long periods of silence about the mother's feelings. In her opinion, a cultural silence on mother love lasted until the closing decades of the eighteenth century – what Badinter calls 'The Absence of Love'. A primary symptom of this absence, according to Badinter, was the regular abandonment of babies. She provides compelling documentation. For example, in 1780 only 1,000 of the 21,000 babies born each year in Paris were breastfed by their mothers.[3] One thousand were wet-nursed in the city, while the rest were sent to wet nurses outside Paris, many dying in transit and many more failing to survive the conditions that awaited them in the countryside; while in eighteenth-century London, the benefactor of a foundling hospital reported that mothers abandoned their babies in gutters and garbage dumps, where they were left to rot.

Badinter argues that abandonment of babies was a cross-class phenomenon, accepted and permitted by society, rather than consti-tuting a response to economic circumstances. All this changed with the development of demography and epidemiology. The study of statistics – population, birth and death rates, and patterns of diseases – was promoted by, and in turn promoted, the view of all human beings as potentially useful to the state as members of the labour force or army. The child thus acquired a commercial value and came to be viewed as a potential economic resource.

The historian Ludmilla Jordanova, writing from a different perspective to Badinter's, has described how, at this juncture, the quality of mothering from pregnancy to child-rearing became a concern on the assumption that the loss of children was prevent-able, and that therefore infant mortality should, as a political obligation, be prevented. She comments:

> those who saw safe, healthy, appropriate reproduction as an important political goal promoted their ideas by trying to cultivate powerful emotions both positive and negative and then invest them in particular forms of behaviour. Infant mortality was an effective focal point for grief and outrage;

good mothering (i.e., producing healthy children who would become responsible adults) was a focal point for idealisation, pleasure, adulation and so on. These were two sides of a sense of loss, where the death of infants could be mourned at both individual and collective levels, and, as a way of offering comfort, the successful mother who reared her children to adulthood giving rewards to herself and her country, could be idolised.[4]

Some historians, while accepting that the significance accorded to motherhood changed during the latter decades of the eighteenth century, believe that those like Badinter and the psychohistorian Lloyd de Mause, who emphasise the normality of maternal indifference prior to that date, have misread the evidence. For example, Valerie Fildes, editor of a collection of papers on women as mothers in pre-industrial Britain, observes that cases of murder, physical abuse and neglect of children under four years do not appear regularly in parish, hospital or quarter session records. She points out that they have to be searched for. Yet it is these isolated examples that are selected by historians who seek to prove widespread cruelty and neglect by mothers and foster mothers.[5]

As far as the mothers were concerned, Fildes writes that notes pinned to the clothing of abandoned babies testify to maternal love and concern. Moreover, women's written works show that they valued maternal experiences highly. Fildes tartly observes that, though historians may find it hard to recognise women's grief at the death of their children, women themselves openly acknowledged it. She cites the seventeenth-century Quaker Rebecca Travers, who wrote that 'none but a Tender Mother can tell what it is to have Hopeful Children so soon taken from them'.[6]

In my view, to a degree Badinter and Fildes are both right. Some mothers doubtless distanced themselves from their children as Badinter describes, and some mothers painfully mourned their loss as Fildes points out. What the historians of motherhood could focus upon, and what the history of motherhood does display are the sets of social, economic, political and religious circumstances which either condoned or condemned ambivalence on the part of the mother.

A historical study by John Boswell, of the abandonment of children in Western Europe, does indicate how historical trends and social forces interact with the ambivalence of the parent–child relationship to produce a variety of institutions, from foundling hospitals to departments of social services.[7] Reviewing Boswell's book in the *International Review of Psycho-analysis*, Paul M. Brinich commented that it teaches us that 'the symptoms of elemental ambivalence that we see around us in the guise of child abuse are, at root, nothing new.'[8] Brinich went on to suggest that the 'symptoms' may reflect our current failure to develop ways – intrapsychic and social – of managing ambivalence. He concluded that the history of the abandonment of children challenges psychoanalysts to extend their intrapsychic understanding of the elemental ambivalence of the parent–child relationship.

The Enigma of Motherly Misery

Sociological investigations of the implications of changing patterns of mothering are, like much of the historiography of motherhood, limited by a failure to foreground ambivalence. In her book *On Being a Mother* Mary Georgina Boulton provides a useful summary of social research in the field since the 1950s.[9] During the 1950s and 1960s research focused primarily upon marriage and reflected the assumption that 'motherhood was intrinsically rewarding and not problematic'.[10] A second theme of early studies was the employment of women with children, and the possible effects that this had on the children, while a third focus was on patterns of child-rearing typified by the work of sociologists John and Elizabeth Newson who, Boulton observes, 'asked only what the women enjoyed about their children, a question which presupposed that enjoyment was a fundamental feature of the relationship and which neglected their frustration and irritations altogether'.[11]

The re-emergence of feminism in the 1960s initially focused on the conditions of motherhood and wifehood in books such as Betty Friedan's *The Feminine Mystique* in the USA, and in Britain with the work of Michelene Wandor, Lee Comer and many others. These writers explicitly recognised ambivalence as at the heart of the experience, although the source of ambivalence was seen primarily as the material conditions of society. Lee Comer wrote:

> They [mothers] cannot talk about what being cooped up all day with their children does to them (and, of course, to their

children), nor can they speak of the precarious ambivalence of their situation – the sometimes overwhelming love they feel for their children which has to vie with their feelings of violence. The difficulties of their situation are tailor-made to breed resentment which is made all the more intolerable by the social pressure not to give way to it.[12]

The feminist challenge to the idealisation of motherhood and the definition of women by their reproductive capacity was, perhaps inevitably, misunderstood by a culture with real difficulties in regard both to feminism and to the concept of ambivalence. Thus the women's liberation movement's campaign of the 1960s and early 1970s, to change the material conditions of motherhood, believed to be at the root of ambivalence, was simply seen as the desire to abandon children, home and husband. Thus, the fourth demand of the women's movement in 1970 for '24-hour nurseries for all under 5s' was taken *not* as a response to the needs of night workers (which is what in fact it was) but as meaning that children were to be dumped for twenty-four hours at a time by their uncaring mothers.

Nevertheless, the impact of feminism on sociology led to a greater interest in the actual experience of mothering. However, although studies began to signal both the frustration and the rewarding aspects of motherhood, the findings are somewhat disjointed and inconsistent. Ann Oakley, whose pioneering work on housewives and motherhood has been enormously influential, acknowledged the contradictory nature of her own findings. She found that two-thirds of her sample of housewives were satisfied with childcare, but added that 'behind this general concept of "satisfaction" with child-care lie more subtle differences to do with *ambivalent* feelings about children and the demands of the mother role'.[13]

It is some measure of how hard ambivalence is to grasp that the majority of social researchers responded by splitting their findings, so that on the one hand there is the *work* of childcare which is described as overwhelming, isolating and stifling, and on the other hand the *mother–child relationship* which is seen as providing immense emotional rewards. Mary Georgina Boulton tried not to split institution and experience, and her solution is appealing. She identifies two main themes in women's accounts of relationships with their children. The first is the pleasure or irritation/frustration that women feel in the course of their daily lives looking after children. The second is the sense that their children give a purpose to their lives and thus provide their lives with meaning. The experience of motherhood is itself broken down into two modes: 'the immediate response' to looking after children and 'the sense of meaning and purpose in doing so'.[14] But the essence of the experience of motherhood is its irreconcilably contradictory nature, and hence, although many mothers can doubtless identify with Boulton's modes, her argument in my view pays insufficient attention to the psychological complexities of the mother–child relationship, the intense co-existence of negative and positive feelings towards children within motherhood.

The plethora of studies on the state of parenthood since the 1960s has to a large extent been instigated by the increasing mobility of women's lives and changing patterns of employment. For example in the USA in 1950 28 per cent of women with children between six years and seventeen years were in paid employment; by 1968 the figure had risen to 68 per cent. Today in the USA two-thirds of all mothers are in the labour force. Similar trends may be noted in most Western countries. In Britain a report published by the Policy Studies Institute in 1991 revealed that nearly half the women who stop work to have babies are now returning to work within nine months of giving birth – a figure that has almost doubled in the last ten years.

Faced with the reality of women's employment, commentators on the family may be divided into those who saw full-time motherhood as best for both children and mothers, and argued that mothers should be given the social and financial incentives to stay at home, and those, like the sociologists Rhona and Robert Rapoport, who believed that society needed measures which would facilitate women's participation in the labour force.[15] We can link this discussion of sociological views on changing patterns of mothering to the cultural denial of ambivalence by pointing out that, whatever their differences, most of these commentators have in common a near-obsession with maternal happiness. The Rapoports urge women to 'continue to seek enjoyment even though there are residues of unresolved issues – for example, in relation to how permissive or disciplinarian to be with the children, how egalitarian to be in relation to the domestic division of labour between parents'.[16] Their book *Fathers, Mothers and Others: Towards New Alliances* was published in the USA in 1977. They were convinced that the contemporary predicament of the family 'for parents as well as the authorities who seek to guide them'[17] involved searching for new models. How, they asked, are we to acknowledge variation and diversity without chaos and confusion? How are we to define the optimal relationship between domestic life and work and the life of the occupational world outside the home?

The solution they suggested was based on balance. Women were to be divided between the public and private spheres in such a way as to achieve maximum job satisfaction in both places:

> Parents are expected to participate in the process of their children's development, but not to be the exclusive arbiters of their children's fate. This gives them more leeway to examine and respond to yearnings of their own without feeling selfish and irresponsible.[18]

The overt message is in support of women diversifying their lives. But the very terms of reassurance employed – women are *not* to feel selfish and irresponsible for working outside the home – indicates that women's employment outside the domestic sphere was seen largely as a selfish 'yearning' rather than as a response to economic necessity or a desire on the part of women to pursue or continue with a career.

Indeed, the bright hopes for new alliances held by the Rapoports and others have not been realised. The incorporation of women into the economy has not been accompanied by the changes in practicalities and psychological attitudes that would have permitted women to 'respond to yearnings of their own without feeling irresponsible or selfish'. Behind the lack of response to the needs of mothers as workers is an unarticulated fear that maternal ambivalence has drawn women out of domestic work into paid work. In other words, women are quite simply suspected of wanting to work because they don't want to be with their children. I am suggesting *not* that maternal ambivalence is responsible for women seeking employment, but that denial of ambivalence and an idealisation of motherhood contributes to the way working mothers are viewed and treated as deserting mothers. As far as mothers themselves are concerned, the conditions they contend with as workers, and the acceptance of lower economic returns for their labour, undoubtedly intensify maternal guilt, rendering ambivalence unliveable and hence prone to denial.

Twelve years on from the Rapoports, sociologist Arlie Hochschild coined the term 'stalled revolution' for what has happened.[19] Workplaces remain deaf or unresponsive to the needs of women workers with children. And shared housework and childcare are ideals only rarely put into practice, so that women are left with a 'double day'. She discusses studies which reveal that, although working mothers have higher self-esteem and suffer significantly less depression than housewives, when compared to their children's fathers, they turn out to be more exhausted and more often ill. As Hochschild points out, women work fifteen hours longer a week than men, which means one month more a year. There is both a wage gap at work and a leisure gap at home:

> Women are often the lightning rods for family aggressions aroused by the speed-up of work and family life. They are the 'villains' in a process of which they are also the primary victims. More than the longer hours, the sleeplessness, and feeling torn, this is the saddest cost to women of the extra month a year.[20]

The recent history of motherhood reveals women struggling with social and economic circumstances which of necessity magnify maternal guilt and stretch a woman's psychological and practical resources sometimes to breaking point. Yet the inner-world experience of mothering is not simply a reflection of external-world assaults and assistance. External reality and psychical reality exist in a complex relationship to one another. I want now to turn to the inner world of mothering and to the discipline concerned with it – psychoanalysis.

'Mothers Hate Their Children from the Word Go'[21]

These are the words of the psychoanalyst D. W. Winnicott who is more usually associated with the reassuring phrase 'the good enough mother'. The discrepancy between the good-enough mother and the mother full of hate from the word go reflects a problem psychoanalysis has with mothering. On the one hand, the suggestion is that the mother is inevitably in the grip of unruly and often destructive unconscious and infantile impulses. On the other, psychoanalytic conceptions of mental well-being require of mothers the capacity for controlled, constructive, containing childcare. This has fed into what is popularly expected of mothers in a way that is particularly problematic.

In their book *Motherhood: Meanings, Practices and Ideologies*, Ann Phoenix, Anne Woollett and Eva Lloyd suggest that mother-hood has been professionalised in two senses.[22] Mothers are held 'professionally' responsible for the way their children turn out. Yet, at the same time, the ubiquity of childcare manuals demonstrates how motherhood has been claimed as an area of expertise by 'professionals'. Moreover, as discussed above, today's mother (and father too) is faced with a set of normative prescriptions about what she *should* do coupled with assertions that there are *no* hard and fast rules about mothering, and that child-rearing should be an individual, private affair.

This peculiarly contradictory view of mothers as in need of guid-ance, yet *naturally* capable of mothering if left to their own devices is reflected in and affirmed by object-relations theory – a branch of psychoanalysis that takes the early relation of mother and infant as a focus of study. Though related in many ways to the work of Melanie Klein, a school of British object-relations theory has arisen independently and has gained worldwide prominence. This school of psychoanalysis, in general terms, asserts that the infant's early environment and, above all, the quality of *maternal care* she or he received, are the primary influence on the developing self.

In the light of the mother's formative impact on the infant personality, the improvement of childcare practices became a subject of concern for psychoanalytic theorists. Denise Riley, in *War in the Nursery*, has pointed out that many of the analysts and psychologists who were most influential in Britain during the late 1930s, '40s and '50s were authors of their own popularisation, offering advice to parents in broadcasts on national radio programmes, in news-paper articles and in women's magazines.[23] Even Melanie Klein contributed to a popular book published in 1936 entitled *The Bringing up of Children*. Riley comments on the irony of this, given the usual (though perhaps inaccurate) evaluation of Kleinian psychoanalysis as indifferent to parental behaviour in the outer world.

Perhaps the most active analyst in disseminating guidance – also the most insistent that mother knows best – was D. W. Winnicott, who initially worked as a paediatrician. In his work we can see how psychoanalysis has the potential to illuminate the processes of maternal ambivalence yet labours under particular constraints. First, psychoanalysis invariably views the mother from the child's position, whether current, remembered or phantasised. Second, because object relations theory in particular offers a representation of the mother as terrifyingly omnipotent in her impact on the child, any contemplation of maternal ambivalence provokes not a recognition of the creative potential of the ambivalent state of mind for maternal development, but a profound need to reassure and dampen down anxiety about the very existence of ambivalence.

Before looking in detail at a paper of Winnicott's which specifically discussed maternal ambivalence, I want briefly to outline the salient points in his overall representation of the mother. According the mother specific power to shape the development of the individual, he wrote, 'If maternal care is not really good enough then the infant does not really come into existence.'[24] He spelled out his meaning in an address to midwives: 'The prevention of mental hospital disorder belongs initially to infant care and the things that come naturally to mothers who like having a baby to look after.'[25]

Perhaps it was his hands-on work as a London paediatrician that led Winnicott to criticise Melanie Klein's contemporaneous work on psychopathology for failing to give adequate weight to environmental factors as opposed to the intrapsychic processes of the infant. He attributed a central power for good to the mother, although, as psychotherapist Nina Farhi has emphasised, there is always a dialectic in Winnicott's account.[26] Farhi refers to Winnicott's insistence on 'the interpenetration of two subjectivities', meaning that even the mother's provision is to some extent fashioned by what the infant brings to the situation. Nevertheless, Winnicott's broad view was that, if the mother was good enough, the infant's potentiality to be integrated would be unimpaired. This suggests that a mother's failure to be good enough is more likely to lead, in Winnicott's terms, to failures of development in the baby.

Winnicott considered that the capacity to be good enough was often out of an individual mother's hands: 'Mothers who do not have it in them to provide good enough care cannot be made good enough by mere instruction ... There are those who can hold an infant and those who cannot.'[27] He believed that good mothering meant acting naturally and doing things that come naturally to a mother. In this he is a descendant of a long line of campaigners who attempted to improve standards of mothering through appeals to nature. Indeed, the eighteenth-century theorists of motherhood evoked nature in their call for greater attention and devotion from mothers. They argued that motherhood was a supremely natural state and that if only women would abandon the distorting trappings of civilisation, they would achieve a delightful and successful maternity. Martha Mears, an eighteenth-century midwife, advised women to follow nature and to 'resign yourself with confidence to this unerring guide; and if at any time you should forsake her, check the fatal impulse.'[28]

Similarly Winnicott believed women should attend to nature rather than intellect: 'Some mothers find it alarming to think that what they are doing is so important and in that case it is better not to tell them. It makes them self conscious and then they do everything less well. It is not possible to learn these matters.'[29] Quite apart from the fact that the vast number of different child-rearing practices historically and cross-culturally call into question the existence of 'natural' knowledge, an adherence to the natural obscures maternal ambivalence. The 'natural' is unnaturally associated with mother love not mother hate, so ambivalence will not be part of 'natural' mothering at all. For, as the psychoanalyst Karen Horney observed, seventeen years before Winnicott wrote 'Hate in the Countertransference', we prefer to assume that love is the given factor and that hostility is an accidental occurrence.[30]

Winnicott's mother is huge in her impact. She is responsible for the orchestration of a highly complex developmental sequence from an initial sustaining of the infant's healthy belief in her or his omnipotence to organising a graduated failure of adaptation to its demands. Yet we were told that her capacity to mother is inborn and outside her control. Winnicott once likened her to 'the power assisted steering on a motor bus'.[31]

A mother in control of so much, even in control of her own failures, yet out of control of her own capacity to take control, is a frightening image to contemplate. Perhaps Winnicott felt impelled to be reassuring, and this was why he coined terms like the good enough mother whose maternal devotion would be her saving grace:

I am trying to draw attention to the immense contribution to the individual and society which the ordinary devoted good mother with her husband in support makes at the beginning and which she does simply through being devoted to her infant.[32]

This comment comes from his popular book on child development, *The Child, the Family and the Outside World*. He reserved discussion of maternal hatred for a paper presented to the British Psychoanalytic Society in 1947 when he observed that 'The mother, however, hates her infant from the word go.'[33] Perhaps it was his keen consciousness of maternal hatred that led to his public emphasis on devotion and an undeserved reputation for sentimentality, although he himself deplored sentimentality as a defence against hatred. In the paper 'Hate in the Countertransference' he wrote:

The mother, however, hates her infant from the word go. I believe Freud thought it possible that a mother may in certain circumstances have only love for her baby boy; but we may doubt this. We know about a mother's love and we appreciate its reality and power. Let me give some of the reasons why a mother hates her baby, even a boy:[34]

And following on from the reassuring comment on the power and reality of mother love he provides an extraordinary list of eighteen reasons why mothers hate their babies. It combines imaginative insight with quite mundane observation. It suggests that mothers feel dominated, exploited, humiliated, drained and criticised by their babies. Winnicott's list combines inner- and outer-world events. For example, along with 'He excites her but frustrates – she mustn't eat him or trade in sex with him' is listed 'After an awful morning with him she goes out, and he smiles at a stranger, who says "Isn't he sweet".'[35]

However, the body of the paper does not concern the feelings of an actual mother. Rather, Winnicott's concern is with the centrality of hate in the feelings of an analyst working with psychotic patients:

However much he loves his patients he cannot avoid hating them and fearing them, and the better he knows this the less will hate and fear be the motives determining what he does to his patients.[36]

Winnicott discusses how the analyst's hate is ordinarily latent and easily kept so, but that in certain stages of certain analyses the analyst's hate is actually sought by the patient, and what is needed then is hate that is objective: 'If the patient seeks objective or justified hate he must be able to reach it, else he cannot feel he can reach objective love.'[37]

The genesis of psychosis is considered to lie in the very early mother–infant relationship, hence the significance of maternal hatred for this particular paper. Winnicott writes:

> Out of all the complexity of the problem of hate and its roots I want to rescue one thing, because I believe it has importance for the analyst of psychotic patients. I suggest the mother hates the baby before the baby can know his mother hates him.[38]

This is because, although the small baby experiences excited rage in relation to its mother, the word hate has as yet no meaning for it. As the baby, in Winnicott's terms, becomes able to feel itself to be a whole person, so does the word hate develop meaning as a description of a certain group of feelings. However, the baby needs to encounter hate if it is to make sense of its own hatred. And similarly the psychotic patient in analysis cannot be expected to tolerate his hate of the analyst unless the analyst can hate him. Winnicott offers his work with a nine-year-old as an example of how to meet hate-inducing behaviour constructively:

> Did I hit him? The answer is no, I never hit. But I should have done so if I had not known all about my hate and if I had not let him know about it too. At crises I would take him by bodily strength, without anger or blame, and put him outside the front door, whatever the weather or the time of day or night. There was a special bell he could ring, and he knew that if he rang it he would be readmitted and no word said about the past.[39]

Thanks to his own analysis, the analyst is able to tolerate hatred, to think about it and to use it without acting it out. Winnicott expresses amazement that mothers can tolerate hating their babies without retaliating. 'The most remarkable thing about a mother is her ability to be hurt so much by her baby and to hate so much without paying the child out, and her ability to wait for rewards that may or may not come at a later date.'[40] Slipping into the sentimentality he himself deplores, at this point Winnicott fails to acknowledge how many mothers do act out hatred in ways that range from the surreptitious shake to major abuse.

His description of the maternal response to hatred is determined and limited by his basic conception of maternity as unconscious and innate. His mother may either respond by failing altogether to become conscious of hatred and simply falling back on masochism, or she might sublimate her hatred in the singing of sadistic nursery rhymes 'which her baby enjoys but fortunately does not understand'.[41]

What Winnicott misses is the creative role of the mother's hatred in the development of maternal thinking, not restricted to its role in the infant's capacity to think. The singing of sadistic lullabies illustrates not only a way of safely containing hatred, but also how the unbearable co-existence of love and hate for the baby continually pushes a mother into the creative act of seeking reparatory solutions. In the depth of the night a baby's crying may prompt a mother to fantasise throwing him or her out of the window. The baby projects his or her hate into the mother, where it meets her own infantile hatred mobilised by adult frustrated needs and desires both to satisfy and be satisfied. At such times a mother's love may be overwhelmed by persecutory anxiety, promoting an impulse to attack the persecuting baby, and stymying the reparatory process. It is at this point that, instead of acting on the impulse, the majority of mothers try to help by singing, rocking, soothing or feeding. The painful conflict of love and hate itself provokes the desire to know and answer the baby's needs.

However, although the desire to answer the baby's needs may be motivated by the anguished co-existence of love and hate, distress is not so easily stilled. Feminists have criticised Winnicott for depicting a universe of mothers and babies where love and devotion win out.[42] Parveen Adams[43] has observed that Winnicott can 'produce a theory of what mothers should or shouldn't do in the name of adaptation and mental health, where Freud's theory marks the importance of desire, desire being that which can't be managed'.[44] She suggests that in the light of Freudian thinking the child's psychic health is not in the gift of the mother: 'The desire for the mother will ensure a perturbation that makes the "good enough" mother into a figure that beckons merely to ensnare the real mother.'[45]

As Freud pointed out, whatever a mother may do for her child, she is going to be experienced as denying and frustrating. For Freud is speaking of the mother of the unconscious. What makes a mother's response to her own experience of ambivalence charged and turbulent is that she is dealing with her own unconscious fantasy, not only her baby's. Just as the baby's experience of the mother is mediated by unconscious fantasy, so is the mother's experience of the child. It is on this terrain that mothers seek for creative solutions to the clashing passions of ambivalence.

The psychoanalyst Masud Khan amplified Winnicott's theory of the significance of maternal hatred from the point of view of infantile development in a paper written in 1969 entitled 'On Symbiotic Omnipotence';[46] its subtitle 'Phenomenology of Symbiotic Omnipotence in the Transference Relationship' indicates that the paper, like 'Hate in the Countertransference', was divided between clinical issues and developmental psychology. But, while Winnicott celebrated the maternal capacity to contain hatred, Masud Khan looked at the disastrous after-effects of maternal inability to acknowledge hatred.

He identified a group of patients whose pathology he attributed to their mothers' failure to own their hatred for their children. He writes of these mothers' 'failure to provide the right dosage of aggressive behaviour in the service of the infant-child's developmental and maturational processes'.[47] In brief, the outcome for these patients was an inability to separate. For without the necessary measure of hatred and aggression, 'differentiation, neutralization and structuration of the personality' are severely hampered.[48] In Masud Khan's view the experience of 'objective aggression, hate, separateness and concentration'[49] are needed for differentiation from the maternal matrix to be achieved.

If we turn Masud Khan's thesis around and view it instead from the point of view of the mother, many of the ideas can enrich our understanding of the potentially creative role for her of ambivalence. Just as the experience of hatred and aggression can be a force for separation and individuation for the child, so too does an awareness of her own aggression and hatred prompt a mother to take a distance from the child appropriate to its stage of development, affirming the mother's own boundaries and her separate needs. In making this turnaround I do not want to fall into the trap of making it sound too easy. (In Chapter 5 I discuss issues around ambivalence and separation in detail.) It could still be the case that an awareness of hatred can render a mother so fearful of her own aggression that she will anxiously close all gaps between herself and her child. Or, at the other extreme, she might avoid what she senses as a dangerous closeness.

Masud Khan commented that, despite the obvious importance of maternal hatred, little has been written about the mother's task 'as the provider of phase-adequate aggressive experiences'.[50] The language he himself employs indicates one explanation for the omission. He writes of hatred as 'one of the most important nutrients' to be provided in 'phase-adequate dosage'. To acknowledge the necessary role of hatred in the hands of a mother who is as powerful and influential as the mother depicted by object-relations psychoanalysis becomes problematic. Masud Khan uses comforting nutritional-medical terminology and, like Winnicott, offers a reassuring representation of ambivalence shorn of unruly unconscious dynamics. Similarly, when John Bowlby addresses the issue of parental ambivalence, he becomes overtly hesitant and apologetic. Describing parental emotion he observes that 'unfortunately, coupled with delicious loving feelings there comes all too often an admixture – I hesitate to say it – an admixture of resentment and even of hatred'.[51] Maternal ambivalence constitutes the unacceptable face of motherhood even for those who recognise at the same time its positive contribution to the psychological development of an infant.

A Complete Alien

I want to return now to mothers themselves, and to explore the unconscious processes that render the acknowledgement of ambivalence problematic, in particular projection, which can take a variety of forms. Projection provides a benign means of unconscious to unconscious communication between mother and child, fostered by their emotional closeness. But projection can take a more malign form in which unwanted contradictory parts of the self are expelled and projected into other people who are then allocated various roles in the person's internal drama. If a mother unconsciously projects repudiated aspects of herself into her child, she then perceives those repudiated aspects of herself in the child. It could be a weak part of herself to be protected, an aggressive or unruly part to be overtly controlled by discipline and maybe covertly admired. Indeed she may project any aspect of herself that feels intolerable and which she cannot bear dealing with.[52] Of course, the baby also projects its unwanted feelings of rage and confusion into its mother, but once again I want to concentrate on maternal psychology.

Projection on to the baby is established even while the baby is in the womb. But due to our culture's ambivalence towards ambivalence, women can usually only air their negative feelings towards their unborn child in a satirical vein (see Chapter 1). For example, Libby Purves, author of humorous accounts of motherhood, writes,

> A friend of that era (always try to have another first-time pregnant friend: she is the only one who will understand) once said, 'I think I've been hijacked'. That rang true for me, too. Here is this tiny terrorist inside you saying, 'You will go to the baby clinic! Lay off the booze! Leave that cigarette alone! Do your breathing exercises! Clench that pelvic floor!'[53]

Libby Purves ascribes her own punitive internal voices to the growing foetus. Certainly, as psychoanalysts Dinora Pines and Joan Raphael-Leff have pointed out, the mother's experience of the baby at birth is influenced by maternal pre-natal representations. For the mother to abandon the unconscious fantasies she must be able to take back her own projections and identifications with them – but this can be gradually and often only partially achieved.[54]

As I mentioned, projections are not always of problematic qualities. A mother may, for example, ascribe characteristics to the foetus which she enjoys or admires, and subsequently observe with satisfaction that the child manifests those qualities. Most of the time a mother is unaware that she possesses those very traits she admires in her child, until suddenly she glimpses something in a son or daughter she can potentially relate to herself. Miriam commented of her thirteen-year-old son:

> Sam is able to be honest, forthright and absolutely himself, in ways that I find it very difficult to be, and have really never been. He can be himself – irrespective – well, almost irrespective – of the impact on people around him.

Miriam is aware to some extent that Sam is manifesting the forth-right part of herself that rarely if ever sees the light of day. This does not make his honesty any less his own, of course. Her other children manifest their mother's more familiar circumspection and measured way of being in the world. There is a mysterious aspect to mothers' projections on to their children. Some children resist them and some seem to take them on wholesale, becoming almost a lookalike of some aspect of the mother's personality. Jane, an actress, says of herself, 'My feelings are very near the surface. That is where I exist and it is the way I work.' She describes her daughter as a quiet girl who has had a hard time standing up to her:

> I am bossy, domineering and rather overwhelming. She was completely unassertive, particularly at school, and beginning to suffer for it.
>
> I tried to talk to her about it and she would simply leave the room, with me screaming after her, 'Why don't you shout at me?' But things did start to change and I remember her answering back and saying, 'I can't talk to you you're always shouting.' It took a year or two but, finally, she became quite clear about how awful I was being, and she would tell me directly how impossible I was. But the painful thing was I couldn't stop being like that. I just went on shouting.
>
> And then this shocking thing happened. She was about ten years old at the time. She picked up a pudding and threw it at me. I was absolutely speechless – for an instant – I thought, 'How dare you.' And she just stood there and laughed. It was quite extraordinary. Then she said, 'You are always telling me to stand up for myself, and I am.'
>
> Since then she has been very confident with me, able to stand up to me and to just let it float off her. We get on incredibly well at the moment.

Jane's public performance is the other side of a private timidity, and she found it intolerable to observe her lack of self-confidence embodied in her daughter. Many daughters might have persisted in carrying their mother's unacknowledged introversion, but Sue, perhaps sensing her mother's fundamental resilience, quite literally hurled back the projection with the pudding.

Grace has four children, two boys by her first marriage and two by her second. She works as a nurse. Here she talks about traits in her older boys that she finds difficult to encounter:

With Laurie it's the silence, the closed door, the not saying anything. It enrages me. I remember when he was little, actually throwing him to the floor to somehow break through the hostile vibe. With Matt it's that he always wants more. If you offer him a five pound note, he'll eye your ten pound note.

Laurie's withholding silence is experienced by Grace as enormously depriving, while Matt's hunger for more seems to her to embody a sense of deprivation that reproaches her. She provides a possible clue to the projective processes at work between Laurie, Matt and herself when she says,

I always had enormous difficulty in letting someone else look after them. It played on all my fears of what would happen if I was not there.

Grace has an acute fear – both conscious and unconscious – that she will be depriving and in turn be deprived. Hence she felt that if she deprived the boys of her presence by having someone else look after them she would be deprived of them by a disaster occurring in her absence. Her sons manifest Grace's conflicts in relation to deprivation. Grace struggles with her impulse to punish them for it, just as she expects to be punished for depriving behaviour herself. Instead she berates herself. Scrutinizing her mothering, she finds it lacking:

I always felt guilty that I didn't spend *real* time with them – time when I really engaged with them. I've treated them as part and parcel of the package of my life. I've not been fully there for them – not giving enough of me.

Treating a child as part and parcel of life surely could hardly be more 'real'. Behind Grace's self-criticism lurks the maternal ideal and the insistence on mother-child 'oneness' with maternal desire subsumed in the child: Grace feels she has not given enough of herself. We can see how the maternal ideal magnified Grace's unconscious conflicts in relation to being depriving and being deprived. The moment when she threw Laurie to the floor signified not so much unbridled hatred as an attempt to rid herself of a source of profoundly persecuting guilt. Laurie's withholding silence made her feel deprived and convinced her she was being depriving.

The positive outcome of the awareness of the conflict between love and hate can be an increase in knowledge. Grace is now very open-eyed about her sons' ways of being in the world. She loves them deeply *and* feels fiercely critical of them. Grace says she has become clearer too about her own tendency easily to feel deprived. She describes how her conflicts in relation to feelings of deprivation were played out within her family:

> I felt very competitive with Ricky [her husband]. I felt he did it better than me, that he was more interesting to the boys and won their attention and love. Then I would feel competitive with the boys and feel that Ricky wasn't giving me enough attention. Conversely, if Ricky did nothing for the boys I'd get furious. He used to become enraged when I got badly into feeling deprived. And sometimes I do feel like a child shouting 'Me Me Me Me.'

In Chapter 6 I shall pursue the important point Grace makes that mothering can make a woman feel profoundly childish, but here I want to explore further the workings of projection between mother and child. Grace says of her sons, with affection and exasperation, 'They are both as bad as one another.'

Maeve, a librarian, with twin daughters aged ten, faces a very different but very common dynamic. Maeve's twin girls Cathy and Coral embody dramatically different aspects of their mother's personality. When her daughters were born, Maeve looked at Cathy and thought to herself, 'Here is a member of my family', but her daughter Coral appeared 'like a complete alien'.

> I had a very instinctive rapport with Cathy from the start. We've always been able to negotiate with each other and understand things from each other's point of view. Even if we have rows, which we do, and get very angry with each other, which we do, and she feels not supported by me, which she does, and I feel she's not seeing things properly, or that she's demanding too much, we have a row and then it is over. We get on to a different footing.
>
> I feel I can communicate with Cathy in a way that seems impossible with Coral. She and I very quickly get into a position of deep hostility. Sometimes I feel she needs me there in order to have what can feel a rather abusive relationship.

I feel abused by her. I always have done. As a baby if you changed her nappy before she had had her feed, she just got full of rage. Things had to be done in the order in which she wished them to be. She is a terrific critic. Sometimes she makes me feel a complete failure and that I'll never respond effectively to her needs. I know it is partly that she has a very powerful capacity to convince me that her needs ought to come first and that they are simply not being met.

Maeve told me that her daughter Cathy reflects many of the characteristics she strives for in herself. She describes the girl as thoughtful, serious, responsible and generous. She has a tendency to become depressed, which Maeve understands and responds to sympathetically. Coral, however, reminds her of her own mother. She sees born again her own mother's intolerance as she remembers it. She commented that her mother hated her (Maeve's) tendency to question everything and her refusal to accept her mother's point of view. She sees herself repeating the same dynamic with Coral:

It's very complicated. I feel I repeat my mother's behaviour towards me with Coral and that she replicates my behaviour as a daughter. Yet I also think that she appears like my mother to me.

Maeve describes Coral as imperious and thoughtless – aspects of herself that she passionately does not want to acknowledge. It is as if a hateful bundle of repudiated qualities is being handed down the generations – discarded into daughters. Maeve describes the punitive fantasy her daughter's behaviour evokes in her. The fantasy employs the same denial and deprivation she found intolerable in her mother – and finds insupportable in her daughter.

Sometimes I fantasise locking her up in a bare room – taking everything away, just removing everything from her grasp, and leaving her in this empty room. And then, if she behaves in a sort of all right way, then she can have one thing, and if all goes well another thing, and then a few more things back.

She contrasted this fantasy, which embodied both how she had felt treated as a child by her mother, and her response to her own child whom she experiences as robbing and draining her, with her reaction to becoming angry with her other daughter:

I would make sure she was safe in her cot or playpen when she was a little girl, and then leave the room until I had calmed down and could cope.

She protected Cathy from herself, but felt she had to protect herself from Coral. She locates everything in herself of vulnerable value in Cathy and everything relating to unacceptable rage and rapaciousness in Coral.

Maeve is painfully conscious of the predicament she is in with Coral. She recognises that she and Coral share a capacity for rage. 'I think she's frightened of my anger, and she's frightened of her own anger, and they get compounded.' Despite her insight, Maeve has a sense of being drawn helplessly into conflict against her better judgement:

> You become this monstrously hateful figure. You find yourself becoming the person you feared you would become; angry, rigid, reproachful. There seems to be no way out. A simple inquiry like, 'Did you have problems finding the street where your Aunty lives?' is received by Coral as a criticism – and she immediately fights back.
>
> Then there is the amazement of realising that you are dealing with someone who is only ten, yet so well defended. You think, what on earth are they defending themselves against? And it seems to be you. It is very alarming.

In fairy tales help for the hated daughter comes in the form of magical external intervention. But, like psychoanalysis, fairy tales focus on the daughter's well-being and development, and not on the (wicked step-)mother's. Both Maeve and Coral in their different ways long for a transformation in the relationship. They do in fact achieve moments which manifest the affection that co-exists with animosity between them. They share a love of dressmaking which promises for them some of the moments of mutuality I described in Chapter 2 – moments which affirm the aspect of love in ambivalence but which can also highlight the distress of hatred:

> One of the things we do together is dressmaking – although rarely in the same room. I start off by showing her how to do it, but as soon as she can do anything by herself she goes off and does it on her own.

Maeve describes here the way ambivalence can act as a positive, though not problem-free, spur towards independence for both mother and daughter. She feels genuinely ambivalent towards her daughter leaving her with what she has just learned from her mother. There is resentment in Maeve's tone, but also a pride at Coral's stubborn independence. I suspect that had not Maeve been so open-eyed about the dynamic between her and her daughter, the two might have been too fearful of their destructive feelings towards one another to allow any space to exist between them. It could have glued them together rather than opening up a creative distance. Another key reason why conflict has its productive aspect for them is that both are aware of a reliable level of affection:

> I know there is a terrific vulnerability in her. To listen to her she simply does not need me. In fact, I am the person she can most do without, and her life would be a whole lot easier if I was not around. Sometimes I do get demoralised and begin to believe it. Then something happens which demonstrates that she actually needs me to be there very much.

An important outcome of Maeve and Coral's relationship is that each has faced and survived her own and the other's capacity for rage. Maeve considers that her feelings for Coral have forced her to face what she terms her 'extremism' while, compared to the 'good' sister Cathy, Coral is significantly less fearful:

> When Cathy was learning to read, she would never read any- thing with a giant or witch in it. She couldn't, for example, even open a book with Little Red Riding Hood in it. I bought her a lovely version of *The Water Babies* but she found it too scary, and so I gave it to Coral. She loves it. She can go to the most terrifying films without turning a hair. Wicked witches hold no horror for her – they never have.

Maeve has split off aspects of herself she least likes – her aggression, criticalness, her hunger – into her daughter, who has *used* hate to develop familiarity with the feelings grouped under the heading 'hatred'. She has become something of a fighter, resilient and resourceful. The witch holds less fear for her than it does for Cathy – the bearer of maternal goodness.

Undoubtedly the dynamics within the family will change over time, facilitated by the girls' development and their evolving feeling for both parents. I have excluded the father from this account to focus on the mutual projections between mother and daughter, but he of course plays an important role in the day-to-day dynamics between them – often enlisted as an ally by his daughter Coral.

For Grace and Maeve, motherhood and an acknowledgement of ambivalence forced them to become familiar with aspects of themselves they were loath to know existed. Maeve reached the point of realising that, in her relationship with her daughter, she was re-experiencing aspects of her relationship with her own mother. Mothering is a multi-generational process. Maeve recognised traits of her mother's she found difficult to acknowledge in herself, in her daughter. She then reacted as if she were her daughter's daughter, while observing with distress that she was behaving like her mother. Through the mechanisms of mutual projection, she experienced her mother's problematic traits in both herself and her daughter. However, in the depressive position (see Chapter 1) the other is loved in spite of 'bad' parts. As we have seen with Coral, this can give a child a sense of security, and give a mother greater belief in her capacity to love. In Margot Waddell's words, 'Emotional honesty is an essential commodity for the growth of the child even though it can involve recognition by parents of aspects of themselves they might rather *dis*own'.[55]

The Mother's Mother

Maeve illustrated the familiar sense in which women feel they are either repeating or repudiating their own mother's treatment of themselves in their mothering. Yet the mothers they invoke, the mother who haunts them and often reproaches them for their ambivalent feelings towards their children, has a complex relationship to their own flesh and blood mother.

Anna Freud pointed out that even the most devoted mother will be felt to be rejecting at times by her child because its demands are limitless, because life outside the womb is unavoidably frustrating. And in its anger a child will in the mind transform the mother into a wicked, harmful witch. Anna Freud cautions that 'We must guard against the error of confusing the inevitably frustrating aspects of extra-uterine life with the rejecting actions or attitudes of the individual mothers'.[56] In other words, a woman's image of her mother is determined by her experience of being a child – an experience powerfully evoked by the presence of her own son or daughter – and she all too easily sees herself as the denying, disappointing, frustrating mother of her own infancy.

Jung, in arguing that our experienced image of our mother must necessarily involve a metaphorical dimension, wrote that

> a sensitive person cannot in all fairness load that enormous burden of meaning, responsibility, duty, heaven and hell, on to the shoulders of one frail and fallible human being – so deserving of our love, indulgence, understanding, and forgiveness – who was our mother. He knows that the mother carries for us that inborn image of the *mater natural* and *mater spiritualis*, of the totality of life of which we are a small and helpless part.[57]

Jungian analyst Andrew Samuels has elaborated the intricate relationship between the metaphorical and the literal levels in depth psychology. In his terms, the literal and metaphorical realms do not like each other very much, though they cannot shrug each other off:

> Metaphor asserts that there is no original literalism at all, that the notion of a flesh and blood parent, and even the idea that there are direct personal experiences, are themselves metaphors. Literalism seeks to say that the original raw material for the metaphor remains imprisoned within the metaphor, and will continue to shine through the layers of metaphorical elaboration, thoroughly infecting the metaphor.[58]

If we seek to explain the anguish attached to ambivalence simply in terms of our distress at repeating what our actual mother actually did or didn't do to us, we simplify and flatten an intricate situation. Yet what Andrew Samuels terms the raw material of the metaphor – in this instance, the flesh and blood mother of our experience – is undeniably important. For example, research suggests that a woman whose mother has died before she was eleven years old, that is before she was able to establish a post-pubertal identification with the mother, is liable to feel a sense of sadness and loss when she relives her own infancy in that of her child,[59] while the social reality of having no mother to call on in times of need is exacerbated if she lacks a good mother in her internal reality as well. Joan Raphael-Leff gives her view of the potential outcome for a woman lacking a positive representation of mothering in her inner world:

> If she carries around an internal image of a hated, denigrated mother, she cannot identify with her, and mothering becomes a competitive experience of rivalry and one-up-womanship. If she had defensively glorified her internal experience of her neglectful mother, she herself will become over anxious, and non-ideal by comparison.[60]

Dinora Pines, who has written extensively on the subject, described how pregnancy may reactivate a woman's intensely ambivalent feelings towards her own mother.[61] On the one hand, pregnancy fosters an identification with a powerful, generous, nourishing maternal figure. On the other, pregnancy can constellate a terrifying sense of unity with her opposite image of her mother – the witch-like, murderous mother. Joan Raphael Leff, however, cites a study of pregnancy which found a 'pattern of reconciliation with the mother in all but extremely ambivalent women'.[62] From being seen as benevolently omnipotent or malevolently responsible for all ills, she may now allow her mother to seem simply human – fallible, a woman like herself.

This feels perhaps over-optimistic, given the complexity of the representation of the mother in the unconscious. For example, as Freud commented, 'under the influence of a woman's becoming a mother herself, an identification with her own mother may be revived, against which she has striven'.[63] In other words, a woman can feel herself drawn *back* into an identification with a being from whom she may have long struggled to separate – with all the contradictory feelings that inevitably entails. Everything in her may react against feeling once again the little girl who wanted to be like Mummy. Long-buried fears, desire and resentment in relation to competing with her mother may be reactivated by her own motherhood. Her sense of identity and autonomy may have developed in determined opposition to the person with whom she now feels drawn inexorably into identification. She may have hoped that becoming a mother herself would free her from the bonds of being a daughter – only to feel fresh ties to her mother. In sum, the complex intrapsychic and interpersonal relationship between a woman and her mother when she herself becomes a mother undoubtedly carries the potential for reconciling transformation, but I suspect that reconciliation often remains in the realm of the ideal rather than becoming a reality.

While acknowledging the impact of her own mothering on a mother, I do not believe it determines in any straightforward way the nature of her mothering. The notion that the recipient of real and recognisable bad mothering will inevitably repeat the pattern with her own children is, in my view, a punitive and pessimistic understanding of mothering.[64] Yes, her feelings towards her mother and towards her infant-self will inflect a woman's mothering, but not in any predictive fashion. A whole clutch of circumstances in fact combine to affect a woman's response to mothering, ranging from her unconscious processes, her physical health, her economic, social and family situation, the availability of emotional support and, of course, the specific psychological contributions of her own children. We may, for example, speculate as to what it was about Coral in her own right that led her to be the recipient of Maeve's negative feelings towards her own mother.

To provide a sense of the unpredictable and diverse responses to remembered mothering, I shall compare the experience of a woman, Frances, with good and loving memories of her mother to two women, Sylvia and Naomi, whose memories are of angry, critical, ungiving mothers.

Sylvia described her mother as constantly cross, oblivious of her children's needs and ceaselessly agitated. Sylvia felt that her mother gloried in her children's misfortunes and envied them their advantages. She herself now has four children. She describes her response to the birth of her oldest daughter, Sarah:

> I could have coped with a doll. I was good at all the changing, feeding and bathing. What I couldn't cope with was the emotional side. That Sarah was a person – that frightened me – that was horrible. I was frightened she would be horrible to me. And I think I was frightened I would be horrible to her. When she looked at me I felt constantly challenged. She was so clever and quick, and like Mummy, she went on and on. And just as I wanted to scream at Mummy to stop, so I wanted to put a pillow over Sarah's head.

Just as Maeve saw her critical mother in her daughter, so did Sylvia. But, whereas Maeve engaged in battle with her daughter, Sylvia responded by becoming a tirelessly loving mother. But to a large extent the care she bestowed on her children was a false reparation, and they sensed it. As she puts it, 'I think I reacted rather than acted, and when I did act it was more in the spirit of performance.' Sarah, her daughter, raged and rebelled – and finally forced her mother to own the reality of her ambivalence and anger towards both her mother and her daughter. Sylvia comments that now, 'since I've been able to acknowledge the range of my feelings for Sarah, I feel I've stopped performing the loving mother and I've stopped reacting to her with hurt and rage'.

Unlike Maeve and Sylvia, Frances remembered her mother as warm, loving, always present and able to provide not only love but also camaraderie for her daughter. She looked forward to reproducing the relationship with her own children. She now has a son, Ian aged nine, and a daughter, Ann aged eleven. She loved her children but was utterly unprepared for the ambivalence that assailed her when they were babies. In her words it made her feel useless, unlovable and unloved. She was swamped by guilt, which fostered hatred for the baby, which in turn magnified the guilt.

Looking back, she says, 'I suppose what I wanted from my children was my mother.' At an unconscious level she wanted to be 'fed' by her children, but instead found herself more often than not deprived and depleted.

Melanie Klein wrote that the first object to be envied by the baby is the feeding breast. The baby 'hates and envies what he feels to be the mean and grudging breast' but equally 'the very ease with which the milk comes – though the infant feels gratified by it – also gives rise to envy because this gift seems something so unattainable'.[65] We can adapt Klein's understanding of infantile envy and view it from the mother's perspective. At an unconscious level Frances experiences her baby as easily capable of providing, but choosing to withhold from her, her feeling of motherly bliss and plenitude and she becomes filled with a destructive envy specific to maternity. Maternal psychology does have infantile components but there is also something else. Frances felt deprived of her own identity, of time and space for herself, and robbed of the sense that she was good enough to be entirely loved.

As with Maeve, the experience was different with each baby. Ian, a baby who cried a great deal, provoked far more painful feelings in Frances than Ann, who was relatively placid. And over the years her ambivalence has become manageable:

I enjoy their company now. I like talking to them and listening to their stories. I still get feelings of hatred and anger towards them, but there's a difference between being angry in a parental way, and being enraged, panic stricken and at the end of one's tether. I know it could get difficult for me again. I can see that if I get really worried about one of them to the point that it interferes with my needs, it can set up the cycle of guilt and explosion again.

Frances's experience of unmanageable ambivalence when her children were babies has given her a greater awareness of her needs and limitations as a mother. Her envy of her babies and her persecutory anxiety during their infancy were undoubtedly coloured by an idealisation of her mother who had died some years before she gave birth to Ian. Although Naomi also experienced her children as persecuting and depriving, unlike Frances, she remembers a mother who was punitive and profoundly critical. She describes her response to pregnancy:

I was really prepared for the worst when I decided to get pregnant. I dreaded damaging the child. I worried that I would be like my mother – become her, in a way. But to my surprise I got immensely excited during pregnancy, I had this tremendous sense of potential. And when Jonathan was born I found I had something to offer. It seemed magical to me that I had milk the baby could make use of. I could satisfy the baby. It was such a pleasure.

Precisely because Naomi found satisfying her baby so affirming and gratifying, she experienced his discomfort and neediness as quite intolerable. She feels the demands of her now older children entirely outstrip her capacity to answer them:

I can't bear the endless demands, the sense of there being nothing good enough, the impression of a bottomless pit. I feel that I am going to be devoured; that there will be absolutely nothing left of me. Jonathan is now eight and Leah is six. I scream and shout at them in what seems like an awful confirmation of actually being like my mother. At times I feel she is encapsulated around me – that I am actually enveloped by her. She'd throw things and scream and shout. And now I do.

The testimonies of Maeve, Sylvia, Frances and Naomi all demonstrate that it is basically impossible to predict precisely how a woman's experience of being mothered will influence her way of being a mother. Sylvia did not mirror her mother's way of being but rather continued with her daughter the placatory, measured defensive behaviour she had adopted with her mother. Maeve, on the other hand, found herself as a mother enacting what she considered her mother's critical, aggressive way of being – but with just one of her twin daughters. Frances, who enjoys memories of having received good mothering, experienced her hostile response to her babies' needs as a betrayal of her remembered mother's goodness, while Naomi enjoyed contradicting the maternal behaviour she had experienced when it came to her own babies, only to find herself drawn into repeating it when her children manifested discontent and dissatisfaction.

Where these women's experiences flow together is in their shared belief that their mothers had a formative influence on their style of mothering. Thus images of their own mothers dominated their experience of mothering as a reproving presence or cautionary tale – making them feel they were either reproducing the mother they hated or letting down the mother they loved. Above all their 'mother' – meaning the mother inside each – admonishes them for their ambivalence.

Just Like Your Father

Focusing on the impact of a mother's relationship with her own mother tends to obscure the extent to which other factors determine a woman's relationship with her children – for example her feelings for her brothers and sisters. Melanie Klein writes that

> Certain difficulties in these past relationships may easily interfere with her feelings for her own child, especially if it develops reactions and traits which tend to stir these difficulties in her. Her jealousy and rivalry towards her brothers and sisters gave rise to death wishes and aggressive fantasies in which in her mind she injured or destroyed them.[66]

Frances, on the other hand, feels the difficulties she experienced with mothering have been provoked precisely because she had no siblings:

Being an only child, I had less occasion to compete for my mother's attention. Juggling competing demands, putting my own on hold and so on, is something I have had to struggle to learn. Hence my resentment of a baby whose demands impinged so dramatically.

By contrast, Sylvia who experienced her daughter at birth as replicating her nagging mother, had an older brother who bullied her. She responded by becoming his little slave, and to *both* mother and brother showed a willing, placatory face, while nurturing a secret defensive sense of contempt for them. Her response to her angry baby was to repeat behaviour that originated in her relationship with her mother and brother. Another interviewee, Kitty who has two daughters, similarly remembers herself as docile and submissive, yet secretly resentful in her relationship with a dominating older sister:

> I can always control my anger and irritation in relation to Laura, the little one. I think it is because she is like me in the family position. While my hostility towards Melanie when I get angry seems totally outside my control. I know it has to do with my older sister and how I hated her bossiness, her grasping ways and her determination to control me. I recognise what is going on with Melanie but I can't stop it.

Of course, the manner in which a child evokes past sibling dynamics need by no means be malign. Margaret, for example, perceives aspects of a loved brother in her son Jim:

> My brother was my dearest and closest friend until I was ten years old. I see his best traits flowering in Jim – his kindness and his concern for others. But I think my brother was stunted by my father who was a difficult and powerful man, and particularly hard on my brother.

Even while celebrating aspects of her brother in Jim, Margaret finds herself incarnating the impatient, ambitious father in relation to her easygoing son:

> The conflicts we have are when I find he is too offhand. He doesn't work hard enough sometimes. He doesn't make an effort and he doesn't have high enough standards. These things just drive me round the bend.

Just as a child can evoke past sibling relationships, so a mother can consciously perceive herself as a child in her offspring. We have looked at the mechanism of unconscious projection of repudiated aspects of the self into a child – but more often than not a mother is acutely conscious of a child's mirroring of herself. And if her level of self-hatred is intense, she often dislikes what she sees. Claire, an infant teacher on maternity leave, says of her oldest child:

> There are ways in which she is too like me. She is a bit of a ninny. She is physically not at all daring and not a bit adventurous. She'll cling to me and be a mother's-girl type of child in ways that I was. It annoys me. I want to peel her off and send her out there to be assertive. At the same time I entirely sympathise. I wanted to huddle to my mother's skirts. Yet I find it quite hard to deal with, I mean the child is under your feet all day.

One further crucial factor in relation to the dynamics of maternal ambivalence is the mother's response when a child reminds her of its father. Sometimes, a child's resemblance to a loved partner is straightforwardly gratifying. Other times, traits desired in a partner are troublesome in a child. I spoke to Sandra, who married a man who manifests the ambition, aggression and desire to control she feels unable to express herself. When her son began to manifest the full repertoire of a typical two-year-old's grandiosity and defiance, Sandra reacted violently. While she can accept her husband's domination, the child who was once part of herself is not permitted to be controlling. Moreover, her social position as a mother allows, even forces, the denied desire to dominate to emerge in her. A complex dynamic has evolved in which she struggles both with her son's assertiveness as her own – and with her own. Reflecting on the battles that wage between herself and her son she observes, 'I had no idea I was capable of such ferocity.'

Melanie Klein wrote that, 'At bottom our strongest hatred, however, is directed against the hatred within ourselves.'[67] I think this is particularly true of mothers, for the object of their hatred is so deeply loved. Klein continues: 'We so much dread hatred in ourselves that we are driven to employ one of our strongest measures of defence by putting it on to other people – to project it.'[68] Hence perhaps the moments when mothers perceive their children as their malevolent opponents:

I felt the baby hated me. He would bite me, but not with a twinkle in his eye. He would be breastfeeding and he'd just bite me.

4

Beyond Endurance

I support pacifism. I'm opposed to all forms of violence and yet I know there's violence in me. My children have shown me that I am capable of it. Yesterday I slapped Sam. He had promised to take Sally to her piano lesson and there he was still in bed. I poured a cup of cold tea over him and I slapped him. I do feel really terrible about it.

Kathleen, idealistic, hard-working with a strong sense of personal responsibility, lives with three children who all, in different ways, express her denied disorder. She wept when she described how her son's behaviour had goaded her beyond endurance into the violence she abhors. In order to gain an understanding of the dynamics of hatred in maternal ambivalence, I have explored the mechanics of projection. I want now to turn to look at those moments when irritation is acted upon – when hatred erupts as violence.

First, I think it is necessary to distinguish between hatred and aggression. In her book on motherhood Ann Dally groups distaste, anger, jealousy, envy, hate and malice under the heading of hostility.[1] She describes distaste as relating to aspects of a child's being and behaviour: 'Thus a mother may find distasteful such things as her baby's crying or his dirty napkins, her toddler eating wood-lice in the garden, her older child's table manners or behaviour, or her adolescent's appearance, unwashed smell or choice of friends.'[2] Anger she defines as a short-lived response to the child provoked by frustration and anxiety, whereas hate is more enduring. It is a composite emotion which is by no means always – and sometimes never – conscious, while malice is an active wish to injure or destroy. Of malice she writes,

Mothers are not infrequently distressed by sudden desires to injure or torture their babies, and they are not necessarily bad or unsuccessful mothers. Other mothers have similar thoughts but are unable to acknowledge them as their own. The hostile ideas seem to come out of the blue and from elsewhere. Such mothers usually feel a great need to reassure others that they love their babies, that such thoughts are 'utterly alien' to them and so on.[3]

Malice is frequently repressed, denied or displaced or reversed, manifesting as excessive solicitude. But Dally concludes that all forms of hostility may be converted into active forms of hostility. Some people convert their feelings into action easily, 'because that was the way in which their own parents behaved'.[4]

Although both are felt in the body, violence is a physical experience as well as a state of mind. It implies action and short-circuits reflection. The conversion of hostility into violent acts is clearly not the prerogative of those who experienced aggression at the hands of their parents. For example, Kathleen, with whom the chapter opened, was never physically punished by her parents. I want to look at the process which prompted another interviewee, Frances, to act out physically her aggression towards her son. Frances, readers may remember, maintains loving and positive memories of her mother. A personnel manager who gave up her job when her oldest child was born, she describes what happened when her son was a baby:

> I feel as if no one has been as bad a mother as I was on occasions. I remember a time with Ian when I was on my own at home with him. He was very little and had just started to eat solid food. It had been a bad day. By that I mean he had not had his morning nap, and I desperately needed him to sleep. I was starving for some time for myself. It was terribly important to me that he slept, and he just would not drop off. I remember producing baby food that I had made myself, and just as he wouldn't sleep, neither would he eat.
>
> I remember taking the spoon and literally forcing him to eat – forcing the food into his mouth. I didn't beat him, I just made him eat. I couldn't bear it – it was all too much. I was tormented with guilt – but just desperate to have some time to myself. It produced a blind rage in me. The more guilty I felt

in relation to Ian, the more I wanted space for myself, and became unable to bear the demands of this baby.

The intense intimacy of a mother and baby – the unconscious to unconscious communication that is constellated between them – can bring her own baby-self to the forefront of a woman's being. Her own infantile neediness merges with needs as a mother, intensifying the feeling of not being met. There is more going on than a search for mothering that is to be met by the baby. There is also a search for the satisfaction that accrues to mothering itself. Frances is reduced to feeling a bad mother as well as a frustrated child. To feel unlovable was torment to Frances. As Melanie Klein writes:

> The reason why some people have so strong a need for general praise and approval lies in their need for evidence that they are lovable, worthy of love. This feeling arises from the unconscious fear of being incapable of loving others sufficiently or truly, and particularly of not being able to master aggressive impulses towards others; they dread being a danger to the loved one.[5]

Frances's suffering was a combination of guilt, anxiety and enormous frustration. She wanted to be able to experience herself as a loving mother producing good food for a flourishing baby. Instead she was gripped by guilt, fear, anxiety and, crucially, frustration. The child would neither eat nor sleep. Both Winnicott and Fairbairn postulate that the hate arises from excessively frustrated need – in Frances's case, the need to feel an adequate mother. Maternal frustration led to the hatred that impelled Frances to force food into the baby's mouth.

She experienced the baby as judging her. As Klein put it, one's projection of a grievance rouses in other people a counter-feeling of hostility: 'Few of us have the tolerance to put up with the accusation, even if it is not expressed in words, that we are the guilty party.'[6] A child's cry easily sounds like a reproach to a mother. For example, in D. H. Lawrence's *Sons and Lovers*, Mrs Morel acknowledging that due to her relationship with her husband, she had not wanted her son Paul, looks down at her baby and feels fear:

> Did it know all about her? When it lay under her heart, had it been listening then? Was there a reproach in the look? She felt the marrow melt in her bones, with fear and pain.[7]

Aware of her ambivalence, she resolves to compensate for hatred with passionate love.

For Frances the sense that the baby was reproaching her combined with the dominant image of the ideal mother she received from the culture, to punitive effect. As she said,

> A mother is a provider. I felt mothers were supposed to satisfy, soothe and make children happy, contented and fat. I had a baby who refused food and who cried and cried. It tormented me beyond endurance. It was intolerable to feel useless, unlovable and unloved.

As I mentioned in Chapter 1, Joan Raphael-Leff has coined the term 'primary maternal persecution'[8] for the state of mind Frances describes – a corrective allusion to Winnicott's primary maternal preoccupation, which constitutes a kind of benign madness in contrast to the malign madness of primary maternal persecution. Frances retreated from the depressive position, adopting what Klein termed a paranoid defence against excessive guilt. The baby became a persecutor in Frances's eyes, with herself as the helpless victim. She experienced herself as 'done unto'. Her sense of persecutory anxiety swamped her capacity to think about the situation. She lived only for the moment and the brief gratification of revenge. The ability to anticipate the outcome of her action – the baby's increased distress – entirely deserted her.

The Safety Catch

Many texts on motherhood focus primarily on what constitutes good mothering and what makes for bad mothering. Briefly, the two extremes are presented as follows. The good mother has experienced a mother able to live with a baby's aggression, rendering states of rage bearable for the baby. She, in her turn, is capable of containing both her own aggression and her baby's destructive impulses. She can transcend her own response to deprivation and frustration, thus enabling her child to tolerate its own rage by taking the anger into herself, making sense of it for the child, and demonstrating to the child that she survives attack and continues to be loving in the face of all manner of aggressive behaviour.

The bad mother, on the other hand, responds to her child as her own bad parents did to her. Instead of containing her baby's aggression, she retaliates. She identifies the baby with the bad-baby part of herself that her parents could not tolerate. Punishing her baby to make it behave is also an attack on the unacceptable baby she feels inside herself, and expresses the full force of long-suppressed infantile rage she may or may not have dared unleash against her parents.

There is, however, a spectrum of maternal feeling from thoughtful containment to retaliatory abuse; a spectrum from pulling up a zip roughly to outright acts of violence. It is perhaps reassuring to think in neatly bifurcated terms of those mothers who contain and those mothers who retaliate, but small moments of aggression will well up and pepper even the most caring of mothers. Although Frances felt no one had ever been such a bad mother as she, she did not systematically abuse Ian. On that one occasion she forced food into his mouth. Most mothers can remorsefully recall a moment when they 'lost control' or 'reached the end of their tether'. A patient of mine described the state of mind that keeps exasperation from flaring into outright violence as 'a safety catch'. Winnicott wondered why more women do not pay out their children for the way they treat their parents. I am suggesting most mothers *do* indulge in small acts of revenge. The question is, what keeps these acts in check? I want to look at the nature of the safety catch – the restraining force on maternal hate that enables mothers to maintain ambivalence rather than losing sight of the fact that the baby they hate is also the baby they love, and becoming violent.

Naomi, a self-confessed 'anger merchant', compares the times when the safety catch holds to the times when it, so to speak, slips – or almost slips:

> Sometimes I can step back and see things from the children's point of view and understand how it feels to reach a point where nothing satisfies. If I can unhook from feeling the source of their frustration, I can feel saddened rather than maddened. At those moments I can respond with 'I haven't got what you need' (nice and gentle) rather than 'I haven't got what you need' (through clenched teeth).

Like Frances's, Naomi's feelings of hatred for her children are generated by a sense of the child's insatiability, swamping her own needs. And like Frances, a primary need is to experience herself as good mother, capable of responding constructively to her children's needs. When nothing seems to satisfy the children, a sense of deprivation grips her along with intense frustration that she feels helpless to help. Importantly, she distinguishes the two states of mind that come into being at such moments – the 'I haven't got what you need' (nice and gentle) and 'I haven't got what you need' (through clenched teeth).

Naomi compares feeling a bad mother to feeling that her children are bad. The difference between moments of maternal remorse and maternal indignation can be understood in terms of Melanie Klein's description of persecutory and depressive anxiety.

Maternal persecutory anxiety involves a mother's phantasised experience of herself as punished and tormented by her infant – no matter the difference in power between them, no matter that it may mostly be due to projections. She can literally feel annihilated, devoured and decimated by a child's apparently wilful determination to humiliate her and to frustrate her needs. She struggles not to attack her persecutor.

Maternal depressive anxiety, on the other hand, relates to a mother's usually unrealistic worry that she will have damaged the baby by her destructive impulses towards her or him. This is the meaning behind Naomi's saddened observation, 'I haven't got what you want (nice and gentle)'. However, following Klein, I want to say that these two kinds of maternal anxiety are intricately related and can alternate. We could regard Naomi's desire to hit out at the children as a reaction to maternal persecutory anxiety (getting rid of the child who hurts her) or as the very cause of maternal depressive anxiety (what will happen if I let go?). While 'I haven't got what you want (nice and gentle)', rather than indicating a profound desire to make it all right for the children, could simply be placatory – a maternal false self. Commenting on the alternation of depressive and persecutory anxiety, Klein writes that 'the desire to repair and revive a loved object may turn into the need to pacify and propitiate a persecutor'.[9] In mothers of small children the two states of mind or positions rarely exist in a pure culture.

Perhaps the safety catch on anxiety is constituted by the capacity to *feel for* the child rather than *feeling one* with the child. This is Naomi's view and it is an important distinction. Feeling for the child comes about when the desire to understand the child is produced by the pain, conflict and confusion of the co-existence of love and hate. Feeling one with the child constitutes an identification with the child's aggression – as identification with the child's projection. It involves a loss of a sense of separateness, a loss of relatedness altogether.

Grace contrasts her behaviour towards two of her sons. She never hit Matt but she did smack Laurie:

> I used to get much angrier with Laurie than with Matt. He wouldn't allow me to get angry. He would stand there and say, 'Don't hit me, don't hit me'. When he said that it made me aware that I didn't want to hurt inside, and I didn't want it to happen to him either.

Matt asserted his separateness from his mother – he refused to be treated as an extension of herself to be done with as she wished. His action maintained him as whole object in his mother's eyes – a loved and hated other whom she could feel for. Love outweighed the hate: in other words, Matt's behaviour managed to maintain mutuality between mother and child, circumventing the dynamics that lead to smacking.

Once a child reaches adolescence, mothers often feel that if only *they* could receive recognition of their separate subjectivity from their children, the conflagrations could be avoided. Felicity describes an incident with her daughter Emily when she felt her daughter's *recognition* of her feelings prevented the familiar descent into mutual paranoia:

> I expected Emily to be home by eight. She said she'd be in by eight. At ten when she wasn't home I went over to the funfair and there she was sauntering out of the gates. I lost my temper and started shouting at her. She told me to stop. So I explained to her that I was shouting because I was so anxious – the funfair is a dangerous place to be in the evening. To my amazement, instead of the usual stand-up fight, she apologised. I think she saw that my anger and anxiety belonged to me and wasn't an attack on her which she had to fight off. It made me realise that she had stood back, and that I ought to stand back. But it's difficult when it's your thirteen-year-old daughter.

Helen, whose eighteen-year-old son lives at home, finds his attitude towards their shared life intolerable; she says he contributes nothing in terms of help around the house, he is uncommunicative, untidy and erratic. Again she feels that some gesture from him towards a relationship with her would keep her ambivalence manageable:

> I do feel an enormous fondness for him and I know what he is having to go through at the moment – that he needs to separate from me. It would demand so little from him to keep my irritation within bounds – even agreeing to have a meal once a day at the same time as me.

As we have seen, ambivalence acknowledged can promote reflection and communication. In Grace's case she was able to work through the mutual intense ambivalence that had rendered relations between her older son and herself so persecuting:

> Laurie came to see me. We had two days of misery and agony, but we sorted it out, and finally had a really lovely time together. He thinks I'm horrible, judgmental and dissatisfied with him – which I am. But I also think he's wonderful, and I don't feel him to be as bad as he thinks I do. The fact that we could speak it was an amazing thing.

During her child's adolescence a mother has to contend with the distress of seeing that child adopt a way of being in the world which is often diametrically opposed to her own. This aspect of the adolescent separation process can goad a mother not into violent behaviour but into vicious dislike, if, up to this time, she has experienced her child as a source of narcissistic gratification. Betty, a mother who has struggled ceaselessly to, in her words, 'improve herself', says of her sixteen-year-old daughter,

> She used to be a little lady. There's really no other word for it. But yesterday I saw her standing at the bus stop and she looked as hard as nails. She's become someone I don't like.

Differences which emerge between mother and child at adolescence can mellow, can be negotiated – or become entrenched. Mavis is seventy-two years old. Her daughter Netty is fifty-three and lives in Canada. Once a year she comes to visit her mother, staying with her for a couple of weeks. Mavis describes what happens:

> I so look forward to her visits, but I breathe a sigh of relief when she goes. She's so terribly clean and tidy. She's forever polishing, plumping up the sofa cushions and washing dishcloths.

She suggests I do the shopping so she can do some hoovering with me out of the way. To be honest, it drives me mad.

The adult daughter and elderly mother appear to be manifesting a role reversal of a familiar adolescent pattern. The untidy mother feels oppressed by the tidy daughter. This raises the question of whether ambivalence changes with age. Once again it is tempting, but dangerous, to generalise. Where Mavis is concerned she responds to the grown-up Netty with the same mix of remorse (I should be tidier) and rage (she's too tidy) that the toddler evoked in her. But, now that her daughter is adult, and more her 'equal', Mavis is open about the irritation that she previously bit back.

Age does not necessarily alter ambivalence, but the issues change. For example, an elderly mother who expects care and concern from adult children can be hurt and outraged almost beyond endurance when it is not forthcoming. As more women choose to have children later in life, mothers do increasingly find their adult daughters preoccupied with young children, rather than available to them. And the conditions of old age, the frustrations and discomforts, can prompt a mother to break the internal and external silence she has enjoined on hostile feelings towards her children. Sometimes the ensuing honesty can enhance her relationship with them – sometimes it simply breeds bitterness.

Creative Aggression

Clearly the splitting and the violent acting out of aggressive impulses under the pressure of persecutory anxiety can occur with a child of any age, but in describing moments when maternal ambivalence intensifies and the 'gap' between love and hate widens, I have focused primarily on the relationship between mothers and babies or young children, because I think proximity to infants does draw mothers into violent oscillations and extremes of feeling.

In her book *Motherhood and Sexuality* the psychoanalyst Marie Langer describes how 'The small child projects his hunger onto the mother and experiences it as if she ate and destroyed him from within as a deliberate aggression and punishment for his greediness.'[10] In the grip of such projections a mother feels simultaneously starved, devoured and accused. Above, I described Naomi who contrasted moments when her children made her feel maddened and moments when they made her feel saddened. She struggled to prevent her children's neediness, hooking into and drawing out and igniting her own 'infantile needs'. Through clenched teeth she combated the spiral of guilt, anxiety and rage that can be provoked. She fought to remain concerned rather than descending into the morass of persecutory feelings.

In the grip of maternal persecutory anxiety a mother does not interpret the experience, but reacts to it, trying, as it were, to defeat it. Once Naomi was able to think about her children's frustration, she ceased to experience herself as her children's victim and a broader range of emotional responses became available. She became aware of the fear of losing the children's love, she was conscious of herself as an adult relating to a small child, rather than feeling a child herself at the mercy of manipulative, malevolent, withholding beings. Love, once more, outweighs hate. Naomi comments:

> What amazes me is the speed with which hate erupts and as suddenly dissipates. It's gone – and we're chatting lovingly to each other. I think to myself, 'Wait a minute, did I dream this? Was she just screeching "I hate you! I hate you!" and I was thinking "And I hate you too! I hate you too!"?' Both of us in full throttle! And then suddenly we'll turn a corner. Peter, their father, helps me. I see him dipping into the same quagmire of rage and I think it's not just me, I feel sad because I know what he is experiencing, but I also have a sense that we are in this together and can help each other unhook.

In Chapter 7 I shall connect moments when mothers 'hit out' to the tension between feeling powerful and powerless. But here I shall pursue further the links between the recognition of ambivalence and creative care of a child.

Melanie Klein wrote:

> Ambivalence carried out in a splitting of the imagos enables a small child to gain more trust and belief in its real objects and thus in its internalized ones – to love them more and to carry out in increasing degrees its fantasies of restoration of the loved object.[11]

Here, Klein is pointing out a role for ambivalence in a child's development of a sense of confidence in his or her capacity to make good damage done to the mother in phantasy. We can transpose Klein's understanding of the constructive nature of the child's ambivalence on to maternal experience in which splitting her representation of her child into the good child and the naughty child would be regarded as part of normal maternal development – not regressive or pathological – and essential for the building up of an image in the mother's mind of the essential goodness of her child, and her belief in herself as able to shape and raise an increasingly 'good' child. And, just as a child gains confidence in its 'constructive tendencies' as it grows up, enabling it to begin to bring closer together its external, internal, loved and hated images, so a mother, as she gains confidence in her mothering, makes steps towards the unification of her images of the child with, in Klein's words, 'mitigation of hatred by means of love'.[12]

If the good child and the bad child remain too far apart in her mind, there is a danger that she will resort to idealising or denigrating the child, with all the attendant dangers to both herself and her child. But with the necessary lessening of splitting comes an awareness that the loved child can be harmed by hatred. In Chapter 1 I referred to Klein's theory that 'side by side with the destructive impulses of the unconscious mind, both of the child and the adult, there exists a profound urge to make sacrifices in order to help put right loved people who in fantasy have been harmed and destroyed'.[13] Klein related her theory of reparation to mothering, observing that, just as a woman made reparation to her own mother for her destructive impulses, so a mother can make reparation to her own children. In this, Klein maintained, she identifies with the mother who loved her – and all she wished her mother had done for her. Ambivalence thus provides the dynamic for creative mothering; sparking impulses to give, understand, construct and mend.

Winnicott elaborated Klein's ideas about love, guilt and reparation. His ideas take us a step further towards understanding what might be called the psychological purposes of the production of maternal ambivalence. His primary focus was on the child's experience, but we can transpose and reframe his description of the transformation of aggression into constructive guilt in infancy in a way that clarifies a similar maternal process. He considered the attainment of a capacity for reparation in respect of personal guilt to be one of the most important steps in the development of the healthy human being, hence his coining of the term 'stage of concern':

The stage of concern brings with it the capacity to feel guilt. Henceforth some of the aggression appears clinically as grief or a feeling of guilt.[14]

He turned his attention to mothers in relation to this 'grief' in a paper entitled 'Reparation in Respect of Mother's Organized Defence against Depression'. In it he describes how the depression of the child can be the mother's depression in reflection. In identification with the mother, the child presents 'a false reparation'. Winnicott briefly focuses on the experience of the mother when he writes,

> Probably I gain a specially clear view of this problem in a children's outpatients department because such a department is really a clinic for the *management of hypochondria in mothers*. There is no sharp dividing line between the frank hypochondria of a depressed woman and a mother's genuine concern. [His emphasis][15]

Had Winnicott elaborated this point rather than devoting the rest of the paper to pathology produced in the child by maternal depression, the childcare texts written under his influence would have read very differently. Instead he simply concluded that a 'mother must be able to be hypochondriacal if she is to be able to notice the symptoms in her child'. He is suggesting here, I think, that if a mother has a keen awareness of her own state of psyche-soma, she will extend a similar state of consciousness to the condition of her child. However, we can draw out other implications from his comment that there is no sharp dividing line between the frank hypochondria of a depressed mother and a mother's genuine concern. Hypochondria may be understood as referring to a state in which the self feels attacked by bad objects, or to a fantasy of good internal objects being attacked by bad internal objects.

Mothers respond to the element of hatred in their maternal ambivalence with a similar sense of loss of an internal good object. This may provoke either persecutory guilt (the problem is he's a bad baby) or depressive guilt (the problem is I'm a bad mother). I want to focus on the depressive guilt. Winnicott, in common with many other object-relations theorists, salutes the attainment of a capacity by an infant to sustain and manage depression as a major developmental achievement. It involves a sufficient degree of personal integration to accept responsibility for the destructiveness that is part of life. But we do not find much in Winnicott about depression in mothers as an achievement. For to valorise depression in mothers in this way would be to permit frank hypochondria! Even though that dividing line is thin, Winnicott does draw it and insists that there is something different from this hypochondria, something that is called 'a mother's genuine concern'. It is a case of so near yet so far in terms of Winnicott's evolving understanding of maternal ambivalence. He almost, but not quite, acknowledges in the midst of a paper on the pathological outcome of the mother's depression for the child, that mothers do *need* to be depressed.

Since Winnicott's day an enormous amount has been written on depression in mothers as an abnormal phenomenon. Depression in different degrees is a recognised feature of three major post-partum syndromes: baby blues, puerperal psychosis and post-partum depression. Obviously a large number of factors determine whether depression remains at the level of Winnicott's creative grief or manifests as a depressive illness. Joan Raphael-Leff makes a useful comment when she writes,

> Were we to delineate the common denominator underlying virtually all post-natal depression, we would be likely to find a sense of being ineffectual and a failure; feelings of profound self depreciation; worthlessness and guilt at not living up to her own expectations, fear of judgement and criticism by others and shame at being depressed rather than elated and joyful.[16]

Underlying the state of mind Raphael-Leff delineates is a profound feeling of helplessness, and it is helplessness that Winnicott believed sabotaged the attainment of the 'stage of concern'. He wrote of the infant that in health he

> can hold the guilt, and . . . is able to discover his personal urge to give and to construct and to mend. In this way much of the aggression is transformed into social functions, and appears as such. *In times of helplessness* . . . this transformation breaks down, and aggression re-appears. [Emphasis added][17]

Applying this to mothers, we can ask what it is that creates 'times of helplessness'. Looking beyond the individual mother who responds to the task of mothering according to her specific psychology, I think there are particular conditions of mothering today which do inflate the guilt associated with aggression and hatred, provoking extreme splitting and overwhelming persecutory anxiety rather than leading to a state of manageable maternal ambivalence. The idealisation of oneness, the representation of mothers as good or bad rather than inevitably ambivalent, the frequent absence of previous experience of childcare, the often sole responsibility, the social isolation, and the eruption of emotions considered unacceptable in mothers, all combine to produce the feelings of helplessness so closely associated with the inability to transform aggression into creative care and attention, not only to the child's needs but also to her own. Ciara describes the depression of early motherhood:

> She wasn't a particularly difficult baby. I just never felt I knew what the matter was. I don't think I felt hostile towards her: I turned it against myself. It was my failure to understand what was needed; my inability to cope. In a way it was easier to blame myself and to think of it in those terms, although it made me terribly helpless.

A degree of depression is an inevitable concomitant of motherhood and implies a recognition of aggression, an acceptance of both responsibility and fallibility. Yet the interplay of the psychical and social conditions of mothering with regard to the component of hatred militate against depression remaining a manageable, creative condition. As Ciara says, she was all alone, and yet expected to understand, and instead she felt totally perplexed. Unable to bear the ambivalent feelings, she was overcome with depressive anxiety and, crucially, quite unable to think.

For Ciara the capacity to think was stymied rather than facilitated by ambivalence. In Chapter 1, I suggested that the theories of W. R. Bion were helpful for understanding the relationship between maternal ambivalence and maternal thinking. However, he employed the mother–child relationship as a model for the thought processes generated between psychoanalyst and patient (see Chapter 7 for the implications of this for mothers). And if we are to use his schema for understanding what goes on between an actual mother and her child, we need to reread his theory of maternal reverie with the full panoply of inevitable maternal passions in mind. Then the model can usefully illustrate the creative role of ambivalence.

In his concept of maternal reverie, Bion depicts a crucial process that takes place between mother and child in early infancy. The baby projects, along with love, unbearable feelings into the mother who 'detoxifies' these feelings, makes sense of them for the baby in her mind, enabling the baby to feel understood, and in turn to develop her or his capacity to understand.

Reverie demands an exquisite receptiveness on the part of the mother. Her mind needs to be in a state of free-floating attention and thus able to receive the full impact of infantile feelings. In Bion's words,

> If the infant feels that it is dying it can arouse fears that it is dying in the mother. A well-balanced mother can accept these and respond therapeutically: that is to say in a manner that makes the infant feel it is receiving its frightened personality back again in a form that it can tolerate.[18]

Bion's view was that the concept of projective identification – which may be defined as to introduce into an other a state of mind, in order to communicate with them about this mental state – explains this process.

For Bion, viewing the mother–baby interaction as a theoretical system intended for the use of practising psychoanalysts, the mother in her unknowing knowingness is essentially a 'receptor organ'[19] and the goal is to remain balanced *vis-à-vis* the storming baby. He describes the link between the containing mind and the contents put into it as manifesting three potentialities, 'L', 'H' and 'K', representing loving, hating and wanting to know about the content. The mother will consciously or unconsciously at times find herself loving, hating or trying to understand what her child is experiencing, feeling and thinking. If the mother fails to take in the child's sensations, the child, instead of having its frustrations made comprehensible, experiences them as stripped of meaning and she or he becomes prey to terror – 'nameless dread'.

Initially this does appear to be a reactive model of mothering. The mother responds, reacts, replies, to the messages directed to her via projective identification. But I want to suggest that the term 'reverie', despite its passive associations, implies an active, albeit unconscious, capacity on the part of the mother to be in touch with her own turbulence.

Taking in a baby's projections can elicit a variety of painful responses: terror, anxiety, anger and concern. What enables a mother to retain Bion's 'balanced' outlook in the face of this flood of feeling is the capacity to be aware of ambivalence – to know, for instance, that part of her wishes to shut the baby up at almost any cost while another part of her passionately wants to make it better for the baby. Hence her 'understanding' needs to be directed not just towards the baby but also to her own feelings – the terror and anger she experiences when she takes in, or perhaps on, the baby's fears. Unless she can acknowledge her internal reality, unless she has the capacity for honest self-assessment, unless she can 'reverie' about herself how can she understand the baby?

The conflict between love and hate – the intense disturbance of maternal ambivalence, as I have commented, can itself provoke and intensify the desire to know and respond to the baby's needs. Instead of acting on violent impulses or succumbing to helpless despair, a mother may look for reparatory solutions. As mentioned above, to the conflict between love and hate Bion added the conflict between knowledge (K), or the desire to understand, and the aversion to knowing and understanding (–K). For a mother, co-existence of L and H urgently mobilises K. If we consider the active processes going on in a mother rather than seeing her as a 'receptor organ', we achieve a richer understanding of the concept of reverie. It is a state of mind achieved by knowing the pain of conflictual feelings.

As we saw in Chapter 1, an essential aspect of the depressive position is the growth of the capacity to distinguish between self and object and between real and ideal object. For a mother, dealing with a distressed baby, struggling to make these distinctions is vital. Otherwise, her own pain and the baby's simply merge and magnify. Recognition of maternal ambivalence, facilitated by reverie, is the basis for self-knowledge. Writing of the depressive position, the Kleinian psychoanalyst, Ronald Britton observes that 'when we acknowledge we hate what we feel to be the same person as someone we love we feel ourselves to be truthful and our relationships substantial.'[20] Without that acknowledgement an untruthfulness can potentially come between the mother and her baby.

I want to return to Kathleen and her older son whom I cited above. Kathleen castigated herself for being committed to a politics of non-violence and yet hitting her son. In reflecting on what had happened Kathleen was compelled to recognise aspects of herself that were concealed by her commitment to pacifism, and, moreover, to glimpse in herself the longing for the 'laziness and irresponsibility' she hated in her son, a sympathy stirred in her for the boy which in future was often to balance irritation.

Hence, mothers need to be able to think about hatred, resentment, panic and aggression, rather than fearing they will be admonished for them. The reproach, as I have suggested, is often embodied in the image of their own mother whom they dread or desire to replicate. I have, however, argued that while a woman's experience of being mothered may be significant, it is in no simple way predictive of how she herself will mother. Indeed to see a woman's present-day mothering reductively as formed predominantly in the past, plays into the culture's denial of the ubiquity of hatred in mothering by finding reasons for it. Once again, we end up dividing mothers into the good and containing, about whom nothing more need be said or done, and the mothers who require explaining. It is hard, but crucial, to hold on to the idea of mothers as necessarily ambivalent.

5

Separation: Both Loss and Release

When Martin was a year old he would only go to sleep if he could hold my hand. I would sit there by his cot and lose all sense of myself. My physical boundaries would feel to be disintegrating. I would want to scream at him 'Give me my space'. I felt desperate for physical space, let alone time for myself. Looking back I do feel tremendously guilty about that. I think the desire to push him away made me feel so terrible because it rekindled my own experience of rejection. I found that the most awful thing to see myself doing.

The relationship between ambivalence and separation from children is intricate and often painful for mothers. Ciara, in this description of her impulse to push her sleeping baby away and to reclaim the hand he held, highlights the co-existence of contradictory feelings in her experience of separation. The desire for release sits side by side with a fear, fuelled by her own experience, that this would lead to a sense of destructive abandonment and loss for her baby.

In a highly praised book, child psychotherapist Dilys Daws elaborated the connection between a child's sleep problems and mothers' and children's difficulties in separating from one another.[1] Daws observes that for some parents separation is a prized goal while for others (like Ciara) it can sometimes be unbearable, evoking echoes of old bereavements and other intolerable losses. I suspect separation is often accompanied by contradictory feelings, and frequently greeted with varying mixtures of *fear* and *relief*.

In this chapter I shall suggest that the existence of maternal ambivalence is, paradoxically, vital for the project of separation, and that the aggressive component in ambivalence is central in the process of parting. But, at the same time, precisely because separation entails a sense of destruction and aggression, ambivalence can supercharge these emotions, making separation too dangerous to contemplate.

Ciara considers that her impulse to retrieve her hand from her sleeping son must have damaged the child. She says guiltily, 'I am sure my rejecting response escalated his desire to cling.' Perhaps she is right. But what she does not consider is the possibility that her desire to pull back, to reclaim her sense of bodily boundaries, may also signify an appropriate and productive move towards separation on her part as a mother. Her automatic self-condemnation is a product of our culture's fascination with the child's separation-individuation process, as named and charted by Margaret Mahler (see Chapter 6). Now, of course, the infant's development is momentous and more dramatic than the mother's, but that mothers undergo a parallel, though different, process of equal intricacy and intensity is not given enough serious consideration in books on separation, save for when the mother is thought to impede the child's development. As I have said, we live in a culture that celebrates the maternal ideal with its image of mother–child oneness. Yet, confusingly, the cardinal maternal sin is nevertheless considered to be a failure to separate.

Feminist revisions of psychoanalytic theory have challenged the significance of separation in individual development. Carol Gilligan, for example, criticises psychoanalysis for exploring human connection in a language grounded in separation.[2] She comments that object-relations theorists have created a language of love unparalleled in its depersonalisation. Jessica Benjamin observes that selfhood is defined negatively as separation from the other.[3] Instead, feminists chart and highlight a pattern of female selfhood characterised not by autonomy and separation but by fluidity and connectedness.

Theorists at the feminist Stone Center in the USA assert that the self–other differentiation of separation theory is not the core of child development, but that the capacity to achieve 'growth in connection' is what counts.[4] They consider conflicts between mothers and daughters to be caused not by the daughter's struggle to get free and the mother's inability to let go, but rather by frustration arising out of disconnectedness which prevents the relationship evolving towards mutual understanding.

I situate myself somewhere between those who privilege separation and those who highlight connection. Although the feminist insistence on growth in connection provides a salutary corrective to an understanding of human development based on progressive separation, I think we can borrow Mahler's term, separation-individuation process, to deepen our understanding of the mother's maturational processes – despite its baby-centred associations.[5] Motherhood does contribute to a woman's individuation and, moreover, it is her sense of individuation that facilitates her capacity to separate (a point to which I shall return). Mother and child face the task of negotiating a sequence of separations from the moment of birth onwards. However, while children move with more or less difficulty towards an ever-increasing sense of themselves as individuals separate from their mothers, women evolve from one maternal identity to another. Thus they move from being a mother supporting a head, to a mother pushing a buggy, to a mother holding a hand, to a mother waving a hand, to a mother waiting for a hand to hold. *But always a mother.* Theirs is a 'vertical' development compared to their children's more 'horizontal' growth away from them.

Naïve Egoism

Within psychoanalytic theory one writer stands out for her acknowledgement that the mother has her own 'separation' process which she pursues for her own sake, relatively independent of her infant's development and often to her offspring's outrage. In her paper, 'Love for the Mother and Mother Love', Alice Balint indicates two stages of maternal development which she terms 'instinctive maternity' and 'civilised maternity'.[6] She characterised the former as a time when neither mother nor child experiences divergent interests or desires. She describes children as in the grip of 'naive egoism' which they retain in relation to their mothers often well into adulthood. She writes that, 'For all of us it remains self-evident that the interests of mother and child are identical and it is a generally acknowledged measure of the goodness or badness of the mother how far she really feels this identity of interests.'[7] It is perhaps an indication of the strength of the maternal ideal that Balint has been understood to be validating the perspective of naïve egoism rather than commenting critically upon its persistence beyond an age-appropriate time. She is quoted out of context, and assumed to be advocating maternal self-abnegation.

In fact she goes on to describe how the mother's developmental processes inevitably come into conflict with the child's naïve egoism:

> The child who has outgrown infancy is no longer so agreeable to the mother (thinking still in terms of instinctual maternity), nevertheless he clings to her and does not know any other form of love but that of his naïve egoism. This naïve egoism, however, becomes untenable, because now there is no mutuality, which was its basis. Thus the child is faced with the task of adapting himself to the wishes of those whose love he needs. It is at this point that the rule of reality starts in the emotional life of man.[8]

In his history of the independent group of psychoanalysts, Eric Rayner situates Balint as a forerunner of Winnicott.[9] But I feel that she differs significantly from Winnicott in her presentation of the ambivalence of the mother–child relationship which, she argues, inevitably contains 'discord which must be resolved'. Both Winnicott and Balint stress the importance of a mother succeeding by 'failing' her child, hence enabling the child to discover her or his autonomy. But Winnicott's mother remains deeply responsive to the child, while Balint's mother responds rather more to her own desires. She depicts a relationship in which the separation processes are rarely simultaneous. Balint's mother pursues 'self-interest' and Balint's child 'hates the mother because she is no longer what she used to be' and no longer finds the child 'so agreeable'.

Found Guilty

Alice Balint considered that those mothers who are unable to progress from 'instinctive maternity' to an acknowledgement of separate interests are victims of society's insistent prolongation of the early mother–infant relationship. Perhaps her view fails to take into account some *unconscious* processes in the mother – as well as the *conscious* guilt to which they lead. Mothers are aware of feeling more or less guilty at separating from their children – whatever the age of the child. The infant within the mother agrees with the child who experiences separation as rejection. At the incontrovertible level of unconscious maternal certainty, the mother suffers from a parallel belief that she should have no concerns other than her child, that she should not desire, as did Ciara, to withdraw her hand from her sleeping son. A sense of betrayal grips a mother who leaves a child at a playgroup or a mother who decides to stop doing her grown-up daughter's washing. Kathleen, for example, feels enormously guilty at no longer wanting to share her home with her late-adolescent son. Now in her late forties, she wants to move away from experiencing motherhood as her primary identity. But she is besieged by doubts about her son's ability to 'stand on his own feet'. He should be old enough to leave home and to no longer need her. But is he? She is gripped by uncertainty. Is she fostering dependence and irresponsibility by letting him live at home? Would she be doing him a service by getting him to move out? Or is such a notion simply salving her conscience? In this case her son provided the answer:

> When Tim came home from college he said, 'Mum, our life styles are not compatible, I think I should start looking for my own place.' It was such a relief. I felt so grateful to him.

Before analysing the sense of badness attendant on separation, I want to emphasise that there are, of course, variations in the experience of separation according to the age of the child and the specific psychology of the mother. Take Margaret, for example. She is a mother who found it less difficult to leave a toddler than to leave an adolescent.

> I think my main experience of ambivalence in relation to Jim has been the desire to go out and do things for myself, and the fear and guilt at leaving him. When he was smaller, it was just a terrible wrench leaving him. But once I had gone I didn't feel particularly worried about him, in fact, I don't think I gave him much thought. Now he is older it's completely different. I worry when I go out. I worry when he goes out. When he was small I felt all right about leaving him with someone I trusted. Now I feel he needs me there – needs *me* particularly. For example, he can't settle down to do his homework unless I'm there. I'm required to provide a context for him to settle down. I've wanted to have a life which carried me away – which involved responsibilities outside home. But I have felt guilty at not being around for him. I've never felt resentful – I'm so grateful to have him – but I have often felt guilty.

There are, however, mothers whose experiences differ markedly from Margaret's. Circumstances permitting, they find separating from a child old enough to do homework perfectly acceptable because separation can be rendered reasonably 'safe' with advanced warning and detailed explanations. While a mother of a toddler in the throes of disentangling herself from a screaming child's grasp may tell herself that she is not the deserting witch her child takes her to be, her sense of internal goodness can easily evaporate in the face of her child's distress. At one level she simply feels 'bad' at causing anguish to the child she loves, but at what I call the level of unconscious maternal certainty it is her belief in herself as a 'good' and worthwhile being that is soured.

We can observe this starkly occurring at adolescence when a child's struggle to establish her or his separate identity can involve a savage critique of almost everything about their parents. A lone mother commented bitterly of her battle with her fifteen-year-old son:

> There's no one to lay down the law at home except me – no one to share the burden of being seen as 'horrible'. His father has never been there for him, never helps or contributes.

While this mother considers that being a lone parent compounds the difficulties attendant on the separation process, others suggest that the absence of a partner can mean that battle lines are less starkly drawn. The mother of a fifteen-year-old daughter and seventeen-year-old son says:

> Of course we have our tussles, but I feel that there is a sense of partnership between them and me – less us and them, less parents versus the children, because there is only me.

Loss of Self-Worth

In order to understand how a woman's sense of internal goodness suffers so severely at moments of parting (I mean both actual separation and psychic distancing), we need to return again to Melanie Klein's theory of infantile development, and to apply it to maternal as well as to infantile experience.

The depressive position can be understood as heralding an infant's recognition of the mother's separate and ongoing existence, of the fact that the mother comes and goes, and that she is both loved and hated. Central to the affects that typify the depressive position is the fear of losing the loved mother. Klein considered the fear of loss and uncertainty as especially significant in relation to the internal good object which is synthesised out of an absorption of experiences with real others and unconscious phantasy structures. In his *Dictionary of Kleinian Thought*, R. D. Hinshelwood offers a clear definition of the good internal object:

> a sense of there being a good, helpful figure inside the personality, felt to reside there, and so closely loved as to constitute the basic primary identification around which the whole of an identity is formed. The good internal object provides the continual internal dialogue of encouragement and self esteem on which confidence and psychological security are based.[10]

What happens to the good object internally is intricately connected with what happens externally. An external rebuff, loss or bereavement may threaten the ongoing survival of a good internal object capable of supporting the person psychologically from inside.

One common psychoanalytic explanation for women who find the work of maternal care particularly difficult is that they are deprived of a sense of good internal object which would facilitate their belief in themselves as able to love and nurture. Less often stated is the view that experiences of mothering can themselves create as well as confirm a woman's sense of having an internal good object. For example, Naomi, whom I quoted in Chapter 3, described 'the lovely wonder that you are so special to the child and that you actually have something to offer. I think I found this business of having milk that the baby could make use of truly magical.'

Naomi had previously experienced herself as lacking in a sense of internal beneficence. She doubted her capacity for sustained nurturance and, indeed, delayed having children until late in life. Her baby's response to her radically changed her sense of self. Similarly, Margaret considers that the experiences of love for her child, and of receiving the child's love, have been profoundly transformative:

> I think it's given me more confidence in myself. I don't think that I grew up with a very great sense of my own value, and having a child, in that children just accept you as a parent, has

been very good for me. Just to be accepted for myself, and for getting on with things, and doing it all right has been extraordinary.

I remember when Jim was very little, five of us organised a crèche. I would come back from work and there he would be in his carrycot absolutely delighted to see me. The others all took it for granted that he would be pleased to see me, but for me to be the centre of somebody's universe – that I could be that important to someone – was truly transforming.

Motherhood can lead to the creation of a sense of there being a good internal object, yet can equally induce a terrible sense of inadequacy, the collapse of self-esteem and the disintegration of the sense of there being a good helpful figure within. Michelene Wandor succinctly sums up this contradictory state of affairs: 'The word you awaited most eagerly from your child, "Mummy", becomes a signal for inner panic – "what now?"'[11]

In different ways moments of separation threaten both the child's and the mother's sense of having an internal good object. The child's sense of abandonment, that fear of having destroyed the loved mother, and hatred of the deserting/rejecting mother, meshes with the mother's own fear of loss of an internal good object if she feels a 'bad' mother.

At heart, most mothers worry that the child will not withstand separation. Perhaps this is a more rational fear in relation to an infant but probably not in relation to a school-age child. Then, something else is going on. Sandra describes her feelings in the morning when she waves the children off to school:

I strap them into my neighbour's car with her daughter. I close the car door and stand on the front steps to wave to them, and every single morning I fear that they will have a car crash and it will be my last sight of them.

There are a number of ways of thinking about Sandra's anxiety. It could be ascribed to unconscious destructive impulses towards her children. Or she may unconsciously fear retribution if sending them to school equates with having rejected them. But in my view such anxieties very often reflect a need to restore an internal image of herself as a good mother in an attempt to stem the ebbing tide as her sense of there being an internal good object flows away. And, indeed, the effort of contemplating her own distress at her children's imagined death does finally turn her into a caring mother in her own mind. She continues, 'Then I go inside and as soon as I close the door behind me I feel fine, stop worrying and get on with my day.'

Once again I have to stress that mothers vary enormously in their susceptibility to the experience of destruction of the internal good object at moments of separation. Frances describes an interaction with her child's nursery school teacher which illustrates the extreme vulnerability of a mother's sense of goodness and self-esteem:

> The time for arriving at nursery was 9.15 to 9.45 but I would always ease myself into our parting by arriving at 9.50. Knowing I had this flexibility was very important to me, particularly at the beginning of term. Until one day the woman who ran the class rounded on me and said, 'I think you owe it to your child to get him into school on time. You don't realize how difficult it is for him.'
>
> I felt totally unable to reply. I felt terribly guilty. I'd been caught out being the inefficient, incompetent mother I fear I am. I wanted to say to her, 'You don't know how difficult it is to leave your son behind.' I wanted to say, 'You have no idea how hard it is to hand him over to you.' But of course I couldn't say that. I was just 'on my knees' and pink, and slightly tearful and incoherent. And then, when I got out of the nursery, I just wanted to beat her up.

Bargaining with Badness

Being five minutes late was Frances's way of saying to her son, 'I don't really want to leave you. I'm not really a bad mother.' In my interview with her Frances acknowledged that the pattern of trying to obtain forgiveness from her children for separating has persisted. They are now aged eight and ten, but she still lives as if separation from them would threaten the survival of her internal good object:

> I think I contain my guilt very badly. I become rather diffident and ask their permission – trying to let myself off the hook. It leaves them in a difficult position. I go ahead and do it but then I endlessly apologise, and put myself forward in a terribly humble sort of way, 'And oh dear me, oh my goodness, that must have been terrible for you.'

Other mothers describe a variety of internal bargains they make with themselves to escape the sense of inner opprobrium associated with separation. Some feel any absence is allowable as long as they are there to put the children to bed, or to take them to school, or to provide a hot meal. Still others experience a kind of role reversal, identifying with the 'abandoned child' rather than the 'abandoning parent'. Jane says, 'John [her partner] and I are terribly clingy. The children end up having to say to us, "It's OK, honestly it is. We'll be fine. You go."' However, the sense of self-reproach a mother can feel in relation to separation can become projected on to the children when it takes the form of conscious or unconscious hatred. After some years in therapy, Sarah has become able to face the hatred constellated by her guilt in relation to separation. She says:

> The children remind me of a litter of kittens. They would rather have a starving dead mother than allow her to go away and feed. It doesn't matter how long that cat has been lying there without eating, when she gets up and moves away, the kittens feel she's a bad mother. And she feels she's a bad mother. As soon as I feel OK about myself by going and doing something for myself, they make me feel I've abandoned them. And the sense they give me of being a rotten, selfish mum destroys whatever feeling of ability I have to do anything besides being a wife and mother.

In fact, Sarah was able to take up a new career when her son and three daughters were in their teens, but not without a considerable struggle. She felt that she and her oldest daughter in particular were locked together in a mutual dependency. She believes it dates from the girl's babyhood: 'I felt like a slave to the baby and that feeling has become knitted into the relationship.' Edith was an active and exhausting baby and Sarah constantly felt that nothing she did was good enough or satisfied the child:

> I remember very clearly standing on the tube platform with her when she was four years old. She was asking me all sorts of questions that I simply couldn't answer. I looked down at her and thought, 'I'm not clever enough to have a child like this.' I had this fear that if it was discovered that I couldn't manage her and that she was too clever for me, I would somehow lose her, that she would be taken away. It terrified me because

though she drove me mad I thought she was absolutely wonderful.

At that moment, standing on the tube platform, Sarah faced both the loss of her internal good object – in this context her sense of self-esteem and belief in her capacity to mother – and also her external good object, the child. It was this threat of loss that turned her into what she describes as a slave to the baby. She slaved to be 'good enough' – to protect both her sense of herself as able to mother, and to protect the child whose loss she feared. Becoming her children's slave created a relationship that knitted them all together.

Sarah's response to her daughter could certainly be explained in terms of her history – the determining power of the past; or in terms of her current life – her relationship with her husband; certainly both of these did shape her sense of herself as a mother. But I am more concerned with the general issues her relationship with Edith raises for our exploration of motherhood.

In a paper entitled 'On Love and Hate' Michael Balint raised some issues in relation to hatred that usefully illuminate Sarah's state of mind when she was overwhelmed by a sense of maternal inadequacy.[12] To combat her sense that she was a bad mother she had created a relationship with her daughter that she likened to slave and despot, with herself as slave. Her resulting resentment can be gauged from her description of herself and the children as a cat with a litter of kittens who would rather have a starving dead mother than allow her to go away from them and feed. Balint's suggestion was that hate constitutes a barrier against dependence, precisely against 'despondent dependence'.[13] In Sarah's case she felt dependent on her children for her sense of well-being because she had corrosive doubts about her ability to mother; thus she hated them, and loved them.

Balint also links hatred to frustrated love. He suggests that we reassure ourselves that those people who we feel do not love us, though important, are bad, that we no longer depend on the love coming from all the important people in our lives. We can do without the love of the bad ones. We see this process under way in Sarah's narrative of the starving cat leaving her kittens, in which both 'cat' and 'kittens' experience the other as responsible for the act of separation, and hence bad. In Balint's terms, both Sarah and her children were erecting a 'barrier of hatred'. He considered hatred as a necessary emotional component of separation, describing it as 'A-not-too-expensive guardian of our maturity, preventing us from sliding back into the archaic object-world, into the infantile dependence on the affection of our environment'.[14] He distinguished, however, between primitive hatred and mature hatred. The former constitutes the barrier to dependency and the latter is a response to specific circumstances. 'The more mature an individual,' writes Balint, 'the less is his need for barriers against regression into primitive forms of object-love, and so the less is his need for hatred.'[15]

Balint's ideas on hatred can be reworked from the point of view of the mother. For a start, we can dispense with Balint's value-laden distinction between good mature hatred and bad immature hatred. In mothers hatred can be simultaneously a reaction to specific circumstances and a constant feature of ambivalence. But, following Balint, hatred can also be a function of frustrated love, a response to the disappointed expectation that with a child a woman will at last experience the unshadowed love she has always longed to give and get. But what of Balint's image of hatred as 'guardian of maturity'? In mothers it can function as a barrier not against infantile dependence but against over-identifying or over-empathising with a child, to the extent that the mother's adult perspective becomes submerged and unavailable either to herself or to her child. But without the element of love in ambivalence, Balint's 'barrier of hatred' can become an insuperable obstacle to connection rather than a constructive boundary. What renders the barrier of hatred permeable is ambivalence.

Earlier in the chapter, I quoted Kathleen expressing her relief when her son volunteered to live away from home on leaving university. She wanted to put a 'safe' distance between herself and her oldest son because

> I only feel good about myself when he is behaving well, and I really hate his current lack of organisation, his unreliability, his disorder and his appalling untidiness. I feel he shows no respect for my values, yet at the same time he is still financially and emotionally dependent on me.

When Tim did leave home Kathleen both wanted to 'organise him' and to know nothing of the mess she was sure he was making of his life, although he surprised her by successfully finding both a flat and a job. In the event, their mutual ambivalence finally helped to construct a creative distance between them, across which they could relate amicably. Kathleen describes them as carefully accepting and establishing limits on what they can expect of one another. She says that she limits her criticism of his lifestyle while preserving some honesty in her relationship with him.

Destruction in the Cause of Separation

The meaning the 'barrier of hatred' carries for a mother will vary with the age of her children. Kathleen felt guilty but justified in wanting her adolescent son 'out' – to a place where he would not consistently turn her into a witch. For the mother of the very young child, the desire to 'get rid of the child' is far more frightening. As Dilys Daws writes, 'The extreme logical extension of putting a baby down and getting rid of it is in fact for the baby to die.'[16] She was discussing parents' responses to the wish to walk away from the baby who cries and cannot be consoled. She suggests that these fleeting hostile feelings and the desire to escape the baby can get fixed as 'death wishes' which themselves get translated into death fears.

> I worry about my sons constantly. Not normal anxieties, such as them falling downstairs. It's more horrendous, more insidious somehow. I was travelling to work one morning when I had a vision of them being thrown down on to the railway track. I stood up in a sweat, before I realised it had been a hallucination. It haunted me all day and by that evening I had decided to give up my job and go freelance.[17]

The narrator is recounting her 'separation anxiety' in an article for a national newspaper, warning against the suffering for mothers induced by full-time work when their children are small. While full-time work obviously would pose certain psychological and practical childcare problems, I doubt that going freelance eased the anxiety of separation, given the power of the aggressive imagery that persecuted this particular mother.

Hester has two children: Diane aged nine, and Jenny who is seven. She distinguishes between constructive and destructive aggression in the service of separation, depending on the ambivalence she feels towards each child. She is very open-eyed about her ambivalent feelings towards her older daughter:

> I feel I rejected Diane when she was small because, quite simply, I didn't like her. I hated the way she tortured her sister – it's exactly as I tortured my sister and my mother hated me for it. I hate her greed and her refusal to see another person's point of view. I hate her lack of thought. Whatever is on the floor she'll simply step on. She's very impulsive just like I am, and that I hate.

Listening to Hester talk about her daughter, it is clear that she has expended an enormous amount of energy on their relationship, and that it has the painful depth so characteristic of a mother's relationship with the child towards whom she feels powerfully ambivalent. Discussing love and hate, psychoanalytic theorist Teresa Brennan points out that both act to bind a person to the other and both constitute giving attention to the other. The attention provided with love is fluid and facilitating whereas with hate 'one's attention fixes the other, and is fixed in turn'.[18] Thus, the co-existence of love and hate for a child can produce a mix of curious certainty and uncertainty about who that child is. It is an uncomfortable state of mind and it pushed Hester into reflecting deeply about her daughter. When she speaks of her other daughter Jennifer, her tone lightens but the description lacks the precision of her portrait of Diane. She says of Jennifer:

> We're very aggressive towards one another. She says to me 'I hate you. I hate you. I'm going to live at Mary's house because she's got a nice mummy.' And I shout back 'Fine, OK, just go and do it.' But there's no sort of guilt. We can just hate and scream at one another and it remains a very easygoing relationship. I feel we can be very aggressive because there is nothing concealed. We don't have fears about each other so we can be nasty. We don't fear separation. She can say what she wants and know that I'm not going to reject her. Whereas with Diane I used to threaten for a long time to send her to live with my sister. And it really was a total rejection – like I don't want you in my life – and that is a terrible thing. With Diane there is aggression and fear. With Jenny there is aggression without fear.

Hester rejoices in the aggression between herself and one daughter but fears it in relation to the other. Here I want to consider Hester's experience in the light of D. W. Winnicott's theory of the use of an object.

Winnicott remarked that there is no such thing as a baby, meaning that a small baby and its mother cannot be considered in isolation from each other, the relationship between them being all-important. His major concern was with the maturational processes of the baby and the mother's facilitation of that development. However, at one point he does touch on the issue of the mother's own development. He writes that 'a normal healthy mother is able to summon up ambivalence in object-relating and to be able to use it appropriately'.[19] The context of this comment is a discussion of a mother who experiences problems around weaning and complains that her child 'will not wean', when in Winnicott's view the mother 'may well be in a depressive phase, in which hate (both active and passive) is not available to consciousness for use in relationships'.[20]

Winnicott's concern with maternal hatred is in relation to its role in 'the disillusioning process', of which weaning is an expression. However, his references to the constructive role of maternal hatred are frustratingly elusive beyond the fact that hatred provides a bastion against maternal masochism, and must be made conscious but not acted out in relation to the baby. I want to suggest that we can try to flesh out Winnicott's references to the role of hatred by taking his description of a specific moment of infant development, which he terms 'use of an object', and reading it thoroughly from the mother's point of view, with the experience of maternal ambivalence as a central focus.

I shall first briefly summarise Winnicott's theory of the process by which a subject accepts that the other is outside the subject's control. He contrasts what he calls 'object relating' with the use of an object. The former implies that the other is a composite bundle of the subject's projections. In object usage, the other becomes an entity the infant can use, one that may inhabit a shared reality but is not nearly so susceptible to manipulation. The process by which a subject places an object outside her or his control involves the destruction of the object. Winnicott writes:

> It is important to note that it is not only that the subject destroys the object because the object is placed outside the

area of omnipotent control. It is equally important to state this the other way round and to say that it is the destruction of the object that places the object outside the area of the subject's omnipotent control. In these ways the object develops its own autonomy and life and (if it survives) contributes to the subject according to its own properties.[21]

Destruction places the object outside the self – outside the self's control. For Winnicott's theory to work, the role of the mother is to survive the destruction, not to retaliate, and hence prove to the baby that separation exists. I would suggest that a parallel process to the infant's is going on in the mother: a maternal use of *infant-as-object*. Now it's the mother who has to cease experiencing the infant as part of herself and to acknowledge its separate reality. And for the mother to do this she has to go through a process of 'destroying' the infant-as-object. Only when she 'destroys' infant-as-object can she be said to have placed the baby outside her area of omnipotent control. Only via 'destroying' her baby can she be said to have achieved the use of an infant, meaning a relationship to the baby as a person increasingly separate from herself. For this destruction to remain benign and non-retaliatory – for the baby to survive – the mother's progress to object usage in relation to the baby needs to be accompanied by love. Once again we see the pivotal importance of a mother achieving a recognition of her ambivalence.

In Winnicott's words, aggression is destruction done that creates 'the quality of externality'.[22] Andrew Samuels's work on the characteristics and psychological purpose of aggressive fantasy usefully amplifies Winnicott's theory of use of an object. Samuels observed that aggressive fantasy promotes a vital style of consciousness (images of tearing things up, dissecting them, controlling them, making use of them). In other words, aggressive fantasy has much to do with our desire to know our world and its objects and hence with object use. Thus aggressive fantasy, as Samuels comments, 'can bring into play that interpersonal separation without which the word "relationship" can have no meaning. In this sense aggressive fantasy may be about wanting to make contact, get in touch, relate.'[23]

If we return to Hester and her children, what she has to say about aggression and separation gains additional meanings. She had described heated exchanges between herself and her daughter

Jenny, aged seven, who declares that she hates her mother and wants to leave home. Hester replies, 'Fine, you go!' and she contrasts this form of aggressive interchange to the way she used to threaten to send her other daughter to live with her sister. With Jenny there was mutual aggression involved in the struggle to separate and mutual recognition that the other could take the fantasised attack and survive it, whereas with Diane, Hester's more painful response to ambivalence made the separation-individuation process and the accompanying aggressive fantasies seem far too real, far too destructive.

Inflamed by guilt in relation to her daughter, Hester confuses fantasy and action. To put it another way, she conflates aggressive fantasy and actual destruction. She feels she has really brutally rejected her. Now, of course, fantasy and action *are* connected and there *are* mothers who act out their fantasies in abuse. But fantasies of a violent kind can in fact circumvent the act of cruelty, although to the mother who experiences a violent impulse towards her child the fantasy feels almost as unforgivable as the act. And for many the prevalence of aggressive fantasy in their lives with their children is simply a source of depressive guilt and they remain quite cut off from any realisation that, as Samuels puts it, the psychological point of aggressive fantasy (as opposed to action) is the promotion of concern. If we reframe the fantasy of sending the child away with these thoughts in mind, we see that it is also about providing a chance to consider the child, to renew the relationship, to free up the stuck quality of the bond between mother and child. In sum, the understandable guilt induced by fantasies of repudiation and rejection can lead to productive concern. Hester tells of how her ambivalence towards Diane focused her thoughts sharply upon the girl:

> Diane became my sole subject – she completely preoccupied me because I was in such a state of turmoil and rage with her, thinking all the time, 'What has gone wrong, what has gone wrong?' as I tried to find a way through the aggression I felt towards her. But I do think it propelled us onwards, and now I believe she'll do very well.
>
> In fact she has never been afraid in social situations. Her first day at nursery school she said 'Bye Mum' and off she went. She goes to a new school and on the first day she makes

four friends. She's Ms Cool – the child everyone wants to play with. She's very solid in the world, although she does have periods of anxiety. Today, perhaps because of all we've been through, Diane and I have a relationship which is very profound.

Hester expresses apparently contradictory beliefs about her daughter and how her relationship with her has affected her. On the one hand she believes she has 'broken her spirit' and on the other hand she observes that she is 'very solid in the world'. I think this is in part because aggressive impulses are in themselves quite contradictory. The distance created is both a 'safe distance' and punitive move. As American psychoanalyst Harold Searles put it, 'At one moment a violet urge may express a striving to be free and the next a desire to relate.'[24] I would add that where mothers are concerned such an urge also provides a cathartic release from the often unbearable passions of ambivalence.

- I want to really hurt them, and to hurt them in the way which is most hurtful – getting rid of them, rejecting them, pushing them away.

- When I'm really furious with them, I fantasise squashing them, like pancakes, annihilating them.

- I have wanted to hurl her across the room – to erase her.

- When we have arguments over his homework, I reach a point of total frustration. I think my reaction is to just leave, to walk away and freeze him out.

- It's the desire to push him away that I find most upsetting. It usually happens when I'm tired.

- I never hit the children, but I imagine it. I imagine beating them into silence.

These moments that mothers describe – moments when they want to 'rid themselves' of their child – share a similar dynamic. In each example, the mother reaches the point where her anger swamps her, asserting her needs and desires in opposition to her children's. In anger she asserts her rights and claims her autonomy.

The recognition by a mother that she has her own needs and priorities is, as Jessica Benjamin has argued, crucial for her child's development: 'A mother who stifles her own longings, ambitions and frustrations cannot tune in empathically to her child's joys and failures'.[25] It is not enough for a mother simply to mirror her child's attainments and accomplishments; she has to offer the child the experience of engaging with another autonomous being if the child is to develop a sense of her or himself as a person in her or his own right. Benjamin concludes:

> Only a mother who feels entitled to be a person in her own right can ever be seen as such by her child, and only such a mother can appreciate and set limits to the inevitable aggression and anxiety that accompany a child's growing independence. Only someone who fully achieves subjectivity can survive destruction and permit full differentiation.[26]

At every stage, development involves baby or child in a conflict between self and other. A parallel state of affairs holds true for the mother. For a mother the recognition of both her needs and her child's desires is a constant and necessary struggle in her development. What prevents a mother from over-submission on the one hand and excessive domination on the other? What maintains an awareness of mutuality in the mind of the mother? Once again we see the centrality of maternal ambivalence. Anger and hate can be a source of a mother's sense of separateness and thus autonomy. Love for the child can contain the anger and hate, rendering it a constructive, rather than destructive, force for separation.

Sometimes it is only when a child reaches adolescence that a mother is able to acknowledge that her anger is an assertion of separateness – that her anger with her child is playing a crucial role in the realignment of the mother–child relationship demanded by adolescence. For anger providing a sense of self – as separate from the child – can provide a space to think. But when a child is still in infancy or latency, anger experienced as a desire to sever connection is felt to be a sin against the maternal ideal. Rather than provoking thought, anger can produce an overwhelming sense of being helpless and powerless in the face of her own rage – and in the face of her child. Culturally, anger is considered the antithesis of care and, although none of the mothers cited above acted out their attack or abandonment, they felt hopelessly culpable.

Some feminists have criticised those clinical practices which encourage anger as a means of separation, arguing that within the mother–daughter relationship rage should not be considered as a means of separation; rather daughters need to be helped to 'bring uncomfortable feelings into constructive interaction in the relationship'.[27] My argument is that hate and rage mobilise *fantasies* of abandonment and separation that can have creative outcomes. The guilt induced by fantasies of repudiation and rejection can lead to productive concern – if these fantasies can be thought about. As Dilys Daws noted, parents who are conscious of such wishes and who can 'own' their angry feelings are in the best position to deal with these feelings and to go on working out how to attend to their child. However, a mother's shocked response to the discovery of her own sadistic separation/rejection fantasies may be to hold the child ever tighter, protecting both herself and the child from the spectre of loss conjured by the fantasies. She may fear not only loss of the child, but loss of the child's love for her, and loss of her love for the child whom she has in fantasy repudiated and abandoned.

Defending against Dangerous Distance

Stepping back from a child does provide a space for a mother to think about her child; but what she sees is not necessarily reassuring for it means facing both her own and her child's ambivalent feelings. Daws suggests that parents who are unable to put their baby down and leave him to protest may ostensibly be worried about the baby's feelings of being left but in fact may be finding any manifestation of ambivalence unbearable. She comments that they 'are upset by the way his cries express a difference of opinion'.[28] This can initiate a deep sense of loss: the loss of the image of the perfect child with the perfect mother. Separation and distance and difference may be necessary for there to be a relationship between mother and child, but the disturbing impulse is often to close the gap by sheer willpower.

Mothers mobilise a number of defences against the anxiety provoked by aggressive differentiation, for example idealisation and/or denigration. In a paper entitled 'Being a Parent', Alan Shuttleworth identifies two different parental styles. There are those who idealise their children and those who just moan about them.[29] As Melanie Klein pointed out, idealisation can be a defence against unconscious death wishes which a child bears towards her mother. These can be carried over to her own child when she becomes a mother. Hence, idealisation can be a means of denying impulses to 'get rid' of the children while denigration can be a means of justifying the desire to 'get rid' of them, thus easing the guilt.

Harold Searles characterised 'incorporation' as a further defence against separation.[30] By this he means a process of incorporating one's self into another person's ego boundaries. In his view it functions to shut out awareness of intolerable levels of hostility 'on the part of the mother towards the infant and vice versa'. He described a mother who employed ridicule as a technique for incorporating her son's personality – the ridiculing of any deviation from her attitude, her tastes, her values. The son tends to be 'driven back into the fold – into his mother's personality – by the potent weapon of ridicule'.[31]

Yet another mechanism of defence against the aggression inherent in separation is to project that hostility on to the outside world. Many mothers, such as Sandra in the following quote, recognise that here their inner-world strategies and fears mesh with external reality in a deeply disturbing and frightening fashion:

> It's ridiculous, but every time I have to go anywhere and leave the kids, I become obsessed with the possibility of them falling through the plate glass window in the kitchen. Even if I leave them with Barry, I still have this vision of shattering glass.
>
> I want to leave London because I am so terrified of the prospect of letting the children go on the tube by themselves. I know hundreds of children travel alone on the tube from when they are quite small, but I don't know how I will cope with the anxiety. I mean, I do look forward to the day when I don't have to take them everywhere – but the thought of them alone on the tube!

Cultural Condemnation and Confusion

Many psychoanalytically oriented writers, such as Lisa Appignanesi and John Forrester, have criticised feminist thinkers of the late 1960s for assuming a direct translation from social reality to the condition of the individual agent or subject.[32] They point out that the essence of psychoanalysis and its contribution to feminist thinking is to interpose psychic reality between the subject and the social order, 'thus making possible the pursuit of the feminist project of revealing the construction of the subject, without necessitating a mirroring relation, in which the constructed subject matches perfectly the roles and categories of the social world'.[33]

In the words of the mothers quoted in this book, I think we have heard here how far the psychic reality of mothers 'deviates' from dominant societal notions of the maternal ideal. Yet external reality does undoubtedly play an enormous part in women's private experiences of motherhood, not only at the level of ideology but in life itself through a whole network of impinging structures, such as the institutions of health and education. Moreover, we do not simply imagine that the world holds terrible dangers for our children; it does. And we do not simply imagine or fantasise that the culture reinforces a guilt-inducing preoccupation with achieving the appropriate closeness and distance between parent and child; it does. But I am not promoting a conspiracy theory of motherhood here. Rather, I am suggesting that the individual mother's ambivalence towards her own ambivalence echoes and is echoed by the society surrounding her.

In *The Modernist Madonna* Jane Silverman van Buren suggests that specific fears underlie society's preoccupation with the mother–child relationship:

> The diverse cultural forms of mother and mother and child in the figures of ancient goddesses, the madonna of medieval Christianity, and the more recent ideology of the domestic madonna attempt to hold and signify deep anxieties about infantile helplessness, meaninglessness and lack of mental organization.[34]

I agree with van Buren that there is in all of us an infantile aspect that dreads annihilation and abandonment. But the current attitude to motherhood in Western countries such as Britain and the USA is shaped by specific historical circumstances. Contemporary Western culture manifests an unflagging concern with (though not a setting aside of resources for) issues such as maternity leave, custody issues, 'quality time', the advantages and disadvantages of day care and so forth. One of the most popular films in recent years in Britain and the USA was *Home Alone 2*, the successful sequel to *Home Alone*. In both films, Kevin, an eight-year-old boy is accidentally abandoned when his family leaves on holiday. The films play on our worst fears of loss and separation, yet interestingly they suggest that both the parents and this son are somewhat relieved to be free. Ambivalence dominates these films. The mother displays unmistakable joy at release from her clever but difficult child. Equally, she is passionately determined to find him when he goes AWOL. The child becomes infinitely resourceful and reassuringly able to survive alone, yet finally wants his mummy. We see the two happily reunited beside the Rockefeller Center Christmas tree in New York City.

Shortly after the screening of the *Home Alone* films, two cases of parents leaving their children at home while they went on holiday caught the eye of the media in the USA and in Britain. Newspaper coverage played upon and fuelled public outrage. In the States the parents were dubbed America's 'most hated couple', while in Britain one tabloid headline read KILL THE BITCH. The lone mother in question played into the hands of reporters by acknowledging her ambivalent feelings towards her daughter, saying, 'She hates me having any fun and is quite jealous and spoiled.'

The journalist and author Suzanne Moore, reflecting on the implication of public response to the case, observed that the sheer hatred projected on to this woman reveals how hard it is for women ever to begin to express their difficulties with their children without being labelled 'wicked' or a 'bad mother'. If the mother had been able to acknowledge her inability to cope, would she have had to take such drastic action? Moore concluded, 'It's hard to say that children can be bloody awkward, demanding little beings and that everyone longs to get away at some point.'[35] One goal of this book is to make a contribution from psychoanalytic and feminist thought to changing the situation of which Moore complains.

While the mother who left her eleven-year-old daughter to go on holiday came in for such opprobrium, no one seemed to notice that the father was signally absent from the family altogether and had clearly abandoned his daughter for far longer than the length of a holiday on the Costa del Sol.

It is not simply that women are still expected to shoulder so much of the responsibility for bringing up children. We also need to understand the strength of feeling evoked by issues surrounding mother–child separation in the context of the extraordinarily rapid changes in the conditions of parenting over the last two centuries. Women are caught between these changing circumstances and our culture's desire that motherhood remain a beacon of order and an emblem of unity in disordered times.

I shall briefly summarise the changes I am referring to in Britain; research indicates that the situation in other Western countries is similar. Legally, the position regarding parental rights has changed utterly since 1839, when fathers had absolute rights over children. The 1925 Guardianship of Infants Act decreed that the welfare of the child was paramount and thus the father could no longer have prior claims over the mother to basic *custody* of the children. Nevertheless, the common-law rule was that parental *rights* were still vested, exclusively, in the father. It was only in 1973, with the Guardianship of Minors Act, that mothers were given full equal rights with fathers in relation to custody and upbringing.

The changed place of women and children under the law co-incided with a dramatic reduction in family size. At the beginning of this century one-third of a woman's life was spent producing babies. But by the mid-1960s the figure was nearer one-fifteenth. In the 1890s a woman lactated on average for fifteen years; during the 1960s the average was four years.

During the nineteenth century, men's lives and identities changed overtly more than women's, as they were increasingly drawn away from agricultural or home-based labour into paid industrial work in factories and cities. Today, as Arlie Hochschild puts it in her study of women's double workload, *The Second Shift*, the economic arrow of change points at women. It is women who are being drawn into waged work, and women who are undergoing changes in their way of life and identity: 'Women are departing more from their mothers' and grandmothers' way of life, men are doing so less.'[36]

Not only have women's work patterns* rapidly changed, but the circumstances of child-rearing have been transformed. A major feature of the 1980s was an increasing separation of marriage and child-rearing.†

---

* Today nearly a third of women in Britain with children under five years are in paid employment. In the USA, 23 per cent of married women with children aged between six and seventeen were in employment in 1950. By 1986 it had grown to 54 per cent. In 1950 it was so rare for women with children under the age of one year to work outside the home that the US Bureau of Labor kept no statistics. In 1991 54.5 per cent of such women work outside the home.

† The number of children born outside marriage in Britain increased from 77,000 in 1980 to 186,000 in 1989.

A resistance to the changing lifestyle of mothers and a longing for an impossibly idealised image of Mother is evident in the extraordinary lack of practical and psychological support for women in their negotiation of motherhood, often so different from their own mother's. In Britain, mothers made it clear that their needs were not being answered.‡ A 1991 Gallup poll revealed that 55 per cent of women wanted tax relief on childcare and 83 per cent wanted crèches at work, while 77 per cent wanted flexible working hours.

Childcare provision became a central issue in the 1992 British general election. The debates that erupted around maternal deprivation in the 1950s were recycled. For example, the work in the USA of psychologist Jay Belsky was evoked. He claims that substitute care for more than twenty hours a week for the infant's first twelve months leads to insecure mother–infant attachment and attendant behavioural problems.[37] In sharp contrast are the findings of the Thomas Coram Research Unit in London: the unit followed a large sample of children whose mothers returned to full employment after maternity leave. At the age of three, the only difference between these children and those who had been cared for by their mothers alone was that the children of employed mothers were on the whole less timid and more willing to share with other children. This was especially true of children in nurseries. Neither group displayed greater aggressiveness or more attachment problems than the other. 'The issue is no longer whether there should be day care for young children, but its social context,' commented Peter Moss, Thomas Coram's senior research officer.[38] He suggests that the quality of the day care available is all-important. He has in mind staff training and pay, child–staff ratios, continuity of care, and parental involvement. However, good-quality, affordable childcare is simply not available in Britain at this time. Only 2 per cent of

---

‡ In Luxembourg in 1991, 75 per cent of single mothers with pre-school children were in paid employment (compared with 18 per cent in the UK). In Denmark, 75 per cent of mothers (with partners) of pre-school children work, compared with 37 per cent of such mothers in the UK. Analysing the discrepancy in these figures, Anna Coote writing in the *Observer* newspaper in September 1992, pointed out that Britain lags behind these other countries as far as childcare provisions are concerned. Britain is the only country in the EC not to have some kind of national policy on this issue. In the USA a tiny 1 per cent of the country's 6 million private companies offer on-site childcare facilities; 10 per cent with ten or more employees offer some childcare assistance, which rises to 55 per cent when large national companies are considered. According to a study carried out by the US Children's Defense Fund, 65 per cent of working mothers with infants reported trouble finalising childcare which affected their decision to return to work.

under-threes have a publicly funded nursery place. So those who argue in favour of quality can offer little comfort to women.

Another group of workers in this field place the onus for the child's well-being on the mother's attitude to day care. Ellen Galinsky co-president of New York's Family and Work Institute, contesting attacks on day care is reported as stating that the impact of maternal employment on young children is highly subjective and linked to the amount of stress and guilt the mother feels.[39] Employed mothers thus have to contend with the feelings aroused in them by those who claim that day care is damaging, those who claim it is damaging unless it is of the highest quality, and those who consider it to be damaging if mothers feel guilty. But, of course, the contradictory, cautionary and frankly admonitory nature of the day-care debates is bound to render mothers anxious and guilty, while the financial and practical problems facing women in need of childcare makes maternity burdensome.

The emotional subtext to the day-care debates can be gauged from the tone of popular press reports on the proliferating surveys of women's attitude to motherhood. For example, take the manner in which in 1992 the *Sunday Times* summarised the content of two such surveys:

> A recent survey found that working mothers are not as guilt-laden as is popularly supposed about the lack of time they spend with their children. And a US *Cosmopolitan* report showed that 70% of mothers who lost custody of their children through divorce were 'extremely happy', and about 7% described themselves as 'euphoric' to have done so.[40]

The numbers of surveys and their sensationalist summaries can be read as a counterphobic response to the dread of maternal abandonment. (A counterphobic response is a psychoanalytic formulation according to which an individual gains satisfaction by pursuing precisely those activities which arouse anxiety in the hope of gaining the reassurance and satisfaction of mastering them.) An example of this is the manner in which *The Times* reported the 1991 survey on attitudes towards motherhood conducted by a pharmaceutical company in conjunction with *New Woman* magazine. BABIES HOLD NO JOY FOR '90S WOMAN, read the headline,[41] and *New Woman* itself blazoned SHOCK REPORT: WHY WOMEN DON'T WANT BABIES ANYMORE.[42] Turn to the report itself and a quite different picture emerges. The women who responded to the questionnaire were not defecting *en masse* from motherhood, but they were voicing *ambivalence*: 80 per cent of the respondents did want babies, 'but one in five *doesn't* including nearly half of those in their early thirties' (their italics). A question asked was: 'Do you ever regret having a child?' The magazine reported the response as follows: 'Hardly ever, say 79% of you. But having had a family more than a quarter of mums in their early twenties and those in their early thirties quite often wished that they hadn't.'

Despite the 80 per cent who wanted babies, the survey was heralded as 'babies hold no joy for '90s woman'. The negative response to motherhood was magnified, rendered preposterous, and thus more easily pathologised. Maternal ambivalence, with its associations of loss and abandonment, is made invisible by the collective counterphobic exaggeration of women's rejection of motherhood.

The culture's response was confronted by Helen Franks in her book *Mummy Doesn't Live Here Anymore*.[43] The emotive title suggests that Franks had played into the hands of those who might be gratified to see their worst fears realised. But in fact Franks deals thoughtfully and sympathetically with accounts of women who for a variety of reasons, ranging from psychological issues to custody cases, no longer lived with their children. She tackles the culture's conception of the abandoning mother and recognises that it militates against the acknowledgement of ambivalence:

> It is easier to regard women who leave their children as selfish, irresponsible and unnatural than to take into account the idea that they might leave but still love them and grieve for them. Once we accept that women can both love and leave, we are into very deep water and uncharted water.[44]

Pondering on the virulent responses evoked in other women by those who actually do leave their children, she suggests that other women fiercely condemn them because they recognise tendencies they fear in themselves. Her explanation of male hostility towards such women is that their actions challenge the sexual division of labour at the heart of our society:

> Women are the people with whom we entrust our children, equality notwithstanding. Like a captive, subservient, but utterly loyal subgroup, they are relied upon to do the job of nurturing, and to do it well. If they are so ambivalent and imperfect, who instead should do it?[45]

The conjunction of women's changing lives and society's resistance to change means that a woman's employment status is seen as *the cause* of maternal ambivalence – and *the solution* to it. Many mothers feel that if only they could get it right the negative component in ambivalence would disappear. Rachel, for example, feels that if only she could be with her son all day – with no guilt-provoking breaks – she would be far more honest and even-tempered:

> I feel immensely guilty at being away from him, so when I get home I want everything to be perfect to compensate for my absence. I know I become unremittingly jolly and loving. He senses that it's not real and becomes an absolute pain.

Other mothers agree. They feel that the element of hatred in ambivalence is exacerbated by the stress of co-ordinating paid work and motherhood, and the difficult moments – the times when resentment flares – are when a mother, tired from her job, has to shift from who she is at work to who she is at home with her child. Yet other mothers flatly disagree. Martha describes how much joy and pleasure she experiences at the end of a working day when she is reunited with her children – feelings that simply would not exist if she was to be with them all day, every day when she is sure they would be 'at each other's throats'. And indeed, mothers who are not in paid employment believe they would be so much better mothers if only they had some involvement, some area of life, independent of their children. Meanwhile, mothers with unsatisfactory jobs wish they could remain all day at home with the children. The emotional heat generated by debates on maternal employment outside the home focuses women's attention on ambivalence in relation to this one area – but not constructively. It detracts from the extent to which ambivalence is a product of inner-world conditions. And it glosses over how few women are psychologically, practically or economically enabled to think about what patterns of work would suit them as individuals, maintaining love and hate for children in a creative balance.

Object Relations and Separation

I want to look briefly at what object-relations psychoanalysis has to say on the topic of mother–child separation, and how this might determine mothers' expectations of themselves and their response to ambivalence.

Issues surrounding separation lie at the heart of object-relations theory. Object-relations theory can be roughly defined as dealing with an individual's interactions with external and/or internal (real and/or imagined) other people, and to the relationships between her or his internal and external object worlds. Internal images are often regarded as constituting a residue in the mind of relationships with significant people in the individual's life, which shape an individual's attitude, perceptions and so on. However, some theorists regard internal images as spontaneously self-generated, mental representations of psychosomatic processes and structures.

W. R. D. Fairbairn is regarded as one of the founders of object-relations theory.[46] His ideas on the shaping role of parents differs significantly from Melanie Klein's. For her 'bad objects' in a child's inner world are derived largely from the child's own inherent and spontaneous destructiveness. For Fairbairn 'bad objects' are aspects of the parents which make them unavailable to the child and frustrate her or his desire for closeness and contact. The implications for mothering are immense. In Fairbairn's view, if the parents respond fully to the child's infantile dependence, ego splitting and the establishment of internal bad objects is avoided, and the ego retains wholeness. If, on the other hand, the original relationship to the mother is ungratifying, depriving and characterised by absence and unresponsiveness, the bad aspects of the mother are internalised and established as an internal object. This internalisation takes place because the child needs to feel the parents are good and loving. In other words, the result of parental failure is that the child conceives of the badness as in her- or himself:

> When the child experienced the 'badness' as outside, in the real parents, he felt painfully unable to make any impact at all. If the 'badness' is inside him, he preserves the hope of omnipotent control over it.[47]

Fairbairn's theory speaks directly to the longing ever present in the child of any age for a loving, fully available mother, but it fails to give sufficient weight to the need for aggression-fuelled separation, the setting of boundaries and recognition of the creative nature of conflict. But we can adapt Fairbairn's ideas to illuminate aspects of maternal experience. His emphasis on the child's inherent longing for relatedness can equally be applied to a mother. In Chapter 1, I described mothers' desire for mutuality in their relationships with their children; a longing for love that gives conflict and separation a constant edge of pain. And often mothers – like Fairbairn's child – tend to believe that the 'badness' lies in themselves rather than in their child, for they feel a greater hope of controlling it in themselves:

> I tell myself that if only I could get up half an hour earlier so that we wouldn't have to rush getting ready for school, I wouldn't be so hateful to them and we wouldn't have such an awful time.

Sandra feels that if only she could master the practicalities of life – get up earlier, get ready for school on time – she would achieve the style of mothering advocated by object relations. She would become a loving, attentive, containing presence. She would be the mother we all long for – and long to be – whereas the passions aroused by maternal ambivalence in conjunction with the timetabling of late twentieth-century life renders Fairbairn's good parent an impossible and persecuting ideal.

The conditions of motherhood are changing faster than psychoanalytic theory about it and nowhere is the discrepancy more evident than in the conflicts aroused by John Bowlby's elaboration of object relations into attachment theory, a blend of ethology and psychoanalysis which gained greater popularity than Fairbairn's complex ideas on the formative influence of frustrated love.

The Occasional Outburst or Slap

The genesis of Bowlby's theory lay in ethology (the study of animal behaviour) and in his observation of children who had a history of repeated placement in care.[48] Attachment, according to Bowlby, is a biologically adaptive mechanism which leads a child to show preference for a specific person, need that particular person, and to protest if they are not present or depart. The attachment bond serves important developmental functions, permitting children to learn from their mothers, and providing a secure base from which to explore and play. According to Bowlby, children in positive, loving relationships to their mother form internal representations of themselves as good and desirable people that persist throughout life. But children who have had poor attachments are considered likely to carry an image of themselves as untrustworthy and un-lovable, and hence be prey to self-destructive or deviant behaviour, or destined not to fulfil their potential.

Bowlby's work has been comprehensively criticised from within the field (for example in Michael Rutter's *Maternal Deprivation Reassessed*) and by feminist sociologists and psychologists (for example, *Motherhood Meanings, Practices and Ideologies*, edited by Ann Phoenix, Anne Woollett and Eva Lloyd). Research carried out since Bowlby's early work in the 1940s has shown that separation *per se* does *not* have adverse effects, unless it occurs in combination with other critical factors. However, it is important to set his work in historical context. Children's homes and residential nurseries were understaffed and inhumane in 1951 when he wrote *Maternal Care and Mental Health*. The improvement in their practices does owe much to Bowlby. Yet the burden of guilt mothers carry for even the briefest absence from their children also owes a great deal to Bowlby.

The influence of the popularisation his work has been immense. As sociologist and psychologist Barbara Tizard points out, it became accepted wisdom among doctors, teachers and social workers that women with children under the age of three, or even five, put them at serious risk by going out to work, and that day care or nursery schooling is harmful for children under the age of three. Until the 1950s it was quite common for British nurseries to take children from the age of two in the belief that communal experience provided valuable socialisation.[49]

Bowlby's consideration of ambivalence concerns the space between mother and child, and their negotiation of distance and closeness, whereas Melanie Klein's concept of ambivalence relates to the splitting of objects. His ideas on parental ambivalence, infantile ambivalence and issues relating to separation can be found in a paper entitled 'Psychoanalysis and Childcare'. Here he recognises the inevitability of ambivalence but considers it to be an *impediment* to attachment. He believed that appropriate childcare techniques would minimise the development of ambivalence in children, who would in turn make less ambivalent parents – less prone to produce ambivalently attached children with attendant behavioural problems. Hence, ambivalence was a problem and its regulation in children was to be achieved by the provision of a constant, beneficent maternal presence which would then limit a child's experience of conflict, rage and thus ambivalence. In Bowlby's words, a child needs loving parents 'who respect his needs and realise that to deny them is often to generate in him powerful forces of libidinal demand and propensity to hatred which can later cause great difficulties for him and us'.[50]

Although most depth psychologists would agree with Anna Freud's observation that no degree of devotion on the part of the mother can successfully cope with the boundless demands made on her by her child,[51] Bowlby believed that a mother could merely by her *presence* minimise a child's experience of conflict. In his view, one of the major effects of mother–child separation is a great intensification of the conflict of ambivalence. Thus if children are excessively ambivalent, in his view this is due to absent working mothers. He writes, 'In days gone by when higher education was closed to them, there was less conflict between the claims of family and career.'[52]

Bowlby is sympathetic, even chivalrous, in pointing out women's immense contribution to the helping professions, and acknowledging that it ill befits a man to criticise, and that society ought to adjust to women's needs. Nevertheless, if children's ambivalence is being insufficiently mediated, it is, he believes, definitely due to maternal absence. Working mothers are less likely to achieve childcare characterised by the 'friendly intervention' which avoids 'stimulating anger and bitterness'.[53] (Of course this begs the question as to whether mothers who are at home all the time are more likely to achieve 'friendly intervention'!)

But what of *maternal* ambivalence? Bowlby's comments on this do at least open up a discussion of the topic but, finally, the clarity of his thought is undermined by his crusading desire to create better parents. He seems well aware that he is breaking a taboo simply by raising the topic:

> But, unfortunately, coupled with these delicious and loving feelings there comes all too often an admixture – I hesitate to say it – an admixture of resentment and even of hatred. The intrusion of hostility into a mother's, or a father's, feelings for the baby seems so strange and often horrifying that some of you may find it difficult to believe.[54]

Bowlby attributes parental ambivalence to the process in which caring for a baby evokes unconscious conflicts in parents that originate from their relationships with their own parents. While accepting that all parents undergo this experience, he nevertheless splits ambivalent parents into two categories. Good ambivalent parents recognise the true nature of their feelings towards their child and adjust their behaviour accordingly. Bad ambivalent parents re-employ the infantile defence mechanisms they developed to deal with conflictual feelings aroused in them by their own parents.

Possibly Bowlby recognised that his discussion of parental ambivalence, aside from changing attitudes to childcare, was in danger of ending up by simply magnifying parental guilt. He offered reassurance:

> Are we prescribing, it may well be asked, that parents should be eternally loving and tolerant and friendlily controlling? I think not . . . and as a parent I hope not. We parents have our angry and jealous feelings too, and whether we like it or not they are going to be expressed sometimes . . . The occasional outburst or slap does little harm.[55]

He suggests that such displays of temper are even useful in that they demonstrate to the children that parents have the same problems that they do. Nevertheless, the underlying message is clear: (1) maternal ambivalence will evoke rage in children; (2) this interferes with the establishment of secure attachment; (3) that produces life-long damage. Admittedly Bowlby emphasises that mothers are not to blame. Their 'mistakes' are due to their inability to regulate their ambivalence, which arises out of the intensity of conflicts provoked in their childhood.

There is so much in Bowlby's paper on ambivalence that I would agree with. Excessive splitting apart of love and hate, so that love can no longer mitigate hate can be destructive. Defence against ambivalence can produce the need to cling in either parent or child (in Bowlby's terms an intense need to possess the child's love). And certainly the aetiology of a failure to tolerate ambivalence can lead us to a mother's relationship with her own mother. I would also agree with his view on the importance of a mother recognising and owning her ambivalence. However, I disagree with the way he believes this can be achieved. He suggests that a child's experience of frustration and hatred should be carefully limited through the constant presence of a mother, thus minimising the development of ambivalence in childhood. In sum, children with a reduced experience of conflict will become adults able to be conscious of and regulate their ambivalent feelings.

Instead of arguing that maternal ambivalence needs as far as possible to be reduced, I have argued that maternal ambivalence is an important element in the necessary separation-individuation dynamic of both mother and child. As I have suggested in this chapter, ambivalence provokes the circulation of passion between mother and child, creating a force for concern, for thought, and for aggressive differentiation. Ambivalence is part of the separation-individuation process, maybe the motor for it, not simply an unwanted by-product of it.

Bowlby's belief that separation provokes frustration which then leads to dangerous intensity of love and hate continues to have an impact on beliefs about the mother–child relationship, through the dissemination of bonding theory which has been subjected to a variety of critiques. In her book *Mother–Infant Bonding: A Scientific Fiction*, the academic psychologist Diane E. Eyer traces a direct line from Bowlby's attachment theory to the rise of bonding theory which has dominated obstetrics and paediatrics for the last decade, to the extent that hospitals in the USA have designated bonding rooms and nurses record bonding times on special charts.[56] Bonding theory – as opposed to common-sense ideas of affectional connection – asserts that post-partum separation of mother and baby interferes with both infant and maternal development, leading potentially to child abuse. Eyer discredits the studies, revealing that they failed to conform to the most basic rules of research design. The original study was of only 28 first-time mothers. The questions they were asked to assess their degree of bonding included, 'Have you been out since the baby was born, and who sat?' A score of 0 was given if the mother had been out, felt good about it, and did not think about the infant while she was out, and a score of 3 was given if she hadn't left the baby or had, but had thought constantly about it. While bonding theory may have prompted more sensitive treatment of mothers and babies in hospitals, it has undoubtedly been responsible for an enormous amount of anxiety and guilt in mothers who feel that ambivalence is evidence of a failure to bond. The journalist and author Anne Karpf, reviewing Eyer's book, made the point that bonding research occurred at a time of growing female emancipation, when women were leaving the home in pursuit of professional opportunities and was perhaps a reaction to those developments.[57] Bonding, as the intellectual backdrop to conservative approaches to women's behaviour, stems from Bowlby's theories of maternal deprivation. The theories have a further ideological root in common in their commitment to maintaining an idealised conception of maternity and femininity during the post-war period.

Bonding theory is also closely allied to the now discredited but still profoundly influential theory that babies and their mothers initially exist in a state of post-natal fusion – 'normal autism' or 'primary narcissism' with their mothers, ideas looked at in Chapter 2. Understandings of the mother–child couple as fused inevitably raises the issue of how they are to separate or unstick from their oneness. Generally speaking, psychoanalysis, including Jacques Lacan's revised narrative of the Freudian Oedipus complex, suggests that the father is needed mainly to rupture this fusionary relationship, to dissolve the superglue mothers use to bind/bond their babies to them.

In his critique of psychoanalytic theory concerning the role of the father, Andrew Samuels observed that the mother–infant relationship is assumed not to contain any capacity within itself for the separating out and subsequent psychological development of the infant. Samuels makes the point that claims by theorists as diverse as Lacan, Mahler and Winnicott that there is a mother–infant fusionary relationship that the father must rupture in order that the infant may attain mental health simply do not recognise that babies themselves desire to grow and separate from their mothers as well as having fantasies of resting in permanent oceanic bliss. And mothers, too, may sense that they have other things to do with their time than remain immersed in primary maternal preoccupation. Samuels concluded: 'Babies and mothers have an investment in separation and to overlook this is to insult babies and mothers.'[58] This investment expresses itself in and is managed by maternal ambivalence towards the baby every bit as much as by the baby's ambivalence towards the mother.

Knowing the Worst

D. W. Winnicott wrote that 'children seem able to deal with being hated', that they 'can meet and make use of the ambivalence which mother feels and shows'. But what they cannot use in their emotional development 'is the mother's repressed unconscious hate which they only meet in their living experiences in the form of reaction formation'. Winnicott concluded: 'at the moment the mother hates she shows special tenderness. There is no way a child can deal with this phenomenon'.[59]

In her study of separation and sleep problems, Dilys Daws cited research that indicates that maternal ambivalence can interfere with a baby's capacity to separate from its mother and thus feel safe enough to sleep at night.[60] And, indeed, a conventional understanding of ambivalence is that it makes separation too frightening to risk. But, like Winnicott, Daws makes an important qualification. In her view the issue is whether the mother is conscious or not of ambivalence. If she lacks self-knowledge, it can carry over to a not-knowing about the range of her baby's feelings and rhythms.

Winnicott's insistence that a child both needs and utilises the experience of being hated is important, but the distinction he draws between conscious and unconscious hatred raises problems. It demands a degree of consciousness that denies how deeply rooted hate is in the unconscious. And it requires a degree of control over hatred that negates the intense conflict between love and hate contained within ambivalence. At a crude level, we could ask what difference it makes to a child if a mother slaps it out of conscious or unconscious hatred. I think we need to dispense with Winnicott's division of hatred into good/conscious hatred and bad/unconscious hatred and to think rather in terms of different expressions of hatred. Hatred without love – hatred outside of ambivalence – can be entirely destructive and can lead to gross abuse. And hatred accompanied by terrible shame and fear, fostered by a culture which cannot bear to contemplate maternal ambivalence, can also lead to the kind of reaction formation Winnicott describes.

Once again what I want to consider is the impact of the experience of maternal ambivalence on a mother's evolving capacity to mother. The issue is not so much that *mothers need to be conscious of ambivalence*, but rather that *ambivalence itself can provoke consciousness* of what is going on between mother and baby. It is the unruly, unacceptable nature of hatred that breeds thought and concern; the aggressive fantasies, the violent impulses bring women face to face with themselves – and with their children. Some can bear it. Some find it unbearable.

Hester, quoted above, went into motherhood wanting to be a 'success' at something and determined to avoid her own mother's mistakes. Her desire for controlled perfection and success collided head on, or perhaps played a part in the construction of her response to ambivalent feelings towards her daughter Diane. In her case the anguish of ambivalence precipitated self-knowledge – as well as an urgent need to understand her daughter:

> I had no idea how much anger and hatred there was inside me. I had always been a nice little person, afraid and rather submissive. I had been in therapy but it didn't give me access to all the feelings of rage and anger at being left out, disliked and resented that surfaced after Diane was born. I've had to work that through myself. Motherhood has made me come to terms with it. I feel now that I can separate from the children a bit more and begin to lead something of my own life, because I have looked the enemy in the face and seen it was me. All the aggression that I hated in my mother and hated in Diane, I can now locate in myself – and I have somehow united with it.

I am suggesting that it is the experience of maternal ambivalence that provides a woman with a sense of her independent identity. The pain of ambivalence, the distress in recognising that the child hates her for frustrating its desires, and that she hates the child for frustrating her independent needs, can be a force for affirming her independent identity. Both mother and child need the mother's affirmation of her own needs, desires, opinions, rage, love and hatred if separateness is to be established – and thus relationship.[61]

6

Unravelling Femininity and Maternity

I feel very guilty about feeling so angry. I feel great remorse.
Even though I wouldn't hit her – the fact that I actually want
to, or feel that violent towards a *child*, devastates me.

I don't know how to deal with my anger. I'm very bad at
expressing it. In our house you were either totally violent and
volatile like my brother and father, or you were nice and peacemakers like my mother and me. It was inculcated in me that rage
was not the appropriate thing for me. I would like Georgina
to be rather better than me at feeling safely angry, but I can see
her becoming like me. If I get irritated with Alan, she gets all
protective and keeps telling me not to be cross with him. I see
her becoming a carbon copy of me – too anxious to please.

Lynette's doubts about herself as a mother appear to be somewhat
contradictory. On the one hand she castigates herself for *becoming*
angry inside herself with her child and having fantasies of hitting
her, and on the other hand she wishes she *could* be angry on the
social level. She fears that her daughter is witnessing and may be
identifying with a passive, conciliatory, weak mother.

Behind the contradiction in Lynette's view of her capacity to
mother – as either too angry or incapable of being angry – lies the
tension of maternal ambivalence. She does not 'see' her ambivalence; instead she understands herself as being either too nasty or
too nice. She cannot conceptualise the co-existence of her hating
and loving feelings. She simply feels inadequate and guilty. She sees
the origin of her acquiescent personality, her inability to process
anger, in her own family history where more muscular feelings
were expressed by the men whilst the women were the passive

peacemakers. Hence she feels at sea when confronted by the powerful passions aroused by motherhood. For Lynette, anger is a shameful foreign body she is ill-equipped to encounter.

Lynette's personal history undoubtedly played an important part in her response to motherhood. And her understanding of her difficulties with anger as a gender issue – men are permitted rage and women are not – is accurate. But there is more to it. As I have pointed out, our culture displays its ambivalence about maternal ambivalence by insisting on adherence to a maternal norm. Mothers like Lynette are, without realising it, always measuring themselves against just such a norm. They have internalised it; what was social and apparent is now subjective and hidden. Mothers are measured, or measure themselves, as either admirably feminine (loving, receptive, sensitive) or disastrously unfeminine (aggressive, phallic, smothering). However, we need to recall that Lynette wishes she could be angry. In her wish, she finds herself in alignment with a parallel discourse on mothering that has developed since the eighteenth century in which mothers are sometimes described as admirably unfeminine (strong, active, resilient) or disastrously feminine (weak, passive, narcissistic). We shall explore both narratives of motherhood in this chapter. Mothers like Lynette struggle to make sense of their tale of ambivalent feelings in a culture characterised by this split, between two different but equally and insistently normative representations of motherhood. The meaning Lynette's ambivalent feelings have for her are thus coloured both by her personal history and by cultural representations of motherhood with which she is in contact. These split representations of motherhood encode the history of our culture's ways of responding to the unpalatable presence of maternal ambivalence.

Healthy Mothers

During the eighteenth century, concern with the quality of mothering was prompted by a desire to avoid the loss of manpower caused by the high infant mortality rate. Motherhood became an overriding issue for both radical and conservative writers. Jean-Jacques Rousseau illustrated the increasing idealisation of motherhood when he wrote (on the importance of breastfeeding) that 'Where mothers resume nursing their children, morals will be reformed; natural feeling will revive in every heart; the state will be repopulated; this first step alone will re-unite everyone.'[1] In 1769 William Buchan, in his highly influential *Domestic Medicine, or a Treatise on the Prevention and Care of Diseases by Regimen and Simple Medicines*, wrote, 'Women are the agents through whom men become either healthy or sickly, through whom they are useful in the world, or become plagues on society.'[2] The women of the rising middle classes, copying the ways of the leisured aristocratic lady, appeared unfit for motherhood. Buchan inveighed against the inculcation of aristocratic femininity: 'Would mothers instead of having their daughters instructed in many trifling accomplishments, employ them in plain work and housewifery, and allow them sufficient exercise in the open air, they would both make them more healthy mothers, and more useful members of society.'[3]

The tension between femininity and maternity attracted the attention not only of those intent on reforming motherhood but also of those concerned with the condition of women. There has been a long tradition of invoking maternal inadequacy as an argument in favour of the education of women. In *Vindication of the Rights of Woman* (1792) Mary Wollstonecraft argued that, as the bearers and educators of children, women played a crucial role – for which they were ill-prepared:

> To be a good mother, a woman must have sense, and that independence of mind which few women possess who are taught to depend entirely on men. Meek wives are in general foolish mothers . . .[4]

Wollstonecraft was opposing the ideology of sexual difference enshrined in eighteenth-century conduct literature which held that women's 'softer' mental qualities *were* of a piece with their function as wives and mothers, and evidence of their natural suitability for a domestic role.

By the nineteenth century, however, Wollstonecraft's opposition to femininity enters the conduct literature itself. Rather than arguing for the education of women, concern for the disjuncture between maternity and femininity became part of the drive to strengthen and affirm the doctrine of separate spheres. Mothers, as domestic guardians of the nation's moral and spiritual well-being, were forbidden frivolous femininity: Mrs Ellis, perhaps the most popular of the mid-century writers of conduct manuals for women, observed that

Notwithstanding all the evils arising out of the unfitness of silly women to undertake the duties of wives and mothers, there still prevails amongst men a popular outcry against women of an opposite character.[5]

Mrs Ellis advocated not education for women, but self-improvement, for 'children seldom love long those whom they are unable to respect, and thus a fond and foolish mother invariably brings upon herself the neglect and often contempt of her family'.[6] Motherhood should, in Mrs Ellis's view, have the 'power to render the feeblest and most delicate of women, unflinching, heroical and bold'.[7]

Mrs Ellis's condemnation of weak mothers and her praise for maternal strength and fortitude continued to characterise texts on motherhood well into the twentieth century. Amongst feminists, Dora Russell, like Mary Wollstonecraft before her, invoked the improvement of mothering, in her call for both education and birth control for women:

There are quite a number of women whose minds and bodies are not fitted or have not been fitted by their upbringing and education to produce and care for children. This is a source of distress to many people who . . . did not think of it at the right moment, when the education of women in public and private schools was being developed.[8]

Russell's arguments in favour of birth control splits the feminine weak women from the worthy mothers: 'Those in whom the courage to create survives when choice is free and all the facts are known are those best fitted to bring children into the world, and breed in them eagerness and intrepidity.'[9]

Dora Russell wrote *Hypatia*, from which I have quoted, in 1925 – prior to the huge impact psychoanalysis was to have on thinking about motherhood. In 1963, when Betty Friedan wrote *The Feminine Mystique*, the influence of the discipline is evident – and in more than her attack upon it. She couches her call for equal opportunities for women in the by now familiar framework of a critique of femininity in the context of motherhood: 'Mothers with infantile selves will have even more infantile children, who will retreat even earlier into fantasy from tests of reality.'[10] While previous writers had thought in terms of mothers' example and influence, Friedan assumes it is the mother's *personality* that will shape the child's.

It might have been expected that psychoanalysis would have been a powerful ally for those, feminists and non-feminists alike, who argue against the elision of femininity and maternity. Indeed, psychoanalysis *has* widened our understanding of motherhood – through decades of debate on the significance of mothering. Yet psychoanalysis has, at the same time, confirmed the link between femininity and maternity and thus the maternal norm which leaves many mothers feeling so abnormal. Competing discourses on motherhood suggest, on the one hand, that the characteristics associated with femininity (sensitivity, receptivity, the capacity to care) render women *fit* to mother: on the other, that the inculcation of feminine behaviour (weakness, passivity, narcissism) has rendered women *unfit* to mother. We see both points of view reflected in the evolution of psychoanalytic theory, with, for example, the psychoanalytic pioneer Jeanne Lampl de Groot representing the latter position in her claim that feminine women make poor mothers.[11] But, at the same time, psychoanalysis brought something new to the elision of femininity and maternity, namely a developmental perspective in which maternity is seen as the developmental goal of femininity. Obviously, psychoanalysis is not a homogeneous entity. There are many different schools, and there is no simple relationship between theory and practice. No analyst or therapist in their consulting room would openly pathologise a mother for 'failing to achieve femininity' or for 'manifesting maternal ambivalence'. But there are particular problems in psychoanalytic approaches to motherhood and to femininity which are embedded in and determined by the history of psychoanalytic theory-making.

The Double Image of Motherhood

Freud's belief in the influence of the lack of a penis on the configuration of femininity is the most 'notorious and popular' version of the Freudian view of women, men and sex.[12] In my view, inadvertently, the concept of penis envy has also been a major force in the pathologising of maternal ambivalence.

Freud described how, for the individual, a route from primary narcissism to object love will be found in the confrontation with a body part, or lack thereof, which is experienced as other to their selfhood, and hence worthy of the term object. For the boy the object is the penis. For the girl, this object will be the penis she comes to recognise she doesn't have. This lack will be supplemented with a series of symbolic equivalences: penis = faeces = gift = baby. Freud named the sequence of events that leads the girl out of narcissism the castration complex.[13]

Freud's theories of penis envy and the castration complex have been comprehensively critiqued and I am not concerned here to evaluate the theory in terms of right and wrong. Rather, my interest is in how his whole way of thinking led to a magnification of the already existing tensions between femininity and maternity. Briefly, according to Freud, the achievement of normal female identity out of an initial bisexuality depends on a girl responding to the impact of the recognition of castration by turning away from her mother. She must suppress her active libido and develop the passive desire that is the only kind that ensures she will be loved by her father. From now on, 'the girl will desire to have the phallus and the boy will struggle to represent it . . . this is the indissoluble desire of their lives'.[14] For a female, the desire for a child, initially from the father, functions symbolically as a pursuit of the penis she lacks. In Juliet Mitchell's words, 'Motherhood purports to fill the absence which femininity covers over.'[15]

Mitchell was referring to the role a baby plays in a woman's attempt to compensate for castration. As she put it, 'phallic potency and maternity – for women and men – came to stand for wholeness'.[16] Thus Freud inadvertently produces a double image of the mother – one that represents her as 'phallic' and 'castrated'.[17]

Freud focused on motherhood and female development in his two papers 'Femininity' and 'Female Sexuality'. He posited that normal development in a girl entailed the movement from her 'masculine phase to the feminine one to which she is biologically destined'.[18] However, he remarks that femininity is not identical with passivity, and to justify this claim he invokes mothering:

> Even in the sphere of human sexual life you soon see how inadequate it is to make masculine behaviour coincide with activity and feminine with passivity. A mother is active in every sense towards her child.[19]

Had the development of psychoanalytic thinking stopped with this remark of Freud's, we could claim that psychoanalysis had indeed achieved the divorce of conventional notions of femininity from maternity, thus opening the way for an acknowledgement of the full panoply of paradoxical emotions and behaviour that mother-hood evokes.

Freud's double image of mother reflects precisely the split repre-sentation that I have suggested constructs – and confuses – women's experience of themselves as mothers. I think that Freud's double image, both phallic and castrated, has a richness lacking in other theories which try to resolve the split. The joint representation of power and powerlessness implicit in his theory of female development resonates with the lived experience of mothers in contemporary Western societies. Mothers find children both draining and a source of plenitude. Being a mother lends a richness and sense of power to a woman's life, but equally she feels devoured and depleted by the all-encompassing demands of motherhood. At the social level, the phallic-castrated mother is writ large in the contradiction between domestic responsibility and a woman's comparative political invisibility.

Freud's description of mother–child interaction, like his represen-tation of the mother, is interestingly contradictory. On the one hand he sees it as an inevitably conflictual relationship. On the other hand, there is Freud's by now notorious observation that the mother–son relationship is the most free from ambivalence of all human relationships.[20] The heart of the mother–child conflict, in Freud's view, offered in the two papers on female development, lies in the child's inevitable insatiability: 'Childhood love is boundless: it demands exclusive possession, it is not content with less than all.'[21] He believed that the disappointment and reproach a child voices with regard to its mother need to be placed in the context of such insatiability: 'it is impossible that the child's reproach can be justified as often as it is met with. It seems, rather, that the child's avidity for its earliest nourishment is altogether insatiable, that it never gets over the pain of losing its mother's breast.'[22]

Freud also attributed a girl child's fear of her mother to the projection of the child's own early aggressive impulses towards the mother. The fear of being killed by the mother then justifies the child's aggressive fantasies about her. In a way that was to become typical of psychoanalytic theorising in this area, Freud focuses predominantly on the child's side of the conflict. But at this point he does turn to the mother and observes that 'It is impossible to say how often this fear of the mother is supported by an unconscious hostility on the mother's part which is sensed by the girl.'[23] Despite hedging his bets with a cautious disclaimer, Freud is here approaching the issue of mutual hostility and mutual ambivalence.

The importance of Freud's recognition of the infant's insatiability and a concomitant maternal hostility is twofold. It allowed for the operation of unconscious fantasy on the relationship, and it indicated that the child and the mother inevitably have divergent aims. The relationship is constantly coloured by contradictory desires, and mother and child rarely want precisely the same thing at the same moment. The mother's desire is of course often satisfied by the child's satisfaction – but what if the child is, as Freud thought it was, permanently dissatisfied?

As I said above, Freud's representation of motherhood does convey the profoundly contradictory experience of being a mother: the power and powerlessness, the sense of fullness and emptiness. Regrettably his followers chose not so much to pursue the tensions and conflicts and contradictions as to resolve them.

Take, for example, the work of American psychoanalyst David Levy, a leading figure in the child guidance movement. In Levy's hands, Freud's mother, 'active in every way', becomes a woman with unresolved longings to express 'masculine' drives, while the child, the substitute for the longed-for penis, must inevitably be subjected to the mother's penis envy. In 1940 he wrote:

> The theory of penis envy helps to explain reinforcing factors in maternal overprotection in regard to the marked predominance of male children and of aggressive mothers in that group. That a high degree of aggression in females is in itself prognostic of overprotection is not to be inferred. Rejecting mothers, whether of sons or daughters, are also more likely to be aggressive than other mothers.[24]

In other words, because the Freudian child is equated with the penis, the aggression Levy's mother feels towards the child must be motivated by her own penis envy. The manifestation of penis-envy-inspired aggression is in either overprotection or rejection. A mother may overprotect in response to her own aggressive impulses, or these impulses may cause her simply to reject. Now, of course, envy *can* magnify hatred within maternal ambivalence. A mother may envy a child the very mothering the child is receiving. But the reading of maternal aggression as driven by penis envy served not to illuminate ambivalence but only to pathologise it.

Angry, irritated, impatient, hating mothers were simply poorly developed unnatural women.

What was extraordinary about the images of the rejecting and the overprotecting mother is that they almost immediately developed a powerful hold on psychoanalysis and hence on psychoanalytically inspired ideas and practices of child-rearing. Anna Freud perceived this, and regretted it. Condemning the wholesale pathologising of mothers as 'rejecting', in the mid-1950s she wrote,

> On the clinical side, more and more of the gravest disturbances ... were attributed to the presence of rejection. On the case-worker's side, more and more mothers were pronounced to be cold, not outgoing, unresponsive, unloving, hating, in short, rejecting of their children. This caused much heart-searching and also much self-accusation, especially among mothers of abnormal children.[25]

The twin daughters of penis envy – the overprotecting and the rejecting mothers – obscure many nuances of maternal behaviour, and certainly cloud over a clear understanding of maternal ambivalence. They are, however, extremely tenacious. Since the 1940s and '50s the focus of analytical inquiry has shifted to pre-Oedipal issues, but, in spite of this, the notion of the overprotecting mother and rejecting mother live on unchanged. Indeed, thirty years after David Levy coined the term, Otto Kernberg wrote of the narcissistic patient that 'narcissistic and at the same time overprotective mother figures appear to be the main etiological element in the psychogenesis of this pathology'.[26]

We should note how later thinkers have reformulated penis envy, viewing it not as a primary force in the construction of femininity, but rather as a defence – the wish for a penis is considered a defence against a devouring or controlling mother.[27] But even in such reconceptualisations of penis envy the understanding of female aggression is associated with the concept of penis envy.

The Great Debate

Of course, I am not claiming that mothers are never overprotecting or rejecting. Mothers certainly resort to either and often to both ways of being with their children. Children undoubtedly experience their mothers as painfully rejecting – the source of all goodness spitefully withheld – or as overprotective – the source of unfair prohibitions. The point I am making is that the splitting and pathologising of maternal aggression produced a specific maternal norm in which the 'good mothers' become equated with a passive, receptive femininity. Women who fail to achieve the maternal ideal are therefore resisting femininity.

I think one reason why psychoanalytic theory fosters an elision of femininity and maternity was the way in which motherhood became implicated in the 'great debate' around female sexuality that began within psychoanalysis in the mid-1920s and reached a peak in 1935. Starting as a debate about the concept of the castration complex, it evolved into a dispute over the status and nature of female sexuality. Those thinkers opposed to Freud saw the concept of the castration complex as derogatory to women. In Juliet Mitchell's words, 'In repudiating it they hoped to elevate women and to explain what women consisted of.'[28] A central concern was to discover what women possessed which was uniquely their own – as opposed to their being classed as lesser men. What they undoubtedly possessed was everything to do with motherhood. As I mentioned earlier, there is a certain ambiguity in Freud's representation of the mother; she is simultaneously powerful and powerless. An expansion of this kind of thinking could well have led to a fruitful flexibility; instead, the struggle to resolve the contradiction led either to the elision that we have noted, or to the splitting off of femininity from maternity as, for example, in the work of Jeanne Lampl de Groot, whom Freud acknowledged in his paper on 'Femininity'.

Amongst all the participants in the debate over women, not one contested the clinical reality of penis envy, although they disagreed as to the interpretation to be put on it.[29] The psychoanalyst Ruth Mack Brunswick, for example, believed that the wish for a child precedes by far the wish for a penis. For both sexes this represents the desire to possess the key attribute of the omnipotent mother – the capacity to produce a baby.[30] In other words, the desire for maternity is originally a search for maternal power and not a search for a lacking penis. Jeanne Lampl de Groot considered femininity to be synonymous with passivity. So when women love men – rather than receiving male love – they, too, are being masculine. Hence, mothers must often be masculine! She writes:

> Just as the little girl satisfies her activity in her play with dolls, so the woman utilizes a bit of her masculinity in nourishing

and caring for her child . . . Feminine, narcissistic women are usually poor mothers.[31]

However, for many whose involvement in the 'great debate' was based on the desire to discover what women possessed that was uniquely their own, to dub mothers as 'masculine' was clearly unacceptable. Psychoanalyst Helene Deutsch attempted a different way of reconciling motherhood and femininity while acknowledging maternal 'activity':

> Motherliness is accompanied by specific active ingredients. Freud has already called attention to the mother's activity . . . D. Levy has particularly emphasised this aspect of the maternal function. This activity is not of an aggressive, masculine character. On the contrary, I believe that it represents that component of motherliness which is closest to the phylogenetic and instinctual.[32]

This quotation is from Deutsch's important work on motherhood which comprises the second volume of her *Psychology of Women*. A somewhat contradictory book, it has provoked rather different responses. Lisa Appignanesi and John Forrester describe it as 'one long paean of praise to the mother, both as privileged first object and as ultimate feminine destiny',[33] while Janet Sayers, author of *Mothering Psychoanalysis* asserted that Deutsch grasped the full complexity of motherhood, stressing its historical, social, biological and psychological determinants.[34]

I think that where Deutsch is not concerned with refuting, modifying or at times even corroborating theories which pathologise maternal ambivalence, she writes movingly and acutely of the constant pressure of conflicting emotions within or experienced by motherhood. She describes motherhood as a world of polarities: activity–passivity, aggression–masochism, femininity–masculinity, love–hatred. As she puts it, 'The frequent conflicts between these forces constantly influencing one another lend depth and richness to the psychology of motherhood.'[35]

Deutsch is perhaps best known these days for her elaboration of Freud's theory of feminine masochism. She suggested that there is a biological foundation for women's masochism in the suffering entailed in menstruation, defloration and childbirth. She distinguishes feminine masochism from perverse masochism in that the latter involves reception of pain and cruelty, while the former employs self-destructive guilt.[36] Where motherhood is concerned she posits a normal, necessary masochism in which 'the narcissistic forces of self preservation and the masochistic function of motherhood must come to harmonious agreement'. In this context, masochism is equated with a maternal willingness to sacrifice. On the other hand, excessive masochistic tendencies lead to a *mater dolorosa* 'groaning under the cross of pregnancy and yet happy in this condition'.[37]

I disagree with Deutsch that there is a biologically determined masochism in women. However, as Winnicott hinted, we can make use of the concept of maternal masochism. We can think of masochistic structures as attempts to deal with and defend against the guilt evoked by maternal hatred. Mothers can pursue an excessively giving, hyper-altruistic mode with their children in an attempt to gain absolution for those impulses which fill them with guilt. Maternal masochism then deals with maternal ambivalence.

As Teresa Brennan points out, Deutsch's definition of masochism was contradictory. While seeing it as biologically determined and hence specific to women, she also described it as 'activity turned inwards'.[38] Deutsch was well aware of the role of aggression in mothering. She wrote, for instance, of the unconscious aggression of the breastfeeding mother who moves between her fear of being devoured and her corresponding self-protective impulse to destroy the child. She suggested that the biblical story in which Moses was hidden in the bullrushes signifies, not protection from paternal aggression, as Freud suggested, but protection from *maternal* aggression. Her analysis of the weakness–strength dichotomy displayed in Freud's dual mother was that maternal weakness reflects passive tendencies in relation to their children (which are the outcome of earliest desires for their father) while maternal strength reflects active tendencies which are the outcome of earliest desires towards their mother. Rather than dubbing good mothers masculine, as did Jeanne Lampl de Groot, Deutsch posited two cores in women: a 'feminine core' and a 'motherly core', the latter being characterised by tenderness and altruism. She comments:

> If this protective, defensive and nurturing activity is accompanied by aggressive masculine components, these do not draw upon the sources of feminine motherliness, but upon adjoining psychic spheres hostile to it.[39]

The tragic irony for Deutsch's standing as a theorist was that her defence of mothers was counterproductive. In her attempt to save mothers from accusations of aggressive masculinity, she inadvertently rendered maternity synonymous with passivity and masochism, which, as Appignanesi and Forrester point out, became widely perceived as the Freudian orthodoxy after the Second World War. She had proposed that maternal aggression is prompted not by *over*protectiveness in response to destructive penis envy, but by protectiveness: 'It is true that the influences of aggressiveness and sensuality are discernible in maternal love, but in the motherly woman the surplus of existing aggressive ingredients is diverted from the child to the environment.'[40] In her desire to defend mothers she is inevitably drawn into producing a maternal norm entirely at odds with the complexity of maternal experience she highlights elsewhere.

She confronts David Levy directly, writing that she considers 'Levy's view that "all maternal over-protection can be regarded as compensatory of unconscious hostility" [as] an excessive generalization'.[41] In her view maternal anxiety is generated not by unconscious hostility, although 'perhaps there is no human relation, not even that of mother to child, that is free of such impulses',[42] but rather by the mother's deep need to preserve her unity with her child. Overprotection is thus generated, not by penis envy and its concomitant hostility, but by separation anxiety. Despite her opposition to generalisations about motherhood, she was herself drawn into producing a monolithic maternal norm. The deep need to preserve unity with the child allows no space for consideration of the equally pressing desires felt by mothers at different moments – such as the wish to push the child away.

I feel that the contradictions in Deutsch's text arise from her engagement with theories that lead to the pathologising of maternal activity and aggression rather than the illuminating of it, and by the difficulty of having, as a primary goal, a description of 'normal' motherhood, with clinical observations of maternal pathology. It is as if two voices sound in the text. She speaks *as a mother*, grasping fully the intricacies and passionate intensity of feeling generated by motherhood, with such observations as 'Mothers always fear for their children and sometimes fear them'.[43] But when she speaks *of mothers*, of maternal pathology, she adheres to the most crude and punitive understanding of the penis envy stance:

There are mothers who transfer their aggressive, envious hatred of men to their own sons. They emasculate their sons by inhibiting their boyish urge to motor activity and drive them into a passive, feminine orientation.[44]

Like Helene Deutsch, the psychoanalyst Karen Horney forged her view of motherhood in the context of psychoanalytic debate around femininity. Unlike Deutsch, Horney abandoned Freud's vision of an initial bisexuality altogether and eventually dispensed with the symbolic equation baby = penis. Disagreeing with the implications of Freud's theory that motherhood is not an innate function, she offered instead her view that little girls display inbuilt characteristics of maternal solicitude; a view which inadvertently pathologises any deviation from the image of mother as domestic madonna. Horney's understanding of motherhood did change during her career but essentially she viewed women as biologically predisposed to mothering, even though their behaviour as mothers was socially determined and informed by their experience of being mothered.

She considered that the equation baby = penis was a theory produced out of male envy of motherhood, and believed it constituted a denigratory attack on women:

This depreciation would run as follows: In reality women simply desire the penis; when all is said and done motherhood is only a burden which makes the struggle for existence harder, and men may be glad that they have not to bear it.[45]

Reacting against the denigration of motherhood that she perceived in theories based on the castration complex, her impulse was to insist on the plenitude of motherhood in its own right:

At this point I, as a woman, ask in amazement, and what about motherhood? And the blissful consciousness of bearing a new life within oneself? And the ineffable happiness of the increasing expectation of the appearance of this new being? And the joy when it finally makes its appearance and one holds it for the first time in one's arms? And the deep pleasurable feeling of satisfaction in suckling it and the happiness of the whole period when the infant needs her care?[46]

This comparatively well-known observation of Horney's has been taken as a general afirmation of women's potential in response to the denigration of femininity that Horney perceived within psychoanalytic theory. However, Horney is equally insisting on the pleasure of maternity in its own right – for its own sake.

While offering a corrective view of maternity by stressing the positive, creative aspect of the experience, she nevertheless had to confront the more negative end of the spectrum. Addressing the issue of ambivalence she observed: 'We prefer to assume that love is the fundamentally given factor and that hostility is an accidental and avoidable occurrence.'[47] She attributed the hostility she perceives in mothers to the fact that 'children may actually and directly revive the images and functions of the parents'.[48] Hence, the conflicts a mother experiences with her child need to be understood as an 'outgrowth' of conflicts with the mother's own parents. Horney writes illuminatingly of the ways in which jealousy, frustration and guilt from the family of origin can be played out between children and parents. Yet, even in Horney we encounter the familiar monolithic representation of the overprotective mother:

> The one form in which the conflict between love and hate may consciously come out is in an over-solicitous attitude . . . [such mothers] are fanatical about their care.[49]

Horney's explanation for maternal overprotectiveness was not that it stems from hostility due to penis envy, but that a son evokes in his mother the ambivalence a woman feels towards her father; she relives this with her son. Janet Sayers has suggested that there is an inexorable drift towards parent-blaming in Horney's work because she locates the aetiology of neurosis in a lack of parental warmth – an account of neurosis as an effect, not of anything internal to the child, but of external abuse alone.[50] I think some understanding of why the representation of overprotection with all its condemnatory crudity surfaces in Horney's work becomes clear at the end of her paper on 'Maternal Conflicts'. Revealingly, she asks, 'Of what practical use are these various insights in our efforts at child guidance?'[51]

The critical, didactic tone that inflects psychoanalytic theorising of maternal experience is in part explained by the move amongst analysts in the 1930s, 1940s and 1950s towards giving advice on child-rearing. As Helene Deutsch put it, 'knowledge of the mother's psychologic processes has become an important part of modern pedagogy'.[52] Accordingly and inevitably, motherhood is viewed less as a relationship to be understood than as a condition to be managed and transformed for the sake of the child. The following comment by Anna Freud is representative:

> There are those who are responsible for their rejecting attitude, who can be exhorted, advised and helped toward a better adjustment to their child, there are also those for whom rejecting is beyond their control.[53]

Once the mother is viewed from the needy standpoint of the vulnerable child she is all too easily seen either to smother or to desert. In the writings of both Deutsch and Horney we observe the same split. When they write as mothers they acknowledge ambivalence and analyse the full ebb and flow of love and hatred in maternal feeling; as clinicians, they view the mother through the selective eyes of the child.

Toxic Hostility

The inability to pursue constructive, non-judgmental, imaginative ways of thinking about maternal ambivalence, inscribed in post-Freudian thought and magnified by psychoanalysis's pedagogic intention, reached its apotheosis in American ego psychology. Theorists of the castration complex identified maternal ambivalence as an outcrop of penis envy and constructed the two linked tropes of motherhood: the overprotecting and the rejecting. In René Spitz's theories we see an example of how psychoanalysis ceased to attempt a description of maternal states of mind; instead, the mother is seen as the origin of practically all infantile ills. Spitz's work illustrates the crude determinism so regretted by Anna Freud. He declared that 'the mother's personality acts as the disease provoking agent, as a psychologic toxin'.[54]

Spitz believed that particular conditions of infancy, for example colic and eczema, were caused by specific maternal behaviour patterns. He listed six major 'damaging maternal behaviour patterns':

1. Primary overt rejection
2. Primary anxious overpermissiveness
3. Hostility in the guise of manifest anxiety
4. Oscillation between pampering and hostility
5. Cyclical mood swings
6. Maternal hostility consciously compensated.[55]

Mothers of children with eczema were considered to manifest number 3. Mothers of children with colic were believed to exhibit number 2. There is little sense of any relationship between mother and child; that colic might produce 'primary anxious overpermissiveness' rather than vice versa.

A glance at Spitz's list of damaging maternal behaviour patterns reveals that the major toxicity was hostility, which then produced anxiety. In other words, you could say that what lies behind Spitz's list are the ordinary passions of motherhood with its flux of love and hate and all the anxiety that such emotions do indeed generate. That these passions should be interpreted wholesale as disease-provoking toxins was due to a need to protect the status of the feminine norm that had emerged from 'the great debate' in psycho-analysis on female sexuality. Good mothering was identified with the achievement of femininity understood as passivity, receptivity, altruism and solicitude. Strong feelings (positive as well as negative) were thus unnatural in a mother and would breed unnatural babies.

The Feminine Paradigm

In Chapter 7 I shall return to the passage of 'overprotecting mothers and rejecting mothers' through psychoanalytic thinking. Now I want to look at how implications of psychoanalytic views of mothering have impinged on the treatment of women during child-birth and pregnancy. There have been a number of differing approaches to this theme since 1970.

The elision of femininity and maternity with the associated pathologising of maternal ambivalence determined understanding of conception, pregnancy and birth. In her book *Women Confined*, sociologist and author Ann Oakley documents the influence of psychoanalytic thinking on health practice.[56] When reproduction and mothering are considered within a framework rooted in a psychoanalytic ideology of femininity, successful conception and birth are equated with successful adaptation to femininity. A woman's feelings about bodily changes during pregnancy, for example, are taken as an index of her attitude to her own femininity. Enjoying the physical transformations is evidence of femininity achieved. Disliking the physical changes, and the reporting to health care professionals of most, if not all, pregnancy symptoms (nausea, vomiting, spotting, headaches, etc.) are considered to express a rejection of motherhood and wifehood as forms of innate femininity. Oakley comments:

> There is a veritable armada of studies that take this line on reproductive womanhood. To regard them seriously as scientific investigation demands a suspension of belief in even the most basic credentials of science, for the central problem is elementary: 'femininity' is a chameleon concept.[57]

Femininity is a cultural product, historically constructed with no fixed referent. As a research variable, femininity cannot be defined in terms of its lowest common denominator because it has none.

Even while the armada of studies attributing women's maternal issues to poorly achieved femininity sails on, voices continue to be raised to assert that, far from being desirable, it is femininity itself that is really the problem. Oakley cites an obstetrician arguing against the insistence on femininity as the prerequisite for good mothering:

> Passivity, dependence, ineptness, emotional lability, and sexual inhibition are so exactly opposite to the requirements of good birth experience and good motherhood that one suspects that they are desired because of a poorly worked through fear of mature women.[58]

Similarly, the psychoanalyst Dana Breen in her 1975 study of first-time mothers found that the least culturally feminine women – in her words 'those who could feel themselves to be . . . active and creative'[59] – are those who enjoy and participate in their childbirth most.

Sheila Kitzinger and others within the Active Birth movement have worked to counteract the dominance of the feminine paradigm for women in relation to childbirth. They have challenged the ubiquity of medical management of childbirth, believing it to be a force that imposes a kind of passive femininity on all labouring women. Such campaigns have successfully changed and significantly improved the conditions of childbirth for women. Yet, inadvertently, a new ideal was created. Mothers in the 1980s seem to have felt that a veritable phallic forcefulness was expected of them. They had to live up to the birth plan they had presented to the hospital. The use of pain relief or surgical intervention was regarded as failure. The muscular fortitude that they felt was expected of them induced, in some mothers, an anxiety about giving birth almost equal to that evoked by the feminine paradigm. Sandra describes her experience of childbirth:

> It was absolute agony. The baby was facing the wrong way. The doctor came in and said, 'I think you are going to need an epidural.' My husband and the midwives all said, 'She can do it, we're sure she can do it.' Months of antenatal training came to the fore in me and I said, 'Give me half an hour.' He left the room and I immediately regretted it, the pain was so bad. I started most unfairly cursing the NCT and screaming for a caesarean. In the end the baby was born 'naturally' though I tore terribly badly. Everyone congratulated me and said how strong I had been, but privately I thought I had been a fool and should have opted for pain relief.

The moralism produced by the elision of femininity and maternity is evident in Sandra's story. Almost from the moment of conception mothers judge themselves, and are judged, as 'good', 'bad', 'strong' or weak.

Feminist thinkers of the late 1960s and '70s in Western countries recognised that motherhood was beginning to be viewed from all sides as the ultimate personality test for women, according to which femininity was either admirably achieved or admirably transcended, depending on ideological outlook. Drawing on their own feelings as mothers, such thinkers began to argue that to experience childbirth as an exam which their sex mysteriously required them to pass or fail contributed massively to maternal misgivings and misery. In Britain Lee Comer combined sociology and maternal 'speaking bitterness' to produce a savage critique of 'the myth of motherhood':

> Their feeling of fear and inadequacy – that they ought to know how to soothe a crying baby but don't, their deep and inadmissible suspicion that they do not love their baby in the way they are supposed to, their total lack of confidence, their knowledge that everyone else expects them to know, conspire to make them feel that they are not real women. Thus each new mother is a link in a chain which preserves the mystique and ensures that the secret is never told.[60]

Many feminist theorists of the 1970's held that the problematic and destructive elision of femininity and maternity was due to the social conditions of motherhood. In 1972, Michelene Wandor wrote cogently on the effects of the isolation of mother and child at home, and the rapidly changing kind of femininity expected of the mother depending on whether she was relating to husband or child. Being with a child alone at home enables a woman to regain some of the 'emotional freedom' of childhood. But replicate this behaviour in an adult context and, in Wandor's words, you are accused of 'being hysterical'. Thus, 'As a mother you have to switch being a child on or off according to who you are with, and often this involves a betrayal of your relationship with your child'.[61]

Rethinking Motherhood

Still other feminist writers turned to psychoanalysis. The 1970s saw a renewal of the earlier psychoanalytic debate on the nature of female sexuality, with the topic of motherhood once again to the forefront – particularly in France and the United States.

Rather than taking motherhood as an outcome of the construction of femininity, these theorists placed the mother at the very heart of its construction. In other words, rather than suggesting that being little girls makes women able to mother 'correctly', women were seen as having been made into little girls by being mothered 'correctly'. In one sense this reversal is a reprise of things said in the debate in the first half of the century and once again we see the 'chameleon'-like qualities of the idea of femininity. British psychoanalytic theorists have tended to view femininity as, in Juliet Mitchell's words, the 'inferiorised psychology' of women.[62] Both Mitchell and later Teresa Brennan emphasise and affirm Freud's view of femininity as observedly true in practice for Western cultures today – in other words that features accurately identified as constituting femininity are not innate but culturally specific.[63] Brennan summarises features of femininity as aggression turned back in on a woman's self, inertia, daydreaming, narcissism, masochism, a weaker sense of justice, less social sense, less capacity for sublimation and greater repression and rigidity.[64] If motherhood is considered the ultimate expression and fulfilment of femininity, the representation of motherhood constructed out of this description of femininity is 'weak' indeed.

Some French theorists, on the other hand, have understood femininity as a subversive power even when the voice that utters it is the mother's voice. In the French writer Hélène Cixous's words, maternal speech is described as 'a song before the symbolic took one's breath away',[65] meaning its pre-existence of a patriarchal social order and its hold on women's lives. American feminists to some extent share the desire of theorists like Cixous or psychoanalyst and author Luce Irigaray to revalue femininity and motherhood as sectors of resistance against the Law of the Father. Rather than taking cultural femininity as synonymous with inertia and passivity, such femininity has been reread through a (somewhat idealised) maternal filter as suggesting an availability to emotionality, a facility for relationship, an admirable absence of aggressivity, and a powerful capacity for receptivity.

Nancy Chodorow's *The Reproduction of Mothering* has undoubtedly had the greatest impact on thinking about mothering of all the feminist psychoanalytic texts of the past twenty years.[66] She explains 'the reproduction of mothering' in terms of object relations theory (see pp. 58, 128 above), demonstrating how the relationship with the mother is internalised differently by children of either sex. Because of their similarities, a girl develops a sense of identity with her mother, making it much more difficult for her to separate from her than for the boy. Thus she is more likely to develop a personal and psychological style marked by a stress on the importance of relationship, emotionality and nurturing – all the conventional maternal traits. The boy, on the other hand, strongly needs to separate and dis-identify from his mother to achieve a sense of being male. So boys grow up fearing close relationships, experiencing intimacy as dangerous, and contemptuous of the maternal traits. The boy has to take on board these attitudes both to separate from the mother *and* to remind himself that he is not like her but is more like his emotionally distant father who has had to toughen himself against the soft and suffocating female world, represented by the mother. The rewards for the boy who sacrifices his potential for human connection in this way are enormous – all the benefits of being male in our society. It is what Andrew Samuels calls the 'male deal'.

From the point of view of mothers-to-be, Chodorow is describing a vicious circle. A girl grows up typically without having established the degree of ego boundaries and autonomy considered essential for a boy. She may lack a firm sense of self, or rather her sense of self involves always being in a nurturing or close relationship with others. When she becomes a mother she will pass on this confusion of boundaries to her daughter. In this view a mother cannot provide her daughter with an experience of differentiation, and will not facilitate her daughter's independence or capacity for self-assertion.[67]

Chodorow introduced research psychologists' accounts of male and female personality traits to provide confirmation of the developmental pathways she has perceived. She cites David Bakan's work in which he claims that male personality is preoccupied with agency (self-protection, self-assertion and self-expansion), while the female personality manifests communion (contact, openness and union).

The significance of Bakan's work is not only that it reinforces Chodorow's account of the birth of a maternally determined femininity, but it positively connotes femininity. Chodorow herself suggests that care and socialisation of girls by women produces attributes which could (and should) be regarded positively: a personality founded on relations and connection, with flexible rather than rigid boundaries, and with a comparatively secure sense of the non-hierarchical nature of gender difference. This provides, in Teresa Brennan's words, a rather gratifying conclusion that 'masculinity is damage'.[68] The claim that connectedness and an absence of spurious and antisocial autonomy figure more in women than men, and the corresponding view that relationships are more important to women, undoubtedly resonates with experience.

As I see it, the problem with the maternally derived femininity Chodorow's theory valorises is that it is based only on a part of maternal experience – love.[69] Hence it is bound to be incomplete and unsatisfactory, hate and ambivalence having been expunged. Jane Flax has suggested that this particular split is characteristic of object relations theory itself which tends to deny and repress aspects of female experience that are not connected with maternity and to overlook the aggression that resides in female sexuality.[70]

Similarly, Andrew Samuels has pointed out how little attention has been paid in psychoanalysis to the study of female aggressive process and fantasy.[71] Maybe it is precisely the absence of aggression and hatred in Chodorow's early and highly influential account of the mother–daughter relationship that alerts us to the need for a deeper understanding of maternal ambivalence. A relationship perceived as constructed out of empathy, identification and 'at-oneness' must involve a denial of the reality of hatred and overlooks the contribution the negotiation of mother–child hatred makes to the personality development of mother and child. Moreover, acceptance of the mother–daughter relationship as one in which separation is problematic more or less demands that we start to recognise maternal ambivalence and its aggressive components as a positive tendency (see Chapter 5).

The conception of the mother that emerged from French theory during the 1970s initially appears to offer ways of thinking about mothering that move beyond the maternal ideal. Feminist theorists Hélène Cixous, Luce Irigaray, Julia Kristeva and Michèle Montrelay, although proposing very different theories, share a voice that contrasts dramatically with British and American feminist work. With French feminist writing we enter a poetical and rhetorical domain which suffers if subjected to an over-literal reading.

In different ways Irigaray and Cixous elaborate the 'maternal metaphor'.[72] They draw on the meanings of maternity and the mother's body to subvert patriarchal values and to confront and revise negative attitudes towards women. Hélène Cixous writes, 'In women there is always something of the mother, repairing, and feeding, resisting separation, a force that does not let itself be cut off but that runs codes ragged.'[73] Cixous here echoes the strand of writing about mothers that has existed since the eighteenth century, according to which mothers are described as admirably unfeminine (strong, active, resilient) as opposed to disastrously feminine (weak, passive, narcissistic). And, indeed, the French feminist employment of the maternal metaphor has been criticised, both in Britain and the USA, for simply reiterating stereotypes. Jacqueline Rose writes of 'the hideous moment when a theory arms itself with a concept of femininity as different, as something other to culture as it is known, only to find itself face to face with, or even entrenched within, the most grotesque and fully cultural stereotypes of femininity itself'.[74]

Domna Stanton, author of works on culture and gender, points out that the strategy of the maternal metaphor provided in the 1970s an enabling mythology. While it may have had an enabling role in relation to women's writing, celebrating the creative, subversive power in motherhood militates against the acknowledgement of the pain, fear, discomfort, weakness, resentment and nastiness encompassed by actual mothering. Moreover, as Stanton puts it, 'the assertion that the maternal constitutes the crucial difference even evokes the stance of the phallic mother, who lays down the Law of the father, rather than lays waste to it'.[75]

Michèle Montrelay manages to avoid the trap of reinventing the phallic mother. She suggests that we need to acknowledge the 'concentric' as well as the 'phallic' character of female sexuality – the former could be described as a more biologically based experience of femininity (a positive femininity) and the latter as constructed out of an experience of lack (a negative femininity).[76] Montrelay contends that the two exist in conflict: they are incompatible and this incompatibility structures the 'feminine unconscious'.

An understanding of femininity as inevitably conflictual – concentric (positive) and phallic (negative) – opens up a space for the recognition of maternal ambivalence. However, the very power that French feminism attributes to maternity leads ineluctably to the desire to minimise or contain the power, rather than to analyse the emotional realities for mothers. We see this, for example, in the evolution of the work of Julia Kristeva.

Kristeva initially acknowledges maternal ambivalence as an aspect of maternal experience that needs further exploration. In her paper, 'Stabat Mater', she analyses the image of the Virgin Mary, highlighting how she both contains and detoxifies the power of maternity, offering women a 'skilful balance of concessions and restraints'.[77] Mary denies man's role in reproduction with the virgin birth, she fulfils women's desire for power in that she is Queen of Heaven, she obstructs a mother's murderous or devouring desires through the privileging of the breast in suckling the infant Jesus, she owns her own suffering in the image of the *Mater Dolorosa*, and finally wields power over death through the Assumption. But, of course, all of this is permitted and obtained through her son.

Kristeva argues that today the myth of the Virgin Mother has lost its power. Hence we need a new myth, encompassing the role of the maternal in female psychology, and crucially, the negative feelings harboured by mothers:

> There might doubtless be a way to approach the dark area that motherhood constitutes for women; one needs to listen more carefully than ever, to what mothers are saying, through

their economic difficulties and . . . through their discomforts, insomnias, joys, angers, desires, pains and pleasure.[78]

Kristeva draws together the strengths and weaknesses, the love and hate potentially contained within maternity. She juxtaposes this text to a description of her own experience of childbirth – suggesting the possibility of a new language and subjectivity that would be closer to the maternal body, its experiences and psychology.[79]

However, Kristeva's writing on the mother changes from the more philosophical nature of 'Stabat Mater' to the more psycho-analytic, for example, in *Black Sun: Depression and Melancholia*.[80] In an earlier hint of this later work – 'Woman's Time' – she adds a note of caution to the employment of the maternal metaphor:

> an archaic, full, total englobing mother with no frustration, no separation, with no break-producing symbolism (with no castration, in other words) . . . But what an unbelievable force for subversion in the modern world! And at the same time, what playing with fire.[81]

Ten years later in *Black Sun* she makes it clear who is in danger of being 'burned' through the celebration of the maternal as a strategy for change. Here she regards the mother no longer from the perspective of a mother but from the position of the child: moving from motherhood as a 'dark area' but one with a potential for illumination, in 'Stabat Mater' to the dark area being synony-mous with death and destruction. In *Black Sun* the text is concerned with depression and melancholia and their relation to a refusal to give up an archaic attachment to the maternal. Kristeva's view is that the symptoms of depression, including the death of speech (asymbolia) are due to a failure by the child to commit 'matricide':

> when it is hindered . . . the maternal object having been intro-jected, the depressive or melancholic putting to death of the self is what follows, instead of matricide. In order to protect mother I kill myself while knowing – phantasmatic and protective knowledge – that it comes from her, the death-bearing she-Gehenna.[82]

From demanding that we pay attention to the maternal voice, Kristeva insists it be silenced for the child's sake. The ambivalent power she perceived in maternity – the love and rage – when she wrote as a philosopher and mother in 'Stabat Mater' later becomes a major force for destruction. Indeed, it is the source of her patients' depression. I noted a similar discrepancy in Helene Deutsch's work between a perspective derived from her experience as a mother and one stemming from a clinical perspective. When both start to write about motherhood as professional clinicians it seems that their capacity to recognise the significance of maternal ambivalence from the mother's point of view deserts them. Instead, maternal ambivalence is deemed the origin of patients' pathology.

In this chapter I have been tracing the evolution of theories of motherhood which mediate mothers' feelings about themselves as mothers. Cultural representations of motherhood depict mother as either 'good' and feminine or 'bad' and feminine, either too passive or too aggressive, either overprotecting or rejecting. That mothers have to learn themselves through these curiously punitive, contradictory images is due, in my view, to the conflation or muddle of maternity and femininity.

If we return to Lynette, whose feelings I recorded at the beginning of the chapter, her view of herself as either too sweet or too angry now makes more sense. She wants to express the sensitivity, receptivity and availability associated with femininity and considered natural in a mother, yet she also repudiates it, longing to be a more muscular mother. Women like Lynette will continue to doubt their capacity to mother as long as maternity is conflated with femininity and seen as a source of subversive strength by some – and as a source of oppression by others.

The linking of femininity and maternity has implications for all women – not just mothers. For it equates becoming a mother with the achievement of full biological and psychological femininity. You are not a real woman until you have had a baby. Women who might in other circumstances prefer to be child-free feel subtly impelled into pregnancy.

A solution – perhaps a utopian one – would be to unravel maternity and femininity. Luce Irigaray argues that this would be achieved only if we could conceive of a maternal genealogy. Margaret Whitford, in her elucidation of Irigaray's thinking, suggests that such a genealogy would

> symbolise the relation between the girl-child and her mother in a way which allowed the mother to be both a mother *and*

a woman, so that women were not forever competing for the unique place occupied by the mother, so that women could differentiate themselves from the mother, and so that women were not reduced to the maternal function.[83]

Irigaray proposes that a reconceptualising of the mother–daughter relationship could enable women to experience a diverse identity. Both Freud and Jung believed that masculinity and femininity are found in both sexes. And within contemporary psychoanalysis bisexuality is becoming more generally recognised as necessary for sexual and psychic integration (see Chapter 9).[84] The time is ripe for a disentangling of femininity and maternity. In tracing the unhappy marriage of the two over the past three centuries, I have tried to show how their association has meant that maternal ambivalence has become equated with unnatural aggression in women.

7

Like a Child

It's as if they press a button and suddenly I'm in there with them – only more extremely there than they are. I behave appallingly, in a way you are not meant to as a mother – without dignity or adulthood.

Alice describes how her children's refusal to comply with her wishes – their defiance – reduces her to helpless rage. It is a moment that is surely familiar to many mothers when their so-called maturity falls away and a woman finds herself behaving as if she were a furious five-year-old. Alice castigates herself for it; becoming a shrieking child is deeply shameful in her eyes. Yet such 'regressing' to child-hood seems to be an inevitable aspect of motherhood. A variety of situations 'press the button', as Alice puts it.

Socially, mothers and young children are frequently (often constantly) isolated from other adults. This induces an intense intimacy in which both mothers and children become the focus of each other's needs and desires. Mutual projective and introjective processes lead both mother and child to experience something of each other's feelings. The baby or child projects her or his rage and frustration into the mother where it marries up with her own infantile feelings of anger and need. A mother's infantile response is mobilised, in part, through the frustration of her needs and wishes (by her recalcitrant offspring) and, in part, by the way the experience of mothering and childcare inexorably lead a woman to re-experience in adulthood aspects of her own experiences in infancy. In other words, the mother's proximity to the child foregrounds the child within the mother.

The sensation of losing control, of adult reticence slipping away, can induce great anxiety and panic in a mother – and sometimes shame. Alice describes how she finds herself becoming more of a raging child than her children. Her adult self reprimands her, urges her to act her age and to behave herself, while her infantile self 'joins in' with the children.

The conflict in a mother's inner world between the voice that demands she be a mature and 'proper' mother, and the child within shouting in chorus with her children is a major source of guilt. These feelings are loud echoes of what is held to be 'proper' for mothers by the outside world. Alice's self-reproach fuses with and is reinforced by cultural representations of motherhood as synonymous with dignity, control and adulthood. Mothers stand for order; children create chaos. Nowhere is this more evident than in the feelings generated by cleanliness and tidiness. A mother feels judged by the state of her child's fingernails. The orderliness of her house is somehow assumed to be an index of her capacity to care for her children. But while it must be tidy, it must not be oppressively neat. Mothers are ideally expected to maintain an environment characterised by cheerful, warm, childish chaos. They are expected to tidy up *and* thrive in anarchy.

Susanah is a mother who finds this particular contradictory expectation of motherhood especially onerous. Fear of her own internal chaos and emotional explosiveness leads her to need external order – at least in her own home. She says

> I hate the disorder children create, and I hate myself for hating it. Sometimes I feel I'll go mad if I have to pick up another sock, yet I am unable to leave it on the floor. There's a mother I see at school, always with hundreds of children milling around her, always smiling, but with never a hair out of place. Why can't I be like her?

Another mother, Naomi, elaborates this particular representation of motherhood:

> I have this picture . . . yes, it's of their childminder. She is able to be a truly adult mother and to control them in a way that is rational, firm, quiet and grown up. I don't feel I know how to do that.

Alice's, Susanah's and Naomi's feelings about themselves as mothers are constructed by the image of mother defined as 'adult' in opposition to 'child'. Naomi stamps, shouts, breaks things and slaps when her children defy her. Her remorse, her sense of being a bad mother, redouble her rage at these moments. Yet it is precisely the ease with which she can regress and become childlike that also contributes to her enjoyment of her children's company, adding to her understanding of them and to her capacity to share their pleasures. She says:

> There are times when there is warmth, there is loving and there is above all fun. I think of it and savour it. I think that when I'm an old woman, I'll have this to remember. It's so full. It's a very full experience to have so much touch.

While Alice and Naomi describe states of mind in which they are able to 'regress' in identification with their children – sometimes to their discomfort, sometimes to their delight – other mothers feel *bad* because they lack the capacity to enter into childish feelings. Lynette, for example, describes herself as singularly unable to play:

> I do enjoy doing some things with Georgina. For example, I really like drawing with her. We sit at a little table and draw together for hours. My worst experience is in the playground. I cannot enjoy that at any level. I push her glumly on the swings. Even her pleasure means nothing to me.

Some mothers told me that they left their childhood behind them with a sigh of relief; they have no wish to revisit it. To be drawn into re-experiencing the powerful emotional world of the child, or even just joining in childhood activities, feels burdensome and sometimes impossible. Hence they too feel that they are bad mothers.

Sometimes the role of 'child' parent and 'adult' parent becomes split between a mother and her partner. Where two lesbians raising a child are concerned, the division can at times mirror the particular capacities of the partners. Thus, for example, one may initially prefer the role of 'playmate' to 'caretaker'. But the division may become institutionalised in the household to the point where each would like to experience the parental attributes denied them. For example, she who becomes the 'child' with the children may long for some 'adult' distance from them.

Within a heterosexual couple, the split may be sanctioned by gender roles, although not necessarily in a predictable way. Sandra comments:

The children see me as one of them and regard Barry as the adult round the house. I think it's partly because he works full time and I am more available. He walks in at the end of the day with an air of world-weary authority, while I'm on my knees under the table hunting for Lego. I think I resent his 'superiority' in their eyes – and resent them for seeing him that way. But I know that I also rather enjoy the sense of *us* against *him*.

The opposite dynamic holds true for other heterosexual couples when it is the father who is seen as another child. A mother beleaguered by the double burden of domestic labour and paid work is often in no mood to play. Coming home does not constitute an end to a day's work, but the onset of the second shift:

The children enjoy Tom more than they do me. He comes home, takes off his jacket and he's on the floor with them in seconds. Whereas I'm starting to load the washing machine and worrying about what's for supper.

The vicissitudes of motherhood for these women are given meaning by a specific split in the representation of motherhood dominant in Western culture. Mothers are expected to be childlike – at one with their children and happily immersed in their world and emotional reality, while at the same time being very mature, and very adult indeed. Now it could be argued that this is simply the human condition; that all of us combine an adult part and a child part which frequently conflict, and that really mothers have nothing special to complain about. But, in my view, mothers do confront specific issues here, which can make ambivalence feel unmanageable.

Having children and being with children sharpens the human conflict between a woman's adult aspect and the residual childish parts of her self. The conflict is potentially creative because mothers need both to identify with and to stand protectively back from their children. How they negotiate this tension is dependent on a host of factors, both practical and psychological. However, a mother's capacity to negotiate the extraordinary emotional mobility demanded of her is hampered and, as we have seen, rendered a source of guilt by the particular split representation of motherhood I have described. Rather than acknowledge the tightrope mothers walk along with everyone else between childlike 'joining in' and adult 'standing back', the culture mediates the experience of mothers as being *either* too immature, *or* too adult and unable to play. Hence, external reality, mirrored by internal conflict, renders women bad mothers *in their own eyes*. This problem is not a universal one.

In Chapter 6, I explored the way in which the cultural elision of femininity and maternity leads to an understanding of maternal ambivalence as abnormal aggression. Here I look at how the conflict mobilised by motherhood, between feeling at once infantile and 'the only adult around', signifies maternal inadequacy for women, rather than a fruitful source of insight into self and child.

The Tandem

Jungian and post-Jungian theory make a particular contribution to this aspect of the mother–child relationship. In a paper entitled 'The Bad Mother', James Hillman[1] uses archetypal psychology to explain why, in the mother–child relationship, either the mother or the child is perceived as, or imagined as, *bad*. He looks first at why mothering makes women feel bad, and then at what it is in the mother–child relationship that renders them *bad*.

Hillman reiterates Jung's idea that there is an archetypal aspect to bad mothering which makes it an emotional inevitability. Even so-called good mothers will often experience themselves as bad mothers. This is because, although the human mother is not the same as the archetypal imago of the mother, she is strongly influenced by it. She is experienced by her child as a mixture of who she is and the archetypal image that the child carries. (An archetypal image is a similar concept to the unconscious phantasy of Kleinian theory.) All archetypal images have a dual nature which is expressed symbolically, as Hillman described:

> You cannot have a good side without the other. The moment motherhood is constellated, both sides are constellated. Nor is it possible to convert the negative into the positive. The empirical mother's experience of her badness is an intimation of the archetypal reality. Kali lurks eternal, so there will always be urges to destroy the child . . . The full experience of motherhood calls forth the urge to destroy the child, to feed off its life, to turn it to stone, drive it mad, abuse or abandon

it. This side of mothering appears in the stepmother of fairy tales.[2]

Hillman makes a further point that is of particular relevance for the theme of this chapter. He suggests that mother and child are differing contents in the archetypal structure of a single tandem. Thus mother and child are not only what they are, but they are what they are because they are locked together in a tandem which affects the nature of each. The tandem is itself subject to oppositional thinking which determines not only the individual's experience, but also how we perceive them. Everything the mother is, the child is not, and vice versa.

Jungian psychology puts forward the view that the image of the child in most cultures is a metaphor – a network of impersonal symbolic connotations or notions that govern our modes of seeing actual children. Qualities associated with the Child include futurity, growth, simplicity, amorality, dependence, joy, spontaneity, creativity, curiosity and imagination. Children connote all of these attributes and carry the undeveloped, infantile, dependent, immature aspects which adults have disowned and placed in the special world called childhood. Mothers on the other hand are expected to move away from the imaginative attitudes and spontaneous ways of being that belong to the Child archetype. As we saw with Alice and Naomi, mothers no longer feel it appropriate to be what they consider immature, undeveloped or infantile.

Hillman's argument is that mothers become separated from their actual children due to their separation from childishness. Hence, he writes that a mother 'may resent her actual child for retaining qualities of which she is now deprived by her position in the tandem'.[3] He paints a horrific picture of the mother constructed out of oppositional thinking within this archetypal structure:

As child is equivalent with imagination, her [i.e. the mother's] language becomes unimaginative, imperative, abstract. As the child is growth, she becomes static and empty, unable to react with spontaneous novelty. As the child is timeless, eternal, she becomes time-bound, scheduled, hurried. Her morality becomes one-sidedly responsible and disciplinarian. Her sense of future and hope is displaced on her actual child; thereby postpartum depression may become a chronic undertone. As her actual child carries her feelings of vulnerability, she may over-attend to it to the neglect of herself, with consequent resentments. Also, her thought processes become restricted to adult forms of reason so that the ghost voices and faces, animals, the scenes of eidectic imagination become estranged and feel like pathological delusions and hallucinations. And her language loses its emotion and incantational power; she explains and argues.[4]

I quote Hillman at length because this description is compelling. Many mothers may see aspects of themselves mirrored in his words. Why do I stress *aspects*? If we take the tandem too literally as between actual mother and actual child, we lose sight of the way motherhood also inevitably constellates the child in the mother. There is an inner tandem to consider, at work in both mother and child. Hence Hillman's 'cure' for his mother marooned in adulthood is a therapy which would provide a *rapprochement* with her inner child, rekindling fantasies, refinding pleasures, releasing spontaneity. Hillman concludes that 'The mother's therapy begins in the tandem with her lost child of imagination, and her therapist is her *actual child*. Though mothers know this and practise it *playing with their children*, even a momentary experience of bad mothering can set a woman back into the adult posture, its separation and loss' (emphasis added).[5]

Hillman suggests that for a mother to experience the tandem as rigid opposition is already to be separated from the 'child'. From the childish perspective that he advocates, the tandem is more of a see-saw. Yet see-saws can be as sickening for mothers as being stuck on the negative (adult) end of the tandem. Far from accessing their 'archetypal' flexibility, fluidity and inventiveness, mothers usually experience overwhelming loss of identity as they are tossed between, on the one hand, occupying the place of time-bound disciplinarian adult and, on the other, feeling at one with the child in all its childlikeness.

Although Hillman's paper is fruitful in its exploration of maternal 'badness', there is a sense in which the 'adult mother' stands condemned. There is no place for her. Her end of the tandem is curiously blank, waiting to be enlivened by the imaginative child. Is there no maternal imagination? Had Hillman pursued further the exploration of the tandem within the mother, it might have led to an exposition of maternal imagination.

Some feminist theorising of the tandem feels equally weighted in favour of the 'child–mother'. Adrienne Rich, for example, ascribes the functioning of the 'adult-mother' to an imposition of patriarchal order. She writes of a holiday in the country with her two sons 'without an adult male in the house'.[6] The three abandon civilisation and clock time. Eating and sleeping cease to happen 'on time', spontaneity rules, inside and outside are no longer distinguished, adult and child mingle in delightful disorder.

The problem with both Rich's Arcadian experience and Hillman's archetypal see-saw is that mothers rarely feel confident or content at either end of the spectrum. Rather, they often experience themselves as stranded in 'no-man's land', cut off from adulthood and childhood alike. It is the image of the park bench that comes to mind rather than see-saws and pastoral paradises. Jane Lazarre describes mothers in a playground:

> The mothers sat on the bench in the sun as long as they could, which was never very long. There was always an injured child to console, a naughty child to reprimand, a whining child to tolerate, an athletic child to plead with as he proudly stood dangerously atop the highest slide in the playground. Very few mothers were content. There was no mistaking their boredom, their shortness of temper, their martyred dedication . . . And each sign of impatience on my part drove me into a new sort of guilt.[7]

French feminism has produced its own version of Hillman's mother-in-touch-with-child-of-the-imagination and Rich's mothering divorced from patriarchy. Luce Irigaray suggested that, if we strip away the Law of the Father, we will tap into a revolutionary maternal life-force. In 'The Bodily Encounter with the Mother', Irigaray wrote that Western culture is founded, not on patricide, but on matricide. She reinterpreted the myth of Clytemnestra as an account of the instillation of patriarchy through the sacrifice of the mother. Clytemnestra killed her husband Agamemnon who had sacrificed their daughter Iphegenia. Irigaray highlighted Clytemnestra's subsequent murder by her son Orestes 'because the rule of God-father and his appropriation of the archaic powers of mother-earth requires it'.[8] She concludes:

> We have to be careful about one other thing; we must not once more kill the mother who was sacrificed to the origins of our

culture. We must give her new life, new life to that mother, to our mother within us and between us. We must give her the right to pleasure, to jouissance, to passion, restore her right to speech, and sometimes to cries and anger.[9]

Irigaray believes that the 'silence' enjoined on the mother perpetuates terrible fantasies and fears – woman as devouring monster, for example – which spring from the 'unanalysed hatred from which women as a group suffer culturally'.[10] To break the silence women need to invent new ways of speaking:

> We must also find, find anew, invent words, the sentences that speak the most archaic and most contemporary relationship with the body of the mother, with our bodies, the sentences that translate the bond between her body, ours, that of our daughters. We have to discover a language (*langage*) which does not replace the bodily encounter, as paternal language (*langue*) attempts to do, but which can go along with it, words which do not bar the corporeal, but which speak corporeal.[11]

Though speaking out of very different intellectual traditions from those of Hillman and Rich, Irigaray was addressing the same phenomenon. She described a maternal role that is potentially 'outside culture'. Like Hillman and Rich, she saw contemporary motherhood as mired in an inauthentic adulthood which silences passion and desire and rage. She asked:

> So what is a mother? Someone who makes the stereotypical gestures she is told to make, who has no personal language and who has no identity. But how, as daughters, can we have a personal relationship with or construct a personal identity in a relation to someone who is no more than a function?[12]

Irigaray's answer echoes Hillman's see-saw solution. She argues that mothers must abandon the pseudo-power of adult motherhood, that mother and daughter need to establish a new reciprocity and flexibility both interpersonally and intrapsychically:

> In a sense we need to say goodbye to maternal omnipotence (the last refuge) and establish a woman-to-woman relationship of reciprocity with our mothers, in which they might possibly also feel themselves to be our daughters. In a word, liberate ourselves along with our mothers. That is an indispensable

precondition for our emancipation from the authority of the fathers.[13]

Yet Irigaray's desire to free women from maternal omnipotence, like Hillman's desire to free mothers from the 'adult posture', would do little more, if realised, than to constrict and constrain mothers to become female Peter Pans. Rather than simplistically re-visioning the pre-Oedipal mother or writing a golden age of mother–child democracy, we need, in my view, to rethink adult motherhood itself, acknowledging the existence therein of contradictory desires and identifications. Naomi describes how this might work psychologically as she tells us of her tandem wishes: to be the mother-in-charge Irigaray and Hillman suggest we dispense with *and* the joyous, unruly mother they appear to favour:

> The ideal mother is calm, patient and rational, at one with the child but firm – not letting them be wild. She is the agent of society. She stops them going into shoe shops and sweeping shoes off the shelves. Yesterday my kids did just that and I was told off for not being a proper mother. I *also* feel that I should be able to control them calmly in a rational way, without screaming at them, without hitting them. Doing it almost by magic. But I don't manage that. I do get freaked out. I do shriek. I do feel like I'm going to explode, and I do feel this imperative from outside to control them.
>
> There are times when I think it would be OK for them to be a bit more relaxed in a public situation – but I feel the pressure. There is the pressure from the children and pressure from the culture. I'm caught in the middle.

Like several of the other mothers I have quoted, Naomi contrasts her personal uncontrollable, regressed rage in the face of her children's defiance and naughtiness with collective representations of motherhood as a repository of rationality and patience. But, despite criticising herself for freaking out, shrieking and reaching explosion point, she acknowledges the wish – and this is truly a political point – that both she and her children could be allowed by society to be less in control. She both does and does not want exclusively to take 'adult' control of the situation.

Naomi understands the tension within her in terms of a cultural imperative she did not originate. She is the one designated to socialise her children – yet they infuriatingly refuse to conform. She secretly sympathises with them, while simultaneously hating them for shaming her. She relates the conflict to her own childhood. She remembers how her own mother's irritation and irascibility was a response to a similar desire to conform to a world of good manners. Naomi describes her mother as 'very, very controlling. It mattered a lot what people thought of my sister and me. It was "don't stare, don't point," all the time.' Thus, when Naomi was reprimanded by the man in the shoe shop for her children's behaviour, part of her rebelliously identified with the 'bad children', while part of her felt humiliated and convinced she was not a proper mother, not adult or orderly enough. Confusingly, but tellingly, at such moments she relates to her children as if *they* were her mother pointing out her unacceptable behaviour and reproaching her for it.

The complicated processes at work in this example of everyday maternal experience highlight the intricacy of adult–child dynamics in a mother's inner world. How this moves between inner world and external reality makes the situation even more intricate. Michelene Wandor has described the split between adult and child in the mother in terms of a public- versus private-sphere division. She describes delighting in the closeness, intimacy, childishness and power in relation to her children, as long as it is in private: 'The liberating effect of this relationship is again defined by the isolated situation in which it occurs. It is a clandestine activity.'[14]

Driving Each Other Mad

Thus far I have focused primarily on intrapsychic issues; on tension between the adult and child parts of the mother, and how what could be a fluidly creative conflict becomes an unwavering source of guilt in a mother's own eyes, thanks to split and normative cultural representations of motherhood. Now I want to look at what happens interpersonally between mothers and children when a mother regresses to the feeling state of a furious child. Sandra told me this story:

> I was driving home with Carl and Lucy. We'd spent the day with friends in Luton. Fifteen minutes from home they started arguing and within seconds it had escalated into full-scale war. They hit, they shouted, they called for me to get involved. I

could feel my exhaustion growing and my rage building up. I completely lost control. I slammed on the brakes and started banging on the steering wheel and shouting at them to go away and to shut up, and to leave me alone. Awful shocked silence followed. Then someone started stroking me and Carl said, 'It's all right Mummy, it's all right.' That precipitated me straight back into adulthood and motherhood. I feel so guilty at the moments when I become the child and sort of force them to parent me.

There are a number of ways of thinking about what went on between Sandra and her children in the car. Employing Hillman's image of the archetypal structure of the tandem, we could say that the dynamic switched from Bad Children–Good Mother to Good Children–Bad Mother. Sandra herself experienced the situation as a moment of unwelcome and uncontrolled regression to childhood which forced a premature adulthood on her children. And indeed, many would agree that Sandra had, at that moment, ceased to function as a secure container for her children's feelings, thus rendering it unsafe for them to live out the feelings.

Andrew Samuels has criticised the ubiquity in psychoanalysis of container/contained to characterise the mother–child relationship. He asked 'Is relationship only about containment? Is that what it is for? What about exchange, bargaining, negotiation, equality – or even torture? Is containment even the characteristic of the mother–infant relationship that it is sometimes claimed to be?'[15]

We could argue that Sandra, by responding as she did, provided her children with a truthful experience in which they recognised the reality of their mother's feelings as well as their own agency and capacity to repair. Harold Searles has written about the immense importance of responding authentically to 'being driven crazy' – a situation which he understands as fundamental to human interaction: 'Desires to drive the other person crazy are a part of the limitlessly varied personality constellation of emotionally healthy human beings.'[16] He is, however, primarily concerned not with benign 'driving crazy' but when the impulse becomes malign; when the technique tends to undermine the other person's confidence in the reliability of her or his own emotional reaction. In Searles's view the key factor is denial. Damage is done if the other denies the child's perception that she is furiously angry. Searles writes:

One of my patients, who throughout his childhood was told 'you're crazy' when he saw through his parents' defensive denial, became so mistrustful of his own emotional responses that he relied heavily, for years, upon a pet dog to let him know, by its reaction to this or that other person who he and his pet encountered, whether the person were friendly or trustworthy.[17]

Searles sees parental denial as an element in the aetiology of schizophrenia, as he has described it in this paper, written in 1959, at the height of the now discredited theory of the 'schizophrenogenic mother'. I cite him not to endorse his reading of the aetiology of schizophrenia but to highlight the importance of owning up to the emotional impact of children, and to suggest how hard it is to do that in the context of prescriptions on maternal behaviour enshrined in representations of the mother as an icon of adult restraint, moderation and thoughtful control.

As we have seen, everything militates against a mother admitting that her child has rendered her helplessly, outrageously angry, and unhappy about it. Mothers are forced into the denial that Searles warns against. This is shown strikingly by what we find in child-care manuals.

Be Happy

An element in the split representation of motherhood I have been describing – mother as icon of adulthood on the one hand, and mother as one of the children on the other – is that it involves a very partial image of the child. This child is almost entirely happy, good and joyful. The infantilised mother and her child share unmitigated fun and happiness. Maternal ambivalence and infantile ambivalence are equally outlawed. In a way this is what we all long for and it is what many women feel they *ought* to find in motherhood.

Of course the equation of motherhood with happiness is nothing new and not wrong in itself; children are undoubtedly a source of pleasure and joy. But the problem with contemporary attitudes towards maternity and happiness is that an imperative has evolved that rules out the inevitable unhappiness associated with motherhood. I want to look briefly at the way the existence of maternal pleasure has evolved into what I call the 'happiness imperative'.

In her paper 'Constructing Motherhood' Cathy Urwin explored how current popular childcare manuals define women's role as mothers 'by giving specific content to their desires, aspirations and daily work and by occluding others'.[18] This observation transforms the widely held view that childcare manuals simply impose things on women. Urwin's point is that the manuals also embody a historically determined set of desires in relation to childcare. These manuals are proliferating; they are now available on video, or in monthly magazine format. During 1993 the *Guardian* started its version in a weekly 'Parents' section.

If childcare manuals are determined by a host of economic and political forces, then it is not surprising that their content changes greatly over time. One example of this is the shift from the parent-centred to the equally prescriptive child-centred approach. It is the latter that has closed the gap between mother and child, producing the 'child mother' and insisting that fun and happiness constitute the heart of the maternal relationship.

Cathy Urwin has illustrated the way in which particular ideas from various schools of developmental psychology have entered into the construction of contemporary motherhood. As far as the happiness imperative is concerned, a source can be found in Winnicott's work, whose ideas, as I detail below, have been a key influence on Anglo-American childcare manuals since the Second World War. For example, he wrote '*Enjoy* being annoyed with the baby when cries and yells prevent acceptance of milk that you long to be generous with. *Enjoy* all sorts of womanly feelings that you cannot even start to explain to a man.' (Emphasis added.)[19] 'The mother's pleasure has to be there, or the whole procedure is useless.'[20] We might speculate which economic, historical and political factors determined the dominance of the happiness imperative in the work of Winnicott and others. Andrew Samuels believes that post-war optimism, commitment to reconstruction, and a general belief in progress played a part in the move from a motherhood of austerity to a motherhood of unrationed happiness and abundance.

In childcare manuals we can see authors struggling to affirm the happiness imperative and align it with what they also know of women's lives – that motherhood is equally about conflicting desires, intense anxiety and unwelcome aggression.

For instance, Penelope Leach writes,

taking your baby's point of view does not mean neglecting your own, the parent's view. Your interests and his are identical. You are all on the same side; the side that wants to be happy, and have fun. If you make happiness for him he will make happiness for you.[21]

The writers of manuals nurture the dream of partnership, reciprocity and mutuality that mothers I interviewed described in Chapter 2. But in the world of childcare manuals these moments are not gold in the dross of the daily grind; they are presented as how life *should* be for mother and baby. Both should feel their needs simultaneously satisfied in mutually pleasing activities. Another childcare manual author, Miriam Stoppard, writes:

> Having read so many baby books which emphasize looking after the baby's needs, I still feel guilty if I occasionally put my wishes on a par with those of my children. I hope no parent reading this will suffer any such shame. I believe that caring for babies should be fun. Happy parents mean happy babies.[22]

While acknowledging that mothers do have adult needs of their own independent of their babies' needs, Stoppard merges mother and baby. We can actually see Stoppard's aphorism 'Happy parents mean happy babies' evolving into an imperative. Nine years after the publication of her book, *She* magazine ran a feature entitled, 'How to Raise a Happy Child':

> One of the best ways to help a child find enduring happiness is to look for it in your own life. Research verifies the value of growing up with happy parents. In addition to taking responsibility for your own happiness, be sure to tell your children about when and why you are happy.

Creative Attentive Playmates

Associated with the happiness imperative is the expectation that mothers will take an active role in their child's play. Since the 1980s, childcare manuals and magazines have increasingly advocated that mothers not be simply 'available' to their children, but actively involved in structuring their time with the provision of creative play.

Cathy Urwin has traced the origin of this development from the child study movement of the nineteenth century, which signalled the importance of play, through the Montessori movement, to the application of Piagetian theory in primary school practice.[24] These theories propose that learning is facilitated through play. Urwin describes how, in the 1960s and '70s, developmental psychologists, using assumptions derived from Piaget, devised educational toys and activities to prevent cognitive retardation in institutionalised infants. She shows how the advocacy of such work with institutionalised children was transposed into domestic settings. Laboratory studies suggested a lack of 'child centredness' or 'attunement to the child' on the part of working-class mothers in particular. Although, as Urwin points out, the artificiality of these experiments has since been criticised, they suggested a link between impoverished homes, lack of parental involvement, and poor school performance. The response, especially in America, was to 'harness or direct the talent of mothers'. Parenting which encouraged learning through play was termed 'scaffolding' by psychologist Jerome Bruner.[25]

How do mothers themselves feel about the command to orchestrate and participate in creative play? Once again there is a wide spectrum of responses amongst mothers. For some it is a welcome concept – a beacon of certainty in the sea of motherhood. They are told, and indeed believe in, their crucial importance to their children's development. But they are unsure how to guarantee the normal evolution of their children's growth. They are convinced that childcare is the most important work in the world and most would agree with Penelope Leach when she writes, 'Bringing up a child is one of the most creative, most worthwhile and most undervalued of all jobs.'[26] The concept of creative play hence provides a mother with a sense of being in possession of a reliable tool of the trade. And for many it is not simply reassuring but also pleasurable. One mother told me, 'At Easter I taught them how to blow eggs and to paint them; we had a wonderful time.' Another commented, 'It keeps me young, it's such fun.' Others see it as a way of enjoying the childhood they felt had been denied them: 'My third son taught *me* how to play.'

For many others, however, the insistence on the developmental importance of creative play is a source of guilt. Feeling bad at play magnifies their depressive anxiety in relation to their mothering

(I'll damage her because I'm bad at playing). It also magnifies persecutory anxieties in that their children are seen as persecutors not playmates in their eyes. An interviewee told me sadly that she was just a poor player: 'Even as a child I felt like an old soul – not playful at all. Now I am hopeless at joining in with the children – let alone initiating games.' Another commented guiltily, 'I'm often distracted and bored, I'm not gripped by dinosaurs.'

In her interesting study of pre-school children and their mothers in London, Mary Georgina Boulton found that middle-class women felt they ought to play with their children – and enjoy it. The women in the study set time aside from housework for playing with their children 'and because play was defined as a duty, they set this time aside even when they did not enjoy it'.[27] Another aspect of this approach to play is the notion of 'quality time', when at least one intensive, planned hour of play, so to speak, excuses parents from playing for the rest of the day!

The injunction to play is itself curiously contradictory. A mother should *enjoy* it but also view it as an important *task*. Amongst the women Rosalind Coward interviewed for her book *Our Treacherous Hearts*, the majority felt they were failing to be the creative playmates they believed they ought to be:

> Most of the middle-class mothers I talked to expressed envy of women who are prepared to devote themselves to 'being creative' with their children. They were often made anxious by other mothers who demonstrated this ability – painting with their children, thinking of stimulating games for them, and generally enjoying them in a way that the interviewees did not.[28]

Coward concluded that it was not lack of time that prevented mothers playing. Surprisingly, perhaps, many of her interviewees simply did not want to play – though they felt they should. Anything was preferable to trying to play. Even cooking and cleaning presented greater attraction: 'At least you can think while you are doing it.'[29]

The women Coward talked to found that their own identities and interests as adults were obliterated by the imperative to play and enjoy. Coward noted the burgeoning provision of creative activities for children as further evidence of this oppressive ideal. Swimming clubs, ballet classes, French clubs, dancing lessons and judo are, in her view, products of the pressure many mothers feel to provide opportunities for creative play. However, I think they may, in many instances, signify rather an escape or respite from the command to join in and become playing children once again. Many of the mothers who sit at gymnastic classes, or next to the judo mats, do not watch their child with rapt attention. Instead, they seem to sink gratefully into conversation with friends – or into their own preoccupations.

Coward considers that women face a new expectation of maternal altruism, in the past perceived in relatively basic terms – a woman would have been expected to give up her own needs in order to feed and clothe her children. Today, altruism is posed in relation to the assumption that children want and need 'deep, exclusive and full attention; they need an adult at their disposal who will listen and hear and play'.[30]

But what is the historical origin of this maternal ideal, this late twentieth-century mother who offers self-abnegating attention to promote the unfolding of the child's self, who maintains the capacity for child*like* spontaneity and imagination but not for child*ish* tantrums? To find the answer, I think we need to turn our attention to the history of psychoanalysis.

Psychoanalysis, and developmental psychology based on it, are as much the product of their specific time, place and culture as they are formative influences. They need to be set in the context of such trends as the reduction of family size in Western societies and the corresponding importance given to each individual child.

The Analyst Mother and the Mother Analyst

What a society wants of its mothers is dictated to a large extent by current understandings of babies' needs, which are in turn influenced by economic forces. Concepts of infancy and the associated expectations of maternal behaviour have shifted with almost every decade of the twentieth century. For example, the infant of the 1920s and '30s was in need of discipline and in danger of being spoiled, while in the 1940s and '50s the infant was in need of constant gratification.[31]

One of the century's most important changes in this area was signified by the publication in 1935 of the psychotherapist Ian Suttie's book *The Origin of Love and Hate*. He proposed that the need for love and companionship was an autonomous force in development. He insisted that his theory differed 'fundamentally from psycho-analysis in introducing the conception of an innate need-for-companionship'.[32] He considered that hatred existed only as a response to frustrated love and declared that 'Earth hath no hate *but* love to hatred turned, and hell no fury but a baby scorned.'[33] As he pointed out, his theory constructed 'the primary, paramount, importance of the mother'.[34] It effectively denied maternal ambivalence altogether. In a world of love and companionship, ambivalence was an unfortunate and pernicious accident.

Suttie worked at the Tavistock Clinic, already a prominent psychotherapeutic institution in London with a worldwide reputation. Before pursuing further the influence of psychoanalysis on society's expectations of mothers, I want briefly to map out how the connection between psychoanalysis and general social ideals of childcare evolved. The Department for Children and Parents – now Children and Families – at the Tavistock Clinic was the model for other child guidance clinics in England. In *The Myth of Bonding*, Diane Eyer has emphasised the importance of these clinics in disseminating and popularising psychoanalytic thinking. She describes how 'social workers attached to child guidance clinics would go into the homes and talk to the parents, looking for unconscious beliefs and wishes, feelings of guilt and disappointment, that might affect the child'.[35]

The only parent available to them was, of course, the mother. It was the mother with whom they had contact, and maternal disturbance increasingly came to be seen as the root of the child's problem. (David Levy, whose ideas on maternal aggression and penis envy were discussed in Chapter 5, was a central figure in the child guidance movement in the United States.)

After the Second World War the mother–child dyad came under yet more scrutiny. John Bowlby became chairman of the Department for Children and Parents at the Tavistock Clinic, where he established a special unit to observe children's response to separation from their mother while at the same time Esther Bick was instituting the discipline of infant observation (see p. 190). Research into the condition of small children, especially in institutions, undoubtedly changed institutional practice for the better, but it was also responsible for endowing paediatricians with far greater authority over the lives of children and their families. In the USA, influenced by the child guidance movement and also by Anna

Freud's work with families, one of the first paediatric departments to develop a family-centred clinic was set up at Case Western Reserve University in the 1950s. It was here that Benjamin Spock, with others, developed 'theories of parent management and child rearing'.[36]

'Dr' Spock was asked to write the famous *Baby and Childcare* because the publishers, Pocket Books, understood that he was the *only* American paediatrician with psychoanalytic training. In the introduction to his book *Babies and Their Mothers*, Spock acknowledged the influence of D. W. Winnicott whose 'writings ... helped bridge the gap between pediatrics and the dynamics of child development'.[37]

Indeed, Winnicott's work not only forms the bridge between paediatrics and the dynamics of child development, but also between psychoanalysis and popular ideals of childcare. He elaborated the emphasis on the early mother–child bond and the central role of maternal devotion that had been foregrounded by Ian Suttie. Winnicott commented on his knowledge of Suttie's work when discussing formative influences on his thinking.[38]

Perhaps more than that of any other psychoanalytic theorist, Winnicott's work was responsible – though inadvertently, of course – for confirming the split representation of motherhood I have been describing: between the spontaneous happy childlike mother and the measured orderly adult mother. His work presents particular problems for those like myself who are both psychotherapists and mothers. As a psychotherapist, I have been enormously influenced by his theories relating to clinical practice. But as a mother I think his representation of mothering is problematic. In spite of his intention of avoiding prescription, he set up a series of ideals, and spelt out the consequences for the child if the mother fails to achieve them. Similarly, the split in his representation of the mother survives his best efforts to overcome it. I think this is perhaps due to the fact that when he writes of the mother from a psychoanalytic viewpoint, he takes mothers as split beings – as the patients of analysts (hence, given psychoanalytic theory, childlike) and as the mentors of analysts (hence, inevitably, as knowing adults). This split served Winnicott well in the short term. If we do not disentangle the problems it makes for us today, our reading of Winnicott will be superficial.

Winnicott was one of a number of analysts in the British school who, in their clinical practice, began to draw a straightforward analogy between the mother's and the analyst's work. As Adam Phillips has observed, mothers were used by the British school theorists 'as though they were a genus, to provide descriptions of what psychoanalysts were supposed to be doing'.[39] Quite what a departure this signified can be grasped by comparing it to Freud's earlier analogy of analyst as surgeon. Freud wrote, 'I have often in my mind compared cathartic psychotherapy with surgical intervention . . .'[40]

The changed conceptualisation of the analytic stance was due in part to the increasing importance attributed to analysing material from a patient's very early infancy, and to the increasing role of transference–countertransference as the central tool for elucidating the primitive material stemming from the unconscious processes of the patient. According to this view, within the transference the patient relates to the analyst or psychotherapist as if he or she were a significant person from the patient's very early life (usually, but not exclusively, the mother) or as a part of the patient's babyself.

Phillips's concern is with the implications of the 'Analyst Mother' for psychoanalytic practice. He considers that the analogy facilitates, yet also pre-empts the transference. My own concern is rather with the impact of the 'analyst mother' on cultural expectations of an actual mother. In Winnicott's writing the juxtaposition of the two is buttressed by a further analogy in which a regressed patient is deemed to be understandable in terms derived from what is known of an actual baby.

Winnicott identifies three major stages of mothering: primary maternal preoccupation, the mirror-role of the mother and the mother of potential space.

Primary maternal preoccupation is described as 'a state of heightened sensitivity, almost an illness'.[41]

It entails becoming preoccupied with the infant to the exclusion of all other interests. It is the maternal requirement of very small babies and thus a temporary state of affairs. Not all mothers can, to Winnicott's regret, achieve this temporary 'illness': 'Some of them certainly have very big alternative concerns which they do not readily abandon.'[42] Winnicott is sympathetic, but his description of the outcome of failure to achieve maternal preoccupation is devastating: 'it is not certain that they [mothers] can succeed in mending the early distortion'.[43]

The subsequent phase, the mirror-role of the mother, is described as follows:

> What does a baby see when he or she looks at the mother's face? I am suggesting that, ordinarily, what the baby sees is himself or herself. In other words the mother is looking at the baby and what she looks like *is related to what she sees there* ... I can make my point by going straight over to the case of the baby whose mother reflects her own mood, or, worse still, the rigidity of her own defences.[44]

In the mirror-role the mother's loving look offers even an upset, scratchy baby a positive, affirming reflection of her or himself. The crucial thing seems to be that the mother has to put aside her own concerns and concentrate her full, undivided, unconflicted attention on the baby – the odd lapse is acceptable but nothing more: 'Of course nothing can be said about the single occasions on which a mother could not respond.'[45]

In the pages from which I am quoting, Winnicott immediately goes on to draw an analogy between the mirror-role mother and the psychoanalyst: 'The glimpse of the baby's face and child's seeing the self in the mother's face, and afterwards in a mirror, gives a way of looking at analysis and at the psychotherapeutic task.'[46]

My evaluation of Winnicott's idea is that, while the mirror-role mother does provide a useful way of thinking about *analytic* attention, in terms of the daily life of the mother and child it demands something more or less impossible on the mother's part – an unachievable hyper-adult degree of self-control and attention. Yet, once again, if the mother fails to provide the required level of attention, Winnicott spells out the dire consequences: the child's 'creative capacity begins to atrophy'.[47] Defenders of Winnicott assert that he never meant it all so positivistically, so causally, in such an oracular, gloom and doom way. But the texts have to be taken seriously or else we end up uncritically canonising Winnicott. Moreover, Winnicott's ideas were in fact widely influential beyond psychoanalysis and psychotherapy.

Just as the mirror-role idea positions mothers as 'therapists', so does the role Winnicott designates mothers in relation to play. Again, it could be argued that this is *not* what Winnicott intended, but it is nevertheless the *effect* of his writing. Following on from her role as 'mirror' the mother is positioned in relation to play which takes place in 'a potential space between the baby and the mother'.[48] Winnicott writes passionately on the importance of play:

> *it is play that is the universal*, and that belongs to health; playing leads into group relationships; playing can be a form of communication in psychotherapy; and lastly, psychoanalysis has been developed as a highly specialised form of playing in the service of communication with oneself and others.[49]

Like any 'therapist', the mother at play combines reticence and spontaneous feeling. She performs a delicate balancing act between 'being that which the baby has a capacity to find and (alternatively) being herself waiting to be found'.[50] Once again everything hangs on the mother's ability to play correctly: 'In the state of confidence that grows up when a mother can do this difficult thing well (not if she is unable to do it)' a baby experiences 'the precariousness of the interplay of personal psychic reality and the experience of control of actual objects'.[51] Winnicott then switches his attention back to the analyst, commenting that 'if the therapist cannot play, then he is not suitable for the work',[52] for it is in playing that the patient is being creative.

Looking back over his life's work Winnicott wrote in 1971 that, in relation to play, he feels his own clinical work achieved a close degree of resemblance to mother–baby work:

> As I look back over the papers that mark the development of my own thought and understanding I can see that my present interest in play in the relationship of trust that may develop between the baby and the mother was always a feature of my consultative technique . . .[53]

However, as Adam Phillips points out, there is 'an uneasy fit – a difference that makes all the difference – between what mothers supposedly do and what analysts are supposed to only say'.[54] Certainly, the analytic relationship can and does resemble a mother–child couple. But the analyst is, as often as not, the reflective, receptive adult mother and the patient is the playing child. But, as I have attempted to show, in the actual mother's experience the adult–child couple is constellated *within* her. Interactions with her child mobilise both her adult self *and* her infantile self. While the image of the receptive, reticent, sensitive mother following her baby's lead with exquisite timing may have provided a creative role model for therapists and analysts, for the mother that same image stands as a reproach in the face of her own emotionality. For the stirring of unconscious content, the reawakening of the child within, is not for all women synonymous with fun and sensitivity but can also signal sadness, rage or destructiveness.

Winnicott had no wish to erect the therapist as a maternal ideal. Indeed, he remarked regretfully that the mother who fails to achieve primary maternal preoccupation must compensate by doing therapy with her child instead of being a parent.[55] Neither would he have wished to banish maternal ambivalence from the mother's emotional repertoire. He wrote that 'To be reliable the relationship is necessarily motivated by the mother's love, or her love-hate, or her object-relating, but not by reaction-formations.'[56] However, the fact remains that each stage of maternity he describes comes with an appended warning – what will happen when mother is not good enough.

In this chapter I have been tracing the cultural split between representations of mother as adult and mother as child. Winnicott does no more than confirm this split. On the one hand, as we saw, he presents the mother as mentor for the therapist (an adult mother) and on the other hand there is the mother he addresses in his clinical or, indeed, his didactic work (a child mother). Addressing the latter mother he says, 'If a child can play with a doll, you can be an ordinary devoted mother.'[57]

Mother Observation

The evocation of the mother–child dyad in analytic work led to a growing interest in what mothers actually do. Phillips comments that 'the study of mothers and infants, which so quickly became the focus of psychoanalytic research in Britain after the war, became the matrix for the study of psychoanalysis'.[58] Similarly, Andrew Samuels termed contemporary British psychoanalysis 'matrocentric'.[59] Today, observation of mothers and infants is an integral part of most training courses in psychoanalytic psycho- therapy and psychoanalysis. Once again I find myself wanting to say that what is probably good for therapists is probably bad for mothers. I found my own experience of infant observation – the observing of a baby at home for one hour a week during the first two years of its life – both a privilege and a useful training in observing. One learns to retain and reflect upon what has been seen and felt. It was, however, only after I had had children that I began to question any assumption that those hours furnished me with truths or even reliable information about what was going on for that baby. Yet observational studies have produced (in Adam Phillips's words) 'canonical fantasies about mothering'.[60]

There are a wide variety of observational studies, some more psychoanalytically oriented than others, some employing technical aids in a laboratory setting, others are home-based. I do not intend to describe the diverse observational studies in any depth, but rather to highlight those aspects which have had an impact on contemporary maternal ideals.

Observational studies have interacted with clinical psychoanalysis to set what is taken to be a scientific seal of approval on the representation of mothering I have been describing. For observational studies have formed a conduit from the imaginative, creative work of Winnicott and Bion – from an awareness of the depth and intricacy of unconscious communication between mother and child – to the simplistic didactic behaviourism of popular advice on childcare of the current 'Be Happy' variety.

In 1959 in the USA Margaret Mahler embarked on a study of the normal steps of development of the self through the daily observation of the interaction of mothers and their babies during the first three years of the child's life. She designated four stages in a child's separation-individuation process, and attributes major personality disturbances in adulthood to difficulties and weaknesses in the maturational process.

Mahler perceived children to be more active and independent in relation to their mothers' failures than had previously been thought. They were observed achieving Mahler's sequences of sub-phases in the face of mothers who found separation at one stage or another largely problematic. Take for example Mrs D., who is described in *The Psychological Birth of the Human Infant*:

> For a long time all the observers of the project considered Mrs D. the perfect mother . . . Only in retrospect did we realize that, unlike most of the mothers who during the period of first active distancing by the infant reacted by giving a 'gentle push to the fledgling', Donna's mother did not.[61]

In the subsequent description of Donna's development we hear next to nothing about the mother's emotional response to motherhood. Mothers are designated helpful – or not – but their more profound, conflicted subjective responses to mothering are largely outside the scope of this influential study.

In the 1970s and '80s observation was intensified and refined. Mothers and infants were observed in laboratory settings. It has been suggested by critics of the findings of infant observation that, as a result, conflicts between the couples were rarely seen; instead 'mutual regulation' was highlighted, and child-centredness and sensitivity were considered the touchstone of successful mothering.

Daniel Stern, perhaps the best known of the contemporary infant observers, combines findings from psychoanalysis and developmental psychology.[62] He identifies four different senses of the self, coming on stream at various points in infancy and childhood, each one defining a different domain of self-experience and social relatedness. Once formed, each 'self' is active in concert with the others throughout life. One of Stern's main stated intentions is to improve clinical reconstruction of a patient's past in order to locate the origin of pathology.

Stern considered that parental behaviour constitutes predesigned responses to the infant's predesigned behaviour. If the parent produces the correct response to the infant, then the infant's predesigned developmental pattern – the unfolding of the four senses of the self – will proceed naturally. The mother's role in relation to her baby is termed attunement. In true attunement the mother exactly matches her baby's state. There are also purposeful misattunements, non-purposeful misattunements, and true misattunements.

Many writers have commented that this is a world of interpersonal rather than intrapsychic events. Stern's baby does not develop images of the mother mediated by its unconscious phantasy, or archetypal imagery. It seems that Stern's view is that as unconscious conflicts cannot be observed in babies, they cannot be taken into account. He writes:

> They [sleeping and eating problems] are not signs or symptoms of any intrapsychic conflict within the infant, however. They are accurate reflections of an ongoing interactive reality, manifestations of a problematic interpersonal exchange, not psychopathology of a psychodynamic nature.[63]

In the absence of an observable unconscious phantasy world of its own the baby is primarily regarded as both an active stimulant and a passive victim of *the mother's* emotional life conveyed to it through her behaviour:

> Through the selective use of attunement, the parents' inter-subjective responsivity acts as a template to shape and create corresponding intrapsychic experiences in the child. It is in this way that the parents' desires, fears, prohibitions, and fantasies contour the psychic experiences of the child.[64]

While remaining very influential – infant observation seemed to contradict core psychoanalytic concepts such as primary narcissism (discussed in Chapter 2) – Stern's ideas have nevertheless been strongly criticised. Philip Cushman challenged the universalism of the theory, asking why we should believe that any of this mutual interactive pattern, which Stern observed primarily in white, middle-class mothers and children, is predesigned and universal.[65] He points out that Stern did not explain how human parents could be predesigned to facilitate the development of a masterful, bounded, autonomous, interior subjective self when only a small portion of the world's population conceives of the self in this way. He concluded that Stern's popularity is due not to his discovery of universal elements of human development, but because his formulation is such a clear psychologically buttressed statement of accepted cultural values and views.

Feminist writers have criticised Stern, not for universalism, but for his reproduction of a sex-stereotypical representation of mother-hood. The ideal mother, according to Sternian infant observation, is quintessentially 'feminine'. She is responsive, receptive and sensitive. *She is definitely not aggressive.* Woollett and Phoenix point out that, though the term 'parenthood' is often used, in practice sensitivity is perceived as a key element in mothering.[66] Insensitivity in mothers is considered problematic, but in fathers the same behaviour is often treated as beneficial, providing a context in which children can learn about unpredictability and excitement and how to express themselves explicitly.

Woollett and Phoenix criticise such work on maternal sensitivity for failing to consider what the cost of it might be for mothers. To behave sensitively, mothers must be prepared to submerge their own needs and interests in those of their children, a degree of self-effacement which in relationships other than the mother–child one would be seen as pathological. Moreover, the degree of sensitivity expected from mothers as a desirable norm fails to take into account the usual context of mothering – the presence of other children, and the practicalities of everyday life.

The concepts of maternal sensitivity and attunement were further refined by T. Berry Brazelton and Bertrand G. Cramer in *The Earliest Relationship: Parents, Infants and the Drama of Early Attachment*.[67] They define a state they name 'contingency' which involves a pattern of appropriate responses to a partner's signals, needs and emotional communications. Inevitably, the existence of contingency produces contingency failures. In their view 'contingency failures' are caused by anxiety, ambivalence, lack of identification with parental roles, or unresolved grief. They consider that 'contingency failures due to even minor forms of depression or depressive behaviour can affect infants', yet they also observe 'resilient resources' and 'self correcting' tendencies in both parents and babies.[68]

The baby of observational studies is growing up significantly different from the baby of clinical psychoanalysis. Stern's baby is pre-adapted to good mothering. The baby's feelings do not have to be 'tamed' but simply enabled to develop. This is in contrast with, for example, the model of mother–baby interaction Bion employed in developing his theory of thinking. He envisaged a baby as a mass of explosive impulses that the mother must make sense of and so to speak remould ('transform'). In this first place the mother is merely guide, in the second case the mother is the container who digests and feeds back in modulated form the child's unmodulated feelings.[69]

Observational studies have certainly contributed usefully to child health and childcare practices. However, there is a difference between the kind of studies pursued predominantly by child psychotherapists in Britain and those emanating from the United States. A collection of papers published in 1989 entitled *Closely Observed Infants*[70] represents the tradition which stresses the role of unconscious and internal processes as well as developmental external ones. Judy Shuttleworth, one of the editors, reviewing Brazelton and Cramer's *The Earliest Relationship*, commented that, for them, 'Phantasy tends to be seen as something that inter-feres with the parents' capacity to know objectively the reality of their baby; an interference by "ghosts" from the past.'[71] There is little exploration of the constructive role of phantasy – its role in enabling a mother to understand both herself and her baby. As Shuttleworth points out, 'This is partly because the model of interaction is not one of mutual projective processes which enable the couple to establish a primitive emotional link.'[72] (Shuttleworth is referring to projective identification and all the processes at work in Bion's theory of reverie outlined in Chapter 3.)

Observational studies that overlook unconscious to unconscious communication 'offer a closed knowable system from which an internal dynamic is absent but which offers the professional an assured role'.[73] Thus Daniel Stern's 1994 Sigmund Freud Lecture in London was entitled 'How Can We Now Understand Mother–Infant Interaction: Implications for Parenting', while Dr Brazelton has been described as 'the Dr Spock of the 1980s'. Professor of Pediatrics at Harvard University Medical School, Brazelton is the author of a number of books and magazine advice columns as well as films on infant development and the role of the parents. In his book *On Becoming a Family: The Growth of Attachment*, he declared that 'The maternal instinct, that capacity to really give and stay on the child's wavelength – is a very precious thing.'[74] Interestingly, Brazelton brings together mother as child, 'on the same wavelength' as the child and mother as adult, with her 'capacity to really give'. Whereas I have suggested that the co-existence within the mother of infantile and adult responses is a constant yet necessary source of tension, he sees it on an assumptive level as nothing more than instinctive.

A theory which dispenses with the unruly influence of mutual unconscious phantasy cannot satisfactorily encompass maternal ambivalence and one in which trauma represents an interpersonal failure due to maternal deficiency lends itself to the behavioural solutions beloved by popular journalism. In the USA, Brazelton was a contributor to the *Redbook* magazine for women. In Britain, *She* magazine during the late 1980s began to devote a regular portion of the magazine to information on the latest theories of child development and guidance on childcare. In June 1992, for example, the section ('Growing Pains') included 'Teaching kids to be kind . . . When his voice is breaking . . . Will baby suffer if you work? . . . Middle children need special care . . . Discipline that works'. As well as advice from the experts on these issues, there was a report on an organisation in the USA devoted to teaching parents successful strategies for dealing with uncooperative children. 'To be successful, say the experts, parents must respond to the problem consistently and appropriately.' Instructions followed.

If parents were not inevitably inconsistent and often insensitive, if motherhood did not inevitably evoke deeply held psychic conflict, the sensitivity/consistency imperatives would be obsolete. Moreover, the conditions of mothering in the USA and Europe – the intensity, the longevity, the sense of lone responsibility – produces precisely the 'misattunement' and 'contingency failure' that, popularised, are believed to spell inevitable developmental disaster.

The magazine advice columns represent the final outcome of the movement within psychoanalysis by which 'mothering was used to understand psychoanalysis'.[75] The resulting need to know what mothers really do led to observational studies of mothers and babies which in turn lent the authority of science to representations of the ideal mother as sensitive, measured, attentive and naturally at one with her children.

We see in relation to what I termed the 'happiness imperative' how science may be employed to didactic ends. The popular piece on parenting in *She* magazine (p. 181) declared that 'Research verifies the value of growing up with happy parents.' Details of this research were not provided. Often a specific project is endowed by the media with universal implications to provide a basis for instructions to mothers. For example, work on the interaction of clinically depressed women with their children is all too easily universalised in support of the 'happiness imperative'.[76]

On Learning from the Therapist

I want to reiterate that, although psychoanalysis has worked to obscure or pathologise maternal ambivalence, it has the potential to provide a crucial means for understanding the workings of it. Therefore, as well as regretting the part psychoanalysis has played in constructing an idealised and emotionally constricted and constrained representation of motherhood, we need to ask if the mother analyst does have anything to offer an actual mother. This is a difficult question to answer without becoming prescriptive or seeming to confirm that mothers should become therapists.

Nevertheless, I do think that the profound, unconscious to un-conscious links that emerge in the analytic framework between patient and analyst or therapist are fruitful to consider in the context of mother–child relating, not to make mothers respond as therapists but to highlight the power of the emotional life they *share* with their children.

Psychoanalytic depictions of mutual projections clarify the sudden dips into intense rage experienced and reported with shame by many mothers. Similarly, Andrew Samuels has drawn on the Jungian tradition to suggest that there is an imaginal world, an alternative perceptual system populated by images, that explains how the experiences of one person crop up in the experience of another.[77] With these ideas in mind, rather than feeling an un-natural mother or a failure, when suffused with an inexplicable rage that in its intensity seems to come from somewhere else, a mother can view it as evidence of her very closeness to the child.

Psychoanalysis has thus deepened our understanding of the intense unconscious communication constellated in the mother–child dyad. A mother introjects her child's rage which, so to speak, marries with her infantile feelings. Such feelings have themselves been mobilised by the frustration of her adult needs by her child's behaviour. Then the turmoil ignites to which mothers confess. The mother I cited at the opening of this chapter who commented, 'It's as if they press a button and suddenly I'm in there with them' can be understood as describing the workings of projective identification and the imaginal world. She continued, 'I behave appallingly – in a way you are not meant to as a mother.' The meaning motherhood has for her – a meaning constructed in part by the culture's absorption of the 'analyst mother' – covers her with shame, which magnifies her rage. She is unable to think about, to question or to respond constructively to the violent feelings evoked in her through her relationship with her children. She is, in her own eyes, simply a bad mother, and an unnatural one at that.

The worsening behaviour of children and their parents is a constant cultural lament. Rosalind Coward, writing in the *Observer*, declared,

> If a child is to grow up with an internal sense of safety, which is necessary to respect others' safety, it needs to have an experi-ence of an adult who can acknowledge and feel for the child's

destructiveness but still be able to look after it. Being able to do this involves confidence to control destructive behaviour without brutalising the child. But it is precisely this ability which is dramatically lacking at the moment.[78]

Mothers are expected to be containing and cognisant in a culture that curtails the range of feelings deemed 'normal' in them, and constructs a split representation of mothers as either children themselves or their children's therapists. Now, of course, the split representation of motherhood does relate to the realities of being a mother – as I said earlier, it is not my intention to suggest a deliberate conspiracy against mothers. Motherhood *does* demand that women be able both to identify with their children's feelings and to take a distance from them. This is terribly difficult to maintain. But it is the state of mind that enables a woman to acknowledge, in Rosalind Coward's words, and 'feel for the child's destructiveness but still look after it'.

I have argued in this chapter that this ability is hampered because our culture does not maintain a representation of motherhood which would enable the inherent conflicts to be experienced constructively. Instead, Western culture categorises maternal conflict as failure, thanks to a split representation of mothers as either at one with the children – one of the gang – or as omnipotently and entirely mature – nothing but Mother. In our world, the internal conflict between their adult aspect and their childish selves has taken on a negative meaning for most mothers. They feel inauthentic or not proper mothers. Hence the culture confirms the split mothers suffer, rather than how an interplay of different states of mind deepens a mother's capacity to mother.

8

Powerlessly Powerful

> When they run away up the road, it's not just that I fear they
> will be kidnapped or hit by a car, I get terrified and enraged
> because they are disobeying my authority, and I feel my
> authority is bound up with my ability to protect them.

Hester, standing on the pavement watching her children, all under
ten years old, tear up the road, is gripped by conflicting emotions.
She dreads losing her children in an accident, she hates them
for frightening her, she has a strong sense of her own power to
protect them, and is simultaneously aware of her helplessness. In
this chapter I shall explore the co-existence in motherhood of
power and powerlessness, control and helplessness in the context
of fear of loss of child and loss of self.

Hester sees the environment as terribly threatening to her
children – and to herself – because the dangers threaten her with the
loss of the children. She is committed to protecting her children,
yet their disobedience, in conjunction with obvious dangers, evokes
levels of rage in her that she fears and sees as almost as destructive
as dangerous drivers and imagined kidnappers. She fears both
losing her children's love – and losing them. She feels powerless to
control either the children or her own anger. She hates them as they
hurtle up the road, to the extent that the fear they will be killed
becomes a guilty wish which she formulates as the fleeting, almost
petulant thought 'and I wouldn't care if they were knocked down by
a bus . . .'

Her observation 'I feel my authority is bound up with my ability
to protect them' signals the issues that need to be addressed in
relation to maternal power. First, she makes it clear how deeply
implicated a woman's identity is in her children's behaviour and

second, she shows how the need and desire to wield a protective and constructive authority can, paradoxically, intensify frustration and hatred, leading not to protection but to greater or lesser persecution of the children.

Many factors render the exercise of maternal authority profoundly paradoxical. Children are smaller, weaker, dependent, and yet necessarily opposed to parental control as part of their individuation process. Mothers are bigger, stronger, adult, and yet socially and politically still the subjugated sex – and emotionally very vulnerable to their children.

Mothers are increasingly accorded the role of authority figures in relation to their children: 'Wait until your father gets home' seems like a saying from the distant past as the numbers of lone parents increase.

Yet even while mothers are accorded overwhelming responsibility for their children's development, their authority is circumscribed, subjected, as they are, to the critical gaze of a network of structures – notably the child's school. The passage of blame between mother and institution often makes it hard to think about what might be best for a child. Felicity is, in her words, constantly 'hauled up to school' to answer for her daughter's disruptive behaviour: 'I think insistently,' "What have I done wrong?"' Feeling blamed and unsupported by the school, she says, 'Surely they should be doing something about her – surely it's up to the school.' The school's response is to phone the mother.

And, whilst society demands that parents – especially women – exercise greater control over their children, dominant beliefs about childcare are contradictory. Where smaller children are concerned there are the opposing ideologies of 'child-centred' and 'adult-directed' care – a permissive versus an authoritarian approach. The split is equally evident in attitudes towards older children. The school suggested that Felicity's sixteen-year-old daughter needed firmer boundaries and stricter surveillance at home, while the Social Services maintained that a sense of responsibility might be fostered if the girl was allocated her own flat.

Of course mothers, too, vary in their response to the contradictions inherent in society's expectations of maternal control. Their own predilections and personalities determine the extent to which they feel they can or should hold power. The issue is obviously inflected by the age of their child, by the social context

– whether docility or defiance is validated by the culture, overtly or covertly – by family circumstances and by the gender of the child. The need to control children is shaped according to whether a mother is mothering in congenial, comfortable, easy and economically secure circumstances, or in practically and psychologically difficult conditions.

In her book *Beloved*, Toni Morrison dramatised a mother's act of power in circumstances of extreme powerlessness. She takes as a setting mid-nineteenth-century America and describes a slave woman's response to the extraordinary cruelty facing her children. Sethe, Morrison's heroine, reflects that 'What she called the nastiness of life was the shock she received upon learning that nobody stopped playing chequers just because the pieces included her children.'[1] Her children are sold as slaves. She kills her daughter to save her from a life felt to be worse than death. Another character in the novel observes sympathetically: 'She ain't crazy, she love those children. She was trying to outhurt the hurter.'[2]

The contrast between late twentieth-century, middle-class Hester or Felicity and Toni Morrison's Sethe is profound, but it highlights the issues I want to explore in relation to motherhood and power: responsibility, terror of loss, and violence. Though these are constant themes – how they are experienced by the individual mother is dependent upon the complex interaction of her psychic reality and external reality.[3]

The nature of a woman's superego plays a significant role in a woman's attitude towards power, control and discipline. The psychoanalyst Janine Chasseguet Smirgel – discussing the commonly held view that women have, at least in appearance, a superego which constantly changes, taking on new aspects, giving up old ones, according to their sexual partner – argues that the superficial impression of being easily influenced and lacking in clear morality conceals a harsher reality.[4] She cites a patient of hers who appears to change her principles with the time of day but who in fact maintains very strong internalised prohibitions. 'One of them dominates all the others, as if it were some sort of 11th Commandment. "You may not have your own law – your law is your object's law".' Chasseguet Smirgel concludes, 'It seems as though many women have internalized this commandment.'[5]

For a mother who tends to follow the law of the other, exercising power and authority over a child can feel simply *wrong*. Grace experiences considerable guilt and a sense of inauthenticity when she tells her children what to do. She describes it as manipulation: 'I hate the sense of manipulating a child to do what you want it to do. It makes me feel horrible.' Hester feels she will be punished by the loss of her children if she relinquishes authority. Molly, on the other hand, is unequivocal in her enjoyment of the power permitted by parenthood:

> They drive me mad: the noise, the mess, the fighting, the way they live in their emotions. But I also like controlling them. You can muck in with them, but there's always a stopping point.

Freud considered that a little girl's doll play constituted an identification with her mother's power and agency and had the unconscious intention of substituting activity for passivity.[6] His colleagues, Ruth Mack Brunswick and Helene Deutsch, pointed out that both boys and girls struggle to acquire an active, independent posture in relation to the mother. Once she becomes a mother herself, a woman reclaims the executive abilities she originally identified with her mother, but within the family at home, a circumscribed and confined sphere.[7] Moreover, a mother encounters in her child a being as intent in acquiring an active posture in relation to herself as she once was in relation to her own mother. Being mothered and being a mother always constitute more or less of a power struggle.

Great Mother and Fragile Container

The curious dialectic of power and powerlessness determines maternity even prior to the moment of conception. A woman may fantasise that a child will endow her with a kind of immortality, yet the fact that the child will outlive her equally signifies her mortality. A woman may hope that conceiving a child will confer adult status upon her, putting an end to her identity as daughter, yet she may equally find that pregnancy and motherhood foster an intense dependency on others and seal her seemingly for ever into a world of daughterhood. Also she may wish to reproduce and reciprocate the kind of good-enough maternal care she herself experienced – only to find herself in the grip of intense unmanageable maternal ambivalence.[8]

Pregnancy itself is a profoundly contradictory state – an enrichment and an injury, as Simone de Beauvoir put it.[9] Similarly, Julia Kristeva describes birth as both deprivation and benefit: 'My removed marrow, which nevertheless acts as a graft, which wounds but increases me.'[10] A woman may see herself as at once Great Mother and Fragile Container.

As discussed in Chapter 3, a good deal has been written on pregnancy from a psychoanalytic perspective.[11] A pregnant woman is known to develop highly complex feelings towards the foetus, largely because during pregnancy and childbirth she repeats more or less intensely her early relationship with her own mother. She may project ambivalent or negative aspects of her internal objects on to the foetus, perceiving it as something bad and voracious within, out to destroy her autonomy and undermine her adulthood. She is identifying the foetus with her own voracious and destructive feelings.

At the same time, in the unconscious, the foetus can represent her mother – particularly her maternal superego – whose retaliation she fears for her infantile destructiveness. Another phantasy in relation to the foetus is that it symbolises something valuable stolen from the mother. Thus she fears her mother will enviously spoil her pregnancy, controlling it, taking it over and making it her own.

On the other hand, a woman may endow the foetus with all the good, lovable qualities she feels her own baby-within-herself possesses and thus fears that she herself will be a danger to a vulnerable, good unborn baby. However, even while pregnancy can evoke fear of destructiveness and retaliation, it also seems to offer the possibility of reconciliation and reparation in identification with a loving, life-giving mother (see Chapter 3).

The contradictions women can experience during pregnancy – the fluctuating identifications with the mother and with the mothered, with the victim and the victimiser, with being creative and with being colonised – can actually contribute to the capacity to mother. Joan Raphael-Leff, analysing the dreams of pregnant women, concluded that the dream material signifies a working through of contradictions. In dreams, elemental opposites in the women's psychic world are confronted and/or reconciled: birth and death, creation and destruction, order and chaos, big and little, strong and-weak, self and other.[12]

A contributor to the anthology *Between Ourselves: Letters between Mothers and Daughters*, addressed her daughter as follows, reminiscing on the child's birth:

> I cried up until the last minute. What if you had a birth defect from my not wanting you? What if I didn't love you? All that weight I had gained! All that hair that fell on my comb! I had created a life but couldn't control my own.
>
> You came on a cool rainy June evening. Not until the last minute did I believe you were here. With your birth some primitive joy was released . . . At the sight of your long legs and dark hair, all my fears died . . .[13]

The letter's recipient was an unplanned baby. Yet, ultimately, compared to her relationship with her other children, Elaine Marcus Starkman's feelings for her fourth child appear more passionate and deeply engaged. I think the extent of her ambivalence during the pregnancy broke through her defences, compelling her to abandon the check she held on her emotions as a mother. It seems, reading the letter, as if it was precisely by acknowledging the full extent of her negativity towards her unborn child that she was able to experience equally powerful love. Curiously, feeling hate – daring to feel hate – gave her the courage to love. During pregnancy she confronted her guilt, fear and intense resentment that this baby was taking away the control she had over her life; she was powerless to control her body and its contents even while creating a new life. At birth, the fact that she was deeply in touch with her emotions enabled the intensity of love and joy at the sight of the baby to outweigh the hate.

Self and Other

Prior to birth, one negative image a woman maintains of the foetus is often that of 'parasite'. Postnatally the picture changes; although in the shifting configuration of mother–child interaction, the imagery of previous phases subtly informs subsequent stages, never entirely fading. Now, in the grip of passionate absorption with another, coupled with the relentless demands of baby-care, the mother can image the baby as both 'tyrant' and 'love of my life'. The issue which will characterise motherhood, throughout her son or daughter's infancy and beyond, is the negotiation of a woman's individuality and capacity as a caretaker with the baby's separate assertiveness.[14] Katherine Gieve, in her edited collection, *Balancing Acts*, appraised the meaning of the conflict for her:

Time passed, my parents went home and John went back to work. I, during my maternity leave, was alone responsible for the baby during the days. The struggle which ensued was not, as I had anticipated, between the baby's needs and my need for my own autonomy and independent identity – but the more complex struggle between my desire for autonomy and my desire and pleasure in satisfying the baby.[15]

Gieve is focusing on women's curiously ambiguous relation to their own power. For some women, the capacity to satisfy – to be able to continue to respond to the apparently unending demands of a loved one – in itself produces a feeling of power, while for others it seems like self-effacement, entirely at odds with their sense of agency.

Possibly 'power' and 'agency' are misleading terms to employ in relation to baby-care for they fail to evoke the ambivalence entailed. The crux of the matter is how women respond to the regression induced by early motherhood. For, just as pregnancy induces regression in identification with the foetus, so does care of a small baby provoke a mother to identify with the baby. As Katherine Gieve put it, 'The anguish of a hungry baby's cry becomes your own anguish.'[16] A new mother feels both one with the helpless baby *and* its omnipotent source of life.

Joan Raphael-Leff has coined the terms 'Facilitator' and 'Regulator' to distinguish between those mothers who respond to the often deeply disturbing feelings of early motherhood by adapting to the baby, and those mothers who expect the baby to adapt to them.[17] She suggests that on an unconscious level the Facilitator is afraid of hating, whereas the Regulator is afraid of falling in love with her baby. I think the distinction she draws well illustrates the way issues of control and authority touch on and mobilise maternal ambivalence. The Facilitator, by going along with the baby, staves off the possibility of distance and conflict. Not only is she attempting to silence her own capacity for hatred, but she is protecting herself from being hated by her child. The Regulator, by refusing to let the baby get the upper hand, keeps passion, intimacy and love at a safe distance. Thus being 'permissive' or being 'authoritarian' are crucially determined by attitudes towards the components of love and hate in ambivalence. I shall return to this point in relation to mothering slightly older children, but here I want to pursue Joan Raphael-Leff's categories somewhat further.

Raphael-Leff emphasised that her model delineates two extreme poles on a continuum. For the Facilitator the inability to fulfil her ideal of exclusive, continuous mothering is extremely distressing. She feels any imperfection, like being unable to soothe a colicky baby, signifies failure and a betrayal of the child. The Regulator fears that her own hard-won independence will be jeopardised, that the baby's helplessness will endanger her by reawakening her own greed and unresolved dependency needs. Both, in their different ways, are wanting to exercise control and omnipotence – to do the right thing by the baby not simply for the sake of the baby but in order not to incur a loss of belief in their own goodness. In the course of her comprehensive and illuminating work on pregnancy and birth, Raphael-Leff went on to designate a third category – the Reciprocator. She represents the experience of tolerating ambivalence and accepting 'both her own and the baby's good and bad aspects.'[18]

Sometimes a mother's orientation, her way of maintaining a sense of her own viability and capability within the demands of motherhood, can change over the course of her mothering. Again, Elaine Marcus Starkman describes how differently she related to her fourth child:

> But I've allowed you to nourish me as I've nourished you. I've allowed that bond between mother and daughter to gradually grow, to reach beyond the limits I've always held. Not that I didn't love your brother and sisters – how they overwhelmed me – but with your birth, the child whom I didn't want but at last proved my worth so that I could say, Enough, I myself began to bloom. Is this my tie with you? That I've finally learned becoming a mother will not change my love of learning, my desire to write?[19]

Elaine Marcus Starkman is, in a way, describing herself changing from being a Regulator who feared a loss of self in loving her children into a Facilitator. With the initially unwanted child, she did not fear being engulfed and obliterated by *loving* the child but rather feared *hating* her and what that hate might do to the child. Thus she allowed the affectionate bond between herself and her daughter to grow beyond the emotional limits on love she had set with her other children. By owning ambivalence she was able to let go of the reins.

It is not unusual for a mother to describe herself as more of a Regulator with her first-born and more of a Facilitator or Reciprocator with subsequent siblings. There are many possible explanations for this. Experience teaches a mother the limits of her omnipotence, and by the time a mother has, say, a third child her personal identity as a mother is less dependent upon any one child's behaviour. But, above all, ambivalence may have become acknowledged and thus no longer needs either to be acted out or fended off through the assumption or abandonment of authority over the child.

> Suddenly I realized that I expected Peter, the oldest, to clean his plate. Daniel, the middle one, didn't have to eat it, but he had to taste it. And little Billy, as far as I was concerned, could do whatever he wanted.[20]

A mother's role in the power relationship between herself and her child is to an extent 'dictated' by the child, its personality and developmental stage. Katherine Gieve describes how her mothering changed when her son was between two and three years old. She began to operate less as a Facilitator and more as a Regulator:

> aged between 2 and 3, [he] began most emphatically to separate himself from me. I was by then used to being on the same side as him in a democratic and symbiotic way. He had created, I felt, a responsive, acquiescent mother, only then to turn me into something quite different ... This time not 'maternal acquiescent' but 'maternal firm and autocratic'.[21]

The maternal firm and autocratic mother whose child is engaged in separating out from her is probably fearful of the extent of her love for it. For separation and independence also connote painful loss. Elaine Marcus Starkman indicates how fear of loss determines her need for a controlled and controlling stance. Addressing her daughter, she declares:

> For my world isn't benevolent. Any moment an evil hand can reach from around the corner, a disease rise within, a young driver screech out of the court mowing down your young life, punishing me for being a wicked mother, leaving me without a small child to keep at center.
> How I worry when I love. I never wanted to give myself fully: I held back so I wouldn't be hurt, so your siblings wouldn't consume me when I was just beginning to know myself.[22]

A mother may fear *loss* of herself in merging with her child; yet she fears being punished for loss of the child if she resists oneness and merging. Felicity was such a mother. She felt that not to subsume herself in her children was to hate them, and to hate them meant to abandon them. Her ambition as a mother was to be entirely loving, to be as giving as she felt her own mother had been withholding, as facilitating and available as she felt her father had been absent and denying. In other words, she wanted to provide her children with all the care and all the opportunities she thought had been denied her. She believed that if she tried hard enough she could totally fulfil her children's needs, as well as protecting them and giving them direction in their lives.

Her expectations of herself as a mother – the extremes of self-abnegation and love she wanted to offer – meant that her children's ordinary insatiability felt like a ravenous hunger she was duty bound but unable to answer. For example, when her son breast-fed, she felt as if he was about to devour her entire breast. His enthusiasm and excitement deeply frightened her, and, with shame and regret, she contrived to cease breastfeeding.

As her children grew up, they sensed their mother's powerful desire to love and give, and her equally fearful sense of being drained. They felt short-changed – and let her know it. Slowly Felicity was forced to realise the necessary limitations of her mothering. The turning point for her in terms of relinquishing maternal omnipotence was when her children reached adolescence. Then their increasing defiance and widening independence forced her to come to terms with the limits of maternal power. She recognised that her compulsion to be an omnipotently powerful mother in itself constructed her sense of herself as an inadequate mother – and led her to resent her children. Once the hatred generated by her sense of powerlessness and helplessness ebbed, she experienced a new ease with them:

> I realised I had changed towards my kids when I stopped minding the way they borrow my clothes. I feel now that they can take what they want, bar a few precious things. I no longer feel ripped off, resentful and guilty. And they have started asking first!

Hitting Out

I want to look again at the process which transforms a mother's anxiety on behalf of her child into aggression against the child (see Chapter 4) . The need to exercise protective control under pressure explodes into violence. A mother loses her temper and hits out. Feeling defeated by the struggle to keep her child safe, a mother brings about the precise state of affairs she has struggled to prevent – the child gets hurt. The dread of loss then becomes a desire to annihilate:

> When I hit her it didn't do me any good. I just wanted to hit her more – it increased my rage and made me feel if I hit her more she might disappear – just not be there.

The majority of mothers I have worked with 'admit' hitting their children. For most it represents, not an expression of power, authority and discipline, but a shameful loss of control over self and over the child, and they remember incidents of violence with painful regret. Grace describes the evolution of the state of mind that leads to hitting:

> In the car Kate won't sit in her booster seat. She insists on sitting on the arm rest, and wearing the lap belt. I insist. She refuses. I know I have right on my side but I can't get her to do what I want. I get angrier and angrier. I start thinking, and if we do crash and she does break her pelvis who is going to have to do all the work of looking after her – me!
>
> I'm overwhelmed by the reasonableness of my position and the intransigence of this small being evoking my fury. I lose control. I feel horrible and miserable.
>
> I think three things are at work in these moments. There is a rigid insistence on control (do what you are told). Then there is true concern (she might break her pelvis) and then there is moral outrage (who will look after her with a broken pelvis?).

In Chapter 4 I explored how a mother's sense of her own frustrated needs can magnify feelings of hatred for her child, rendering her response to ambivalence unmanageable. We saw how creative concern can then become swamped by anxiety. In Chapter 5 I looked at the way aggressive aspects of the separation process can similarly render ambivalence unmanageable, how a sense of helplessness can transform thought-provoking depression into mindless, hopeless despair. Here I want to analyse how the real and/or imagined loss of a child can change manageable ambivalence into ambivalence which provokes unbearable anxiety.

Mothers constantly encounter real and imagined losses in the course of their mothering. Each step of a child's development could be thought of as a loss. Fear of loss means that a mother has to contend with the cultural expectations of maternal power, cultural curtailment of maternal power, her own desire for potency, her conviction of powerlessness, her loving concern to protect her child – and her hate.

In order to gain a clearer grasp of the processes engendered in a mother by this peculiarly contradictory state of affairs, it is helpful to consider again salient points in Melanie Klein's theory of ambivalence – and then, once again to relate such ideas to maternal rather than infantile ambivalence. Klein came to believe that ambivalence exists very early in life, 'being already experienced in relation to part objects'.[23] This implies that the quality of ambivalence is changeable. As the child develops, the nature of ambivalence changes with the increasing *rapprochement* of love and hate. Klein describes

> the all-important process of bringing together more closely the various aspects of objects (external, internal, 'good' and 'bad', loved and hated), and thus for hatred to become actually mitigated by love – which means a decrease of ambivalence. While the separation of these contrasting *aspects* – felt in the unconscious as contrasting *objects* – operates strongly, feelings of love and hatred are also so much divorced from each other that love cannot mitigate hatred.[24]

Klein's phrase 'a decrease in ambivalence' is somewhat confusing. From a developmental standpoint her theory suggests that ambivalence is an achievement – the capacity to tolerate the co-existence of love and hate. Yet here she seems to be depicting ambivalence as a problem to be decreased. To minimise confusion I have avoided referring to ambivalence as increased or decreased; instead I speak of manageable and unmanageable ambivalence. When manageable, a greater trust in love is established and in Klein's words there is 'a decrease in sadism and a better way of mastering aggression and working it off'.[25]

Fear of loss provokes both an increase in feelings of love, and, paradoxically, a decrease in trust in love. Fear of loss is inherent in the very co-existence of love and hate. For it leads a mother unconsciously to fear that her hatred will irrevocably damage her child – that she will be responsible for her child's failure to survive.

Usually, however, a child's evident ability to survive, coupled with their mutual love, reinforces a mother's sense of her own goodness and her capacity to love. As we have seen, guilt then becomes a source of reparatory and creative mothering.

The intricate relationship between the fear of loss, feelings of loss, and fluctuations in love and hate explains the appeal of a particular genre of women's magazine feature. Almost every issue of popular magazines such as *Bella* or *Hello* carries a moving account of a child's serious, life-threatening, illness. A mother reading these features identifies with the parental pain depicted. As she contemplates undergoing the same anguish herself she is filled with love and gratitude for her own child's well-being; 'all is forgiven' and love at least temporarily outweighs hate.

Loss vicariously experienced is, of course, very different to confrontation with actual loss and powerlessness to prevent it. As Klein pointed out, 'splitting under the stress of ambivalence to some extent persists throughout life and plays an important part in mental economy'.[26] When, for example, a child leaps daringly from a high wall, far from feeling an influx of love a mother can be filled with hatred. The bad child appears to be out to hurt her. She can feel momentarily powerless, helpless, angry and anxious. For in mothers, especially, persecutory and depressive anxiety inform and reinforce one another. She is a bad mother for not having stopped the child from jumping; the child is bad to have jumped.

Klein discussed the relation of ambivalence to loss in the context of bereavement and mourning, considering mourning to be a manifestation of a process which is constantly carried out in smaller ways throughout life, whenever losses and rejections of a lesser kind are suffered.

We can reframe Klein's description of a failure to experience constructive mourning and look at it from the point of view of a mother who tries and fails to exercise the desired protective power over her children. Klein writes as follows of those who fail to resolve mourning:

> Feeling incapable of saving and securely reinstating their loved objects inside themselves, they must turn away from them more than hitherto and therefore deny their love for them. This may mean that their emotions in general become more inhibited; in other cases it is mainly feelings of love which become stifled and hatred is increased.[27]

Bereavement threatens the phantasy of there actually being a good thing – a good internal object – inside oneself that nourishes other people. This induces guilt – guilt that harm has been done to a loved person. Too severe and punishing a sense of guilt evokes many defensive evasions. Instead of guilt leading to remorse, mourning and reparation, it calls into play a failure to mourn characterised by paranoid and manic defences. Denial, idealisation, splitting and control are all employed by the ego to counteract persecutory anxiety – and to a lesser extent depressive anxiety. Klein comments, 'When anxiety is paramount, the ego even denies that it loves the object at all.'[28]

If we take a scene familiar on any city street, we can see how mothering institutes at telescopic speed the processes Klein describes in unresolved mourning. A child skips off the pavement. Its mother yanks its arm and brutally slaps the child. For, as the child steps into the gutter, the mother has a terrifying intimation of loss and her powerlessness to prevent that loss. In the slapping moment, she experiences her own destruction of the good internal object that has been nourishing her from within, enabling her to care for her child. She hates the child for threatening her with loss, for turning her into a monster, and obscuring the love that is obviously also there.

A mother who cannot trust her capacity to put things right is a mother who cannot, at least temporarily, manage ambivalence. Then she may resort to manic omnipotence, splitting, and denial of her love for her child. The psychic reality of depressive pain is over-whelming. Her dependence on her relationship with her children is denied and they are omnipotently controlled and treated with triumph and contempt. Thus fears of their loss cannot give rise to pain and guilt.

In sum, a mother faced with a disobedient child whose defiance she feels threatens her with loss experiences an intolerable intensification of hatred. Mounting anger, frustration and anxiety instigate defences against depressive pain. Love succumbs to hatred. The mother experiences herself as wronged and the child as utterly in the wrong. The mother can then feel permitted to be sadistic.

Making it Worse

Moments when mothers' concern for their children becomes swamped by a sense of persecution need to be understood in the context of unconscious processes constellated by the intense intimacy of mother and child. Unconscious to unconscious communication is, as I've indicated, very much present in the mother–child relationship. A mother of a small baby receives massive projections of powerful feelings. In psychoanalytic terms, a mother needs to accept them without undue diminishment through denials or other defences. The mother acknowledges the reality of the baby's feelings while by her reaction she reduces them to a manageable size.

However, a mother's doubts about her capacity to mother can be magnified by her baby's projections. For example, a mother's loss in moments of conflict of an internal good object – meaning here the loss of a sense of herself as benevolent, loving, patient and protective – can be intensified by her baby's projections. After all, even the most apparently facilitating, easygoing and democratic mother is at times perceived by her child as punitive and wickedly autocratic.

Ruth Mack Brunswick described the immense power of the mother in the infant's and small child's mind: 'She is not only active, phallic but *omnipotent*.'[29] The small dependent child faced with the hugely omnipotent mother sustains 'early narcissistic injuries from the mother'[30] which 'enormously increase the child's hostility'.[31] The child projects its destructive feelings deriving from its sense of helplessness into its mother, fears them – and sometimes fights them. Chasseguet-Smirgel observes,

> the child's primary powerlessness, the intrinsic characteristics of his psychophysiological condition, and the inevitable frustrations of training are such that the imago of the good omnipotent mother never covers over that of the terrifying, omnipotent, mad mother.[32]

Just as the baby in her or his powerlessness attributes omnipotence to the mother, so mothers faced with expectations of omnipotence can feel terribly impotent. Paradoxically, the dependent child seems to them a powerful tyrant. Some react by struggling to be omnipotent, others in receipt of projections of omnipotent goodness or badness slip into angry helplessness. At such moments a mother would be enormously helped by having someone present who could metaphorically stand between herself and her child, someone who could 'metabolise' her fears and helplessness just as she does her child's.[33] However, the circumstances of twentieth-century mothering mean that mothers usually process their children's projections in isolation – in private – with no one available to reality-test.

The growing child can at times speak her or his mind in a way that facilitates and allows mutual projections to be thought about and, so to speak, be cut down to size. Mary, a mother whose behaviour is particularly adaptive and anti-authoritarian, describes an incident when her daughter Marcella was five which illustrates this point:

> We were going upstairs because it was her bedtime when she looked at me and said, 'Oh, there's no face in the back of your head.' And I said, 'Oh, there is sometimes?' She replied, 'Sometimes, the other one, the bad one, has her face on the other side.' I wondered at the time if the bad one was about my repressed negativity which I was hardly aware of – but she was.

Flick reported the following incident with her sons, making it clear what a relief it is when feelings can be spoken:

> I was making the kids' supper and they were sitting talking at the kitchen table. I heard Jack who was then five years old say to Tom who was seven, 'Do you think that? I do too!' It caught my attention and I asked them what they were talking about. Jack told me that they both think that after I put them to bed and kiss them goodnight, I go out of the room and remove my mask and clothes, and reveal myself to be a witch. I was a bit taken aback but at the same time it felt that because they could say it we could all know I wasn't really a witch. Sometimes I do feel a witch!

Frances describes herself as a strict and controlling mother – above all with her youngest child. She says, 'I want my children to be likeable; I don't want anyone saying, "there's a brat".' Her son has split off the witch from his mother and located her elsewhere:

> When he was about three years old I left him with a child-minder, and he became a baby again; he used to pee on the floor and refused to speak to the childminder – but with me he was lovely. I worry a lot about him. I know that chaos is something he doesn't associate with our relationship. Somehow, it has to be kept elsewhere.

Once a child reaches adolescence, the process of separation between mother and child inevitably intensifies conflicts over maternal power and authority. Whereas Mary, Flick and Frances are encountering small children's projections and perceptions of themselves as persecuting figures, Grace feels misunderstood and unable to communicate with her practically grown-up children. She believes that now they are essentially outside her control, issues of authority ought to be in abeyance, yet somehow she is still in the wrong:

> My utter failure to communicate with them is indescribably painful. Again and again there seem to be misunderstandings, miscommunication. I think with longing of that wonderful sense of oneness I felt at the moment of their birth. It doesn't continue. Instead I'm seen as a monster and a witch.

The Outside World

Now I want to outline the way external reality both reflects and reinforces a mother's psychic reality, magnifying her guilt in relation to 'keeping order'.

In the public sphere, in the press, parliament and in social and academic institutions, parental authority is subjected to constant scrutiny, and the repeated call is for greater parental authority and control over children. For example, the British 1989 Children Act marks an attempt to shift the balance of power over children's lives away from the welfare state and on to the family. At the same time mothers are viewed with disquiet and issued with contradictory advice and injunctions.

If we look at the plethora of studies of family life produced over the last thirty years, they demonstrate a repeated concern with issues of authority. Take, for example, two well-known studies of family life from the mid-1960s, *Patterns of Infant Care in an Urban Community* (1965) by J. and E. Newson and *The Captive Wife* (1966) by Hannah Gavron. The Newsons noted a new equality between parents and children, evidenced by the fact that, according to their research, 'children these days, it is said, are able to "talk" to their parents in a way which, for a considerable number, seems to have been quite impossible before'.[34] Hannah Gavron interpreted matters differently. Where the Newsons optimistically observed closeness, communication and equality, she saw distance: 'It could be argued that there has been not so much a loss of authority as a loss of contact between parents and their adolescent children.'[35]

Both studies, despite their different findings, grasp the crucial link between authority and closeness. The psychic conflict generated by the dynamics of authority can lead to a mutual 'dehumanisation', resulting in excessive defensive distancing, or to a failure to recognise the discrete individuality of the other. Above all both studies reflect the way parental authority becomes the focus of anxiety about child–parent relationships in response to the extraordinarily rapid changes in the conditions of parenting – especially mothering – over the last two centuries.

A nostalgic longing for a family life shorn of ambivalence has been one upshot of such changes. Family life held up as an ideal takes as its model the bourgeois family of nineteenth-century capitalism. It is this model that Christopher Lasch yearns for in a call for a renewal of parental authority in *Haven in a Heartless World*.[36] As Michèle Barrett and Mary McIntosh observe in their critique of Lasch's work, this type of family has taken on a universal, essentialist and normative character. Within it, fathers dispense authority while mothers offer unconditional love and unflagging attention.[37]

In reality, even when Lasch published his book in the 1970s, only 12 per cent of households in Britain consisted of a working husband and a wife at home with the children. The persistent downward trend continued and the equivalent figure for 1992 was 7 per cent. In other words, out of 19.5 million households only 1.4 million conform to the conventional representation of family life. In 1993, 17.5 per cent of all families were headed by a lone mother and 1.4 per cent by a lone father.

The juxtaposition of the nineteenth-century ideal with twentieth-century reality contributes to the process of scapegoating of parents – particularly in the press. Take for example a series of articles in The *Guardian* during September 1991. For five consecutive days, the newspaper devoted full-page features to 'The Parent Trap'. A headline read: RIOTS, ABUSE, CRIME AND RUNAWAYS: THE MESSAGES OF CHILD-REARING AND FAMILY LIFE ARE CONFUSED AS NEVER BEFORE. There were numerous references to parental isolation, the fragmentation of communities, the arrival of a 'videoculture', and the growth of materialism to provide social explanations for the 'crisis'. Parents were offered tea and sympathy for all they had to contend with. But another message came over equally loud and clear. *Parents* were unquestionably to blame for riots, drug abuse, anorexia and an overall 'anarchic lawlessness among the young which appears increasingly impervious to persuasion'. Parents must toughen up, shape up and take control. With a few nods in the direction of the problem of over-authoritarian fathers, the overwhelming consensus was that parents must exercise more authority; even 'television ought to carry more encouragement to the authority of parents'. We were informed that 'loss of parental authority is a recurrent motif amongst professionals who care for damaged children'. Not only amongst professionals but also amongst parents there is a longing for discipline, certainty and control. Elizabeth Howell, of the psychoanalytically informed community organisation Exploring Parenthood, is quoted as saying that a large proportion of their helpline calls are from 'parents worried about discipline'.[38]

The group of parents most often singled out for blame are lone parents – specifically lone mothers. 'Anarchic lawlessness' and violence amongst the young are laid at their door. Violent crime has undoubtedly increased. Between 1979 and 1986 there were 4,000 more crimes of violence each year than the year before. But since 1987 the rate of increase has tripled to an unprecedented 13,000. The then Social Security Secretary Peter Lilley declared in 1993 that 'We have produced a generation of fatherless children. No father to support them, discipline them and set them an example.'[39] He blamed the rise in violence since 1950 on the absence of fathers.

Lilley cited Norman Dennis's book, *Families without Fathers*, to substantiate his view.[40] It is based on two studies; the first, by Eileen Crellin *et al.*, called *Born Illegitimate* (1971), in fact concluded that lone-parenting did not cause maladjustment: children of lone mothers were actually less likely to be maladjusted than those with two parents![41] The second study, by Israel Kolvin *et al.*, *Continuities of Deprivation*, does indeed suggest that the more the father is absent, the greater the likelihood that the home is a 'deprived' one.[42] However, a crucial issue that creates deprivation is that the absence of a partner and extra breadwinner renders the family economically deprived. Lone-parent families are on average at least twice as poor as two-parent ones. In a critique of Dennis's book, Oliver James commented that 'It is no exaggeration to say that the misuse to which Dennis has put these studies is a scandal.'[43] He offered his own conclusion: 'Being married is not a significant factor in the violence equation; it's being single as a result of an unhappy relationship and the low family income that follows.' This view was substantiated by a study published in January 1994 by the Family Policy Studies Centre which emphasised that the children of widowed lone parents do almost as well as those raised by both parents, indicating that some importance needs to be given to the nature of the family disruption rather than the disruption itself. Similarly, in an address to the UK National Council for One Parent Families in 1993, Andrew Samuels said:

> I simply cannot agree that there are any *inevitable* damaging psychological outcomes from living in a lone-parent family. As a clinician many of the most disturbed people that I see come from absolutely conventional backgrounds with two long-married parents who may even both be alive. The whole situation would be different were lone-parent families to be given adequate resources, approval and support from the community.

In sum, the expectations confronting mothers at this specific historical moment are deeply contradictory. On the one hand, as a socially isolated and politically disempowered group, they are considered incapable of keeping order. On the other, responsibility for the control of children and thus the 'pacifying' of society is seen to reside with them. They are superwomen who are expected to fulfil the fantasies associated with the maternal ideal, fantasies of unproblematic maternal unity and plenitude. And they are scapegoated for the anxieties and disturbances generated by rapid social change and poverty, while, as Jessica Benjamin has argued, 'The real problems that endanger mothers and children – inadequate day care, lack of maternity leave and flexible worktime – hide behind the ideal of motherhood, the vision of a self-sufficient family guarded by an omnicompetent angel of the house.'[44] I have sketched in the social and political position of mothers – blamed, undermined and economically disadvantaged – to suggest that external reality really does militate against maternal ambivalence remaining manageable.

Maternity as Perversity

Intensified scrutiny of domestic life has revealed the extent of child abuse across Western societies. Not only is there a dawning awareness of the prevalence of violent and sexual abuse, but there is the added recognition that, although most perpetrators are fathers, mothers too can abuse. However, although revelations of maternal cruelty have to some extent disrupted the maternal ideal, it is invariably read as outright perversion of the norm rather than as situated on a continuum of 'normality'. I would suggest that much maternal cruelty can be understood as an intensification of love and hate leading to increased splitting and enactment of hatred. The process is exacerbated, as I have suggested, by social and political attitudes towards mothers and children. We cannot fall back on the reassuring thought that all maternal cruelty is perversion – we have to admit that mothers can be cruel. Indeed, those who have experienced abuse at the hands of their mothers describe their immense distress at simply not being believed.

Feminists, however, have long asserted that the social construction of motherhood leads inevitably and inexorably to maternal cruelty. As I discussed in Chapter 2, Simone de Beauvoir in *The Second Sex* presented a particularly jaundiced view of the maternal abuse of power.[45] For her, a mother, forced to recognise that her child is an independent being and ultimately beyond her control, takes out on the child her sense of helplessness and powerlessness in the world: 'Such a mother is often remorseful and the child may not feel resentment, but it feels the blows.'[46] Adrienne Rich, writing thirty years later, makes a similar point but with greater sympathy for mothers:

> Powerless women have always used their mothering as a channel – narrow but deep – for their own human will to power, their need to return upon the world what it has visited upon them.[47]

Whereas de Beauvoir depicts mothers as hateful and hating, infantile and injurious in their powerlessness, Rich constantly affirms that love and anger co-exist, and that when anger provoked by the conditions of motherhood is taken out on the child, that anger is usually accompanied by guilt, remorse and grief.

More recently, maternal abuse has been considered from a psychoanalytic perspective in Britain by Estela Welldon and in the USA by Louise Kaplan.[48] Welldon, placing her psychoanalytic investigation within a political perspective, argues that the idealisation of motherhood has concealed maternal abuse and thus women's capacity for perversion. For, in her view, the seriously abusing mother represents a form of female perversion. She considers that the difference between male and female perverse acts lies in the aim. Whereas in men the act is aimed against an external part object, in women it is carried out against themselves: 'either against their bodies or against objects which they see as their own creations – their babies'.[49] The perverse maternal attitude, she suggests, manifests as a desire to engulf, to dehumanise, to invade, take control of and merge with children.

She identifies both a psychological and a sociological aetiology of the female perversion she sees lived out in maternity. In terms of the former, she considers that the perverse person feels she 'has not been allowed to enjoy a sense of her own development as a separate individual'.[50] Rather she has maintained a profound belief that she is her mother's part object – an important but almost unidentifiable part of her mother's life. Alternatively, she felt unwanted, ignored and undesired. One way or another she felt deeply vulnerable and insecure and developed a profound hatred of the source of her suffering – her mother.

From being victims, such people become victimisers. They humiliate their children as they were humiliated. Welldon emphasises that through her perverse actions such a mother is trying to conquer a tremendous fear of losing her mother: 'As a baby she never felt safe with her mother, but instead at her most vulnerable, experiencing her mother as a very dangerous person.'[51] Her hostile and sadistic acts are a means of asserting power in the service of security.

Welldon writes that motherhood as a perversion occurs as a result of a breakdown of inner mental structures.[52] Feeling profoundly unsupported, the mother falls back on the only *power* available to her. Then we see the perverse behaviour. But this in its turn only makes her feel more *powerless* and unsupported.

Turning to the social aetiology of perverse maternity, Welldon suggests that perversity is a product of the denigration of motherhood and women's powerlessness: 'weakness which they strive to turn into possessiveness and control';[53] she considers that 'being in complete control of a situation provides a fertile ground for some women who have experienced injurious and traumatic events in their own lives to exploit and abuse their babies'.[54]

Welldon describes maternal abuse as a generational issue; an abusing mother is in her experience the daughter of an abusing mother. However, not all children of abusing parents become abusers. Some, it is true, will identify with their violent parents and, as adults, repeat abusive behaviour with their own children; others do not. Perhaps, as Selma Fraiberg suggests, affective memory is the critical factor. If a mother remembers the pain, and resolves that her children will not suffer the same wounds, the children are protected from the repetition. But when the painful affect is split off from consciousness, even though the memory may be intact and active, identification with the cruel parent (and hence abusive behaviour) can result.[55]

Similarly, Louise Kaplan sees abuse in generational terms. Like Estela Welldon she names maternal abuse a female perversion. She believes that perversions are pathologies of gender role identity. In her view, 'women learn to disguise their forbidden masculine wishes behind a stereotype of female innocence, weakness and self sacrifice'.[56] Thus a mother's rage, hostility and destructiveness are often disguised as care. Kaplan concludes that 'the care giving mother shows no compassion or mercy'[57] as she expresses hatred disguised as an act of love.

Both Welldon and Kaplan forge their theories out of their clinical work with deeply disturbed women, and designate their maternal cruelty as perversity. Clearly not all women who ill-treat children can be categorised as perverse. We need a way of thinking about maternal abuse of power that encompasses everyday acts of unkindness as well as gross cruelty. In my view, an understanding of maternal ambivalence illuminates a spectrum of lesser and greater acts of psychological and physical hurt.

To Smack or Not to Smack

The debate over smacking illustrates that violence towards children *is* widespread and in some spheres covertly condoned by our society. The debate parallels the inner-world conflict in relation to hitting – the co-existence of the impulse and shame about it.

Discipline and authority are viewed as moral issues. Thus babies of even a week old are referred to as 'bad' or 'good', 'easy' or 'difficult'. A survey by EPOCH (End Physical Punishment of Children) revealed that two-thirds of babies are smacked before they reach one year old and three-quarters of four-year-olds are smacked once a week. In 1992 more than 90 per cent of British parents admitted to smacking their children.

Attitudes towards discipline and authority coalesce around the smacking debate: to smack or not to smack. Fundamentalist religious groups and right-wing organisations tend to favour corporal punishment. The Bible is often cited as the text which authorises and condones smacking. Dr James Dobson, an American child psychologist and author of *Dare to Discipline* (1972) and *The New Dare to Discipline* (1993), has an enormous following in the United States and is becoming increasingly popular in Britain. He quotes the Bible in favour of smacking: 'Foolishness is bound in the heart of a child; but the rod of correction shall drive it far from him' (Proverbs 22:15) and 'He that spareth his rod hateth his son; but he that loveth him chasteneth him betimes' (Proverbs 13:24).[58]

In 1992 the British magazine *Christian Family* was relaunched as *Parentwise* and the *Guardian*'s report quoted *Parentwise*'s intention 'to reflect the growing demand for advice on childcare'.[59] The first issue carried an article by Dobson. The magazine's editor was quoted as saying, 'We see Dobson as an inspiration. My wife and I try to follow what he sets out.' He did, however, express reservation with regard to Dobson's recommended utensil (or weapon), commenting, 'I have problems with using a wooden spoon to spank my children, but I know some households do.'[60] Bruce Ray, another American Christian whose ideas are gaining ground in Britain, recommends employing the rod: 'A rod may be literally a rod or it may be a ping-pong paddle, the belt around your pants or a ruler.'[61]

Outside these religious groups, voices are not lacking in support of smacking. For example, Stephen Green of the Conservative Family Campaign was reported as commenting in 1992 that, 'Parents must retain the right to mete out physical punishment as a last resort. We do not agree with the anti-smackers' claims that smacking children leads to more serious physical abuse of children.'[62]

The anti-smackers represented by EPOCH monitored 700 families for thirty years. The study established a link between smacking children when young and 'delinquency' in teenagers. Increasing numbers of countries are making it illegal for parents to smack their children. Sweden led the way in 1979, followed by Finland, Denmark, Norway and Austria. Arguing in 1992 in favour of such a ban becoming established in Scotland, Kathleen Marshall, director of the Scottish Child Law Centre, observed that

'Children are the only group in society who have no protection from being assaulted. We need to move away from the idea of parental rights and towards the idea of parental responsibility.'[63] Both pro-smackers and anti-smackers are moved by moral outrage; the former direct it against children and the latter against parents.

In 1994 the High Court ruled that a childminder had the right to smack small children in her care, although 90 per cent of local councils do impose a 'no smacking' policy on childminders, following guidance set forth in the Children Act 1989. The childminder declared the High Court's decision to be 'a victory for hundreds of thousands of ordinary loving mothers whose experience and commonsense is recognised as being of more practical use than the unrealistic and unrepresentative theories of the experts of the anti-smacking brigade'.[64]

Putting aside the rights and wrongs of the case, her comment highlights the culture's attitude towards maternal ambivalence. She insists that hitting a child is an aspect of love, while the defensive opposition she constructs between mothers and experts indicates both how little empathy mothers expect from 'experts', and the extent to which the image of 'experts' express and inflate maternal guilt in relation to ambivalence.

'I carry on like a shrew'

In society's attitude towards smacking – the simultaneous sanction and prohibition – we can see at work the moralism towards mothers that militates against the acknowledgement or even the experiencing of maternal ambivalence. And it is this that leads to the dissolution of creative ambivalence – to the splitting of love and hate so wide apart in the psyche that love no longer mitigates hatred – and a mother strikes out.

Mothers feel terribly guilty if they smack, and some almost as guilty if they feel they are being too 'soft'. Surrounded by pronouncements on their mothering, verdicts that decree them Good or Bad, mothers are rarely in a position to use their ambivalence reflectively. A fictional mother, Pearl Tull in Anne Tyler's novel *Dinner at the Homesick Restaurant*,[65] provides a useful illustration of how the moralism surrounding a mother, in conjunction with the workings of her own punitive superego, transform ambivalent concern into mindless hatred. The book also shows how a woman's expectations of maternal power collide with experiential reality of powerlessness and helplessness. The effects are dire.

Pearl is bringing up three disparate children in the 1950s with no practical or emotional support. The family lives in Baltimore where Pearl lacks relatives and friends. Her difficulties in communicating thoughts and feelings, compounded by shame in relation to poverty and lone parenthood, isolate her. She has only the children. In this passage Pearl expresses a mother's vulnerability to fear of loss in her compulsion to have more children:

> 'I want some extra,' she said . . . But it wasn't as simple as she had supposed. The second child was Ezra, so sweet and clumsy it could break your heart. She was more endangered than ever. It would have been best to stop at Cody. She still hadn't learned, though. After Ezra came Jenny, the girl – such fun to dress, to fix her hair in different styles. But she couldn't give Jenny up either. What she had now was not one loss to fear but three. Still, she thought, it had seemed a good idea once upon a time: spare children, like spare tires; or those extra lisle stockings they used to package free with each pair.[66]

Pearl is deserted by her husband. His absence is relatively insignificant in terms of family life – his presence as husband and father had always been intermittent and tenuous. But Pearl feels acutely the social stigma of lone parenthood. Her self-esteem suffers and she lives in fear of denigration and blame. She conceals his defection and struggles to keep up appearances in the face of poverty. The smallest incident which increases her sense of guilt and helplessness in relation to her children – a guilt she cannot articulate – precipitates her into manic defence. The following incident occurred after her daughter had expressed admiration of another girl's dress:

> Pearl threw the spoon in his [her son Cody's] face. 'You upstart,' she said. She rose and slapped him across the cheek. 'You wretch, you ugly horror.' She grabbed one of Jenny's braids and yanked it so hard Jenny was pulled off her chair. 'Stupid clod,' she said to Ezra, and she took the bowl of peas and brought it down on his head. It didn't break, but peas flew everywhere. Ezra cowered, shielding his head with his arms. 'Parasites,' she told them. 'I wish you'd all die, and let me go free. I wish I'd find you dead in your beds.'[67]

Her intense concern for her children is obliterated. The image of her daughter admiring a friend's dress suggests discontent, ingratitude, and criticism of herself. This increases the intensity of the conflict provoked by ambivalence to the point where it cannot hold, and love and hate split apart so that pure hate and violence cannot be held back. The children are no longer the boys and girl she loves and hates and deeply fears losing. Her love for them gets denied and they are simply parasites she longs to be rid of. She ends up wishing for what she fears the most – their loss.

An important feature of Pearl's attack on the children is her desire for maternal omnipotence. Hatred is induced by the frustrating feeling that, however much power a mother may feel is vested in her, it is never enough. At other times this mobilises not violent rage in Pearl, but a poignant sadness and regret that she cannot make things perfect for her children. As the conflict between love and hate fluctuates in intensity, it can, in the same mother, at times be productive of creative reparation and at other times of manic insouciance and rage. Here Pearl attempts to repair things with her oldest son:

> Pearl sat down on his bed. She was shaking her head, looking stunned. 'Oh, Cody, it's such a battle, raising children,' she said. 'I know you must think I am difficult. I lose my temper, I carry on like a shrew sometimes, but if you could just realize how . . . helpless I feel! How scary it is to know that everyone I love depends on me! I'm afraid I'll do something wrong.'
> She reached up – for the photos, he thought, and he held them out to her; but no, what she wanted was his hand.[68]

Klein's observation that reparation – the act of restoring a person damaged by one's own hate, unkindness or ill-treatment – is not just a defence against guilt, but can have a creative outcome, a going forward, a development, is relevant here.

When her children reach adulthood, Pearl surveys them in her mind and feels that, indeed, she has 'done something wrong'. Jenny, her daughter, is living with her third husband and too many stepchildren. Cody is still utterly dominated by sibling rivalry for Ezra, who in his late thirties is still living at home with his mother.

> Pearl believes that her family has failed. Neither of her sons is happy, and her daughter can't seem to stay married. There

is no one to accept the blame for this but Pearl herself, who raised these children single-handed and did make mistakes, oh, a bushel of mistakes. Still, she sometimes has the feeling that it's simply fate, and not a matter of blame at all. She feels that everything has been assigned, has been pre-ordained; everyone must play his role. Certainly she never intended to foster one of those good/bad son arrangements, but what can you do when one son is consistently good and the other consistently bad? What can the sons do, even?[69]

Pearl struggles with her guilt. On the one hand, she is tempted to agree with society's understanding that, as a lone parent, she is deficient and definitely to blame for how her children have turned out. On the other hand, she realises that forces have been at work that are outside her control. She terms it fate.

Mother Blaming

The dominant cultural belief is that mothers do indeed entirely determine the personality of their children. 'Mother blaming' is a symptom of the power vested in mother. As Estela Welldon puts it, the power motherhood conveys can scarcely be overemphasised. Raised in a society where primary responsibility for childcare is placed in mothers' hands we are, inevitably, marked by our mothers, and inevitably we will blame those mothers when things go wrong. A mother's psychic guilt in relation to the confluence of love and hate she feels towards her children is exacerbated by the social conviction that mothers are truly culpable. Mothers mobilise what defences they can against intolerable levels of guilt. Guilt may, as we have seen, be displaced on to a child who is experienced as terribly persecuting, on to the child's father, on to a school, on to the environment. The mother is then left feeling wronged, weakened and helpless.

The discipline usually held responsible for the ubiquity of mother blaming is, of course, psychoanalysis, which has offered the most persuasive, if controversial, account of the formative impact on adult personality of infantile experience. Clearly, no psychoanalyst or psychotherapist in the consulting room actively *blames* the patient's or client's mother for ambivalence. Most practitioners work towards a shared understanding of the meaning of the levels of guilt associated with ambivalence, especially when working with patients or clients who are themselves mothers. Nevertheless, it is important to explore how psychoanalytic theory can inadvertently contribute to cultural 'mother blaming'.

As discussed in Chapter 5, during the 1940s psychoanalysis took an increasingly prescriptive stance towards mothering, particularly with the popularisation in Britain of the works of D. W. Winnicott and John Bowlby. In his book *The Independent Mind in British Psychoanalysis*, Eric Rayner described the intention of the group of British analysts who wished to understand environmental influences: 'If they could pick out causative foci of developmental disability or agents of destructive potentiality, perhaps they could then have some hand in initiating prevention at source.'[70] He instances Bowlby's success in affecting social policy in relation to institutional childcare as an example.

Winnicott was aware that what Rayner calls 'picking out the causative foci' – the search for aetiology – inevitably would sound blaming, but insisted that this must not deter psychoanalytic inquiry. He wrote, 'We must be able to look at aetiology and be able if necessary to say that some failures of development that we meet spring from a failure of the ordinary devoted mother factor at a certain point or over a phase.' He goes on to say that he has no interest in apportioning blame and that anyway, 'mothers and fathers blame themselves, but that is another matter, and indeed they blame themselves for almost anything . . .'[71]

Winnicott is right: neither he nor anyone is actually interested in apportioning blame, but rather in identifying first causes. Mothers matter where aetiology is concerned. In fact, mothers are neither precisely blamed nor overlooked; instead they are evaluated.

The evaluation of maternal success or failure has changed with changing conceptions of babies' capacities and behaviour. And psychoanalysis itself is also changing. The deployment of causal understanding and the overall influence of the past on the present is, as we will see, being challenged from within psychoanalysis. We need to ask whether this movement within psychoanalysis is opening the way to a deeper understanding of maternal processes – of the psychology *of* the mother, rather than of psychology determined *by* the mother.

Some analytic theorists are increasingly questioning the nature of the impact of past experiences upon present personality and functioning. Instead of working with a model of the mind in which the past *caused* the present, some clinicians emphasise one in which experience builds up and develops within the person, affecting the present in sometimes puzzling and oblique ways.

Thus the developmental framework employed clinically by psychotherapists and analysts, the sequences, for example, oral/anal/genital or symbiosis/separation/individuation, are ways of conceptualising structures of the mind. Moreover, the classically Kleinian view of the *phantasised* qualities of the object are emphasised as being particularly important rather than its actual, historical quality. The child psychotherapist Anne Alvarez comments that 'an adolescent girl may dream of evil crones in the night and fear the ill will of female teachers throughout the day in ways which may bear only some relation to the actual behaviour of the teachers concerned, or, for that matter, of adult maternal figures from the past'.[72]

The role of memory and the place of reconstruction of a patient's past in clinical practice is widely debated within the profession. The spectrum of opinion ranges from those who consider retrieval of the past to be clinically crucial, and believe that the role of the therapist is to bear witness to past wounds – though most would add that, once the external has been fully acknowledged, it is then a question of how it has been elaborated in the internal world of the patient,[73] to those who consider that parents 'encountered' in the consulting room are no longer to be understood as the *actual* parents. Joseph Sandler writes,

> It is the current set of internal object relationships which is externalised in the transference, and it is, as we all know, a mistake to consider these externalised internal relationships as replicas of the relationships to the actual parents, or even to the parents as perceived by the child, for what we are dealing with are internal objects derived from phantasy figures, or from parental images distorted by phantasy, in which projections of one sort or another play a prominent role.[74]

Andrew Samuels presents a useful discussion of these issues in *The Plural Psyche*. He argued that we need a 'diachronic' mode of exploration which makes use of memory and causality organised chronologically as well as a synchronic mode which would 'concentrate on the integrity of the now'. Samuels believes that reconstruction of the past may remain an important therapeutic aspect of psychoanalysis because it can reduce anxiety, hence providing increased space for understanding.[75]

'Mother blaming' has lessened not only because of the questioning of causality and reconstruction from within psychoanalysis, but also because of a new emphasis on the *interaction* of mother and baby. In her book *Live Company*, Alvarez observed that, even in relation to babies themselves, the evidence and the arguments for an interactional object-relations theory makes it clear that the 'cause' of cognitive deficit or emotional withdrawal or both, can 'never entirely be in the mother'.[76] She pointed out that child development research has shown that social and cultural supports (for example the quality of partnership a mother has, as well as her socioeconomic level) all affect development. She stresses, moreover, that the mother–child relationship is rarely fixed or static: 'A depressed mother may be helped to come out of her depression by a lively responsive baby, and a depressed mother may become more depressed with an unresponsive and unrewarding baby.'[77]

The importance of the point that the child puts something into the relationship is underlined by Hanna Segal when she reflects on 'mother blaming'. In an interview with Jacqueline Rose, she said,

> Now, when I look at my patients, you can always see the pathology of the mother or those bad circumstances reflected in the child. But it is not a one-to-one relation at all . . . You don't get a one-to-one correlation. There is always something like resilience, and what comes from inside. It could be that there are such circumstances that no child could come out unscathed. There are also such children that would need almost perfect parents to deal with some inner defect.[78]

Hanna Segal insists 'it is not a matter of blame'. The analyst would never consider the mother of the patient 'wicked', but instead would need to explore her parents, her personality and the interaction between mother and child. She warns against siding with the child. Other psychoanalytic theorists suggest that mothers need to be seen as 'victims' caught in a three-generational process.

Clearly, in terms of its clinical practices, psychoanalysis is not a 'mother-blaming' institution. If, however, we turn to the deployment of specific clinical experience into written case histories, a different picture emerges. In 1991 the *International Journal of Psycho-Analysis* devoted an issue to fifteen different clinical accounts of psychoanalysis.[79] All the papers except one contained descriptions of negative mothers of the patients being presented. Roughly half of these mothers were characterised as depressed and/or anxious and hence unavailable for mirroring, reverie, attunement or contingency. Perhaps the form of the case history all too easily flattens the complexity of the analytic encounter, inferring causality from description.

In this chapter I have been discussing mothers' sense of simultaneous power and powerlessness; the frustration this provokes and the splitting apart of love and hatred it can generate, until a mother is hardly aware that the child she hates is also loved. I have suggested that the impact of psychoanalytic theory on cultural attitudes has inadvertently had a hand in fostering mothers' sense of awful culpability. If we return to Pearl musing on her fault as a mother we can observe a mother struggling with a simultaneous sense of power and the belief that it is circumscribed. She considers that 'there is no one to accept the blame for [the way her children have turned out] but Pearl herself'. Yet she is not convinced: 'she sometimes has the feeling that it's simply fate and not a matter of blame at all'. The concept of 'fate' cuts down to size Pearl's grandiose and guilt-ridden sense of omnipotence in relation to her children. Where psychoanalysis is concerned, some conceptions of the unconscious can be seen as playing the same role as 'fate' does for Pearl. In these theories, it is not the mother's personality or what takes place in the mother–child relationship that are solely responsible for the adult personality the child develops. Rather, the idea is that there is a constitutional side to the unconscious, a sort of inborn personality that the child was always fated to have. This pre-exists anything a mother might do. Moreover, her conscious effort to do the right thing co-exists with unconscious processes between a woman and her child which are essentially outside her control. For some mothers this may seem like an exoneration, offsetting the despair they feel at seeming to be utterly responsible for the psychological development of their children; for others it engenders the despair of powerlessness.

9

Does Gender Make a Difference?

I expected Dean to be like me. I expected him to smile when I smiled, but I realise now that boys are very different. Dean related like a boy and I simply didn't know what boys were like. I expected him to be not simply like me but actually to be me when he was born, and I didn't have a lot of tolerance for the way he was – for the difference. Alice [his sister] is different but she is like me. She's not me but she responds the way I do. She's a member of my species. If you squeeze her hand she'll squeeze back. Dean would hold my hand as if it was a chair – there would be no messages going back and forward, and it would drive me crazy.

A mother's response to her child's gender is determined by a host of issues such as her conscious and unconscious feelings towards her own sexuality, and her expectations and beliefs about gender difference in conjunction with cultural valuations of sons and daughters. Clare realised that she expected the child who emerged from her body to *be* her, and the difference she immediately perceived between her son and herself she attributed to his sex. Hence, perhaps, her belief that this boy was unresponsive because all boys are unresponsive. For she says that, 'Girls smile when they see a smile. Boys don't.'

Martha, on the other hand, was concerned that her son Jack manifested too great a responsiveness. Like herself, he seemed to be over-concerned and too easily rendered guilty in relation to the other. He is too sensitive. She did not add 'for a boy' but it is arguable that her feelings about his sensitivity might be different if he were a girl:

I feel worried about Jack because he is so like me – and like aspects of me I don't approve of. He really easily feels guilty. For example, this morning I was annoyed with him and his sister for being late and I expressed it by withholding love. They came through the door expecting love and cuddles, and larking around while we got ready for them to go out – and instead I was just nasty. I could see Jack really wanting to make it better, sort of trying to get through to me and saying 'Oh you're going to *Thelma and Louise* tonight, that'll be great' and right at the end before they left he said, 'I'm sorry, Mum, we were so late.'

I have juxtaposed a mother who feels her daughter is like her with a mother who feels her son is like her to emphasise that identification, with the pleasure and pain it evokes, can function independently of the biological sex of the child. The sex of the child matters, but often in unexpected and unpredictable ways. In this chapter I shall explore some of the ways gender difference can both intensify and modify the conflicts evoked by ambivalence.

Making a Man of Him

Before exploring the subjective response of mothers to their child's gender, I want to summarise briefly a significant shift of emphasis in psychoanalytic understanding of the role of the mother in the formation of this identity. However we understand this development, whatever mechanisms are seen to confirm the child in her or his gender identity and sexual orientation, the mother is generally believed to play a crucial role.

According to classical Freudian theory, masculinity and femininity evolve through a complex process of development, initiated by the moment of recognition of genital difference. The perception of difference takes on different meanings for the boy and the girl. The mother of a girl, according to Freudian theory, has to contend with her daughter's resentment and disappointment, for the girl holds her mother responsible for her lack of a penis. Repudiating and denigrating her mother, the girl turns to her father and the promise of maternity. Later in his career Freud acknowledged, for the girl at least, that the mother had a more profound and enduring influence than consideration of the Oedipal triangle alone allowed.

He likened her pre-Oedipal relationship with her mother to the Minoan-Mycenaean civilisation hidden behind Greek civilisation.

For a boy, a mother was considered to evoke forbidden incestuous desires. Freud thought that a little boy repressed his desire for his mother because of the felt threat of castration from the father who insists on his possession of the mother. But, as we have seen, whereas a mother was assumed to have a troubled relationship with a disappointed daughter, her relationship with her son was assumed to be free of ambivalence. However, just as the early mother–daughter relationship has prompted a re-evaluation of their link, so too have theorists acknowledged the power of the early pre-Oedipal mother–son relationship. Today psychoanalytic theorists accept the importance of the very early relationship to the mother in the construction of sexual difference for *both* sexes. Mothers are now understood to be threatening not because of what they *lack* but in the *power* they possess.

Acknowledging the importance of the time prior to the development of castration anxiety implies the strength of a different fear – the threat of fusion with the mother, or fear of re-engulfment. Dana Breen, introducing a collection of papers on contemporary psychoanalytic perspectives on femininity and masculinity, suggests that, although castration fears are still considered important, for many the castration complex does not hold the place in psychoanalysis that it did with Freud. Rather it is understood to represent for both sexes the 'acknowledgement of incompleteness, of human limitations, the abandonment of the belief in one's omnipotence and the possession of all attributes including the sole possession of the mother's love'.[1]

While the castration complex has certainly been de-emphasised in some post-Freudian psychoanalysis, the concept of unconscious identification is still considered to play a central role in the development of gender and sexual identity.

In brief, a girl must dis-identify with her mother if she is to gain an independent identity. Yet, at the same time, her sense of gender identity depends on her identification with her mother. A boy is similarly described as needing to dis-identify with his mother. However, his gender identity is understood as dependent upon an identification with his father. The extent to which that is achieved is determined by whether he is able to sufficiently dis-identify with his mother. The conclusion drawn from this schema is that 'men are far more uncertain about their maleness than women are about their femaleness'.[2] Hence, women's certainty about their gender identity and men's uncertainty about theirs are both assumed to be due to their shared early identification with their mother.

While a boy's gender identity is dependent on the struggle to free himself from the mother's grasp, a mother's role is to renounce the pleasure of closeness that their bond provides.[3] Mothers are seen as either promoting or hindering the process of a boy forming an identification with the less accessible father. This view of the maternal role in the formation of gender identity hence provides a significantly different understanding of maternal power. Viewed through the lens of penis envy and the castration complex, mothers are under suspicion of gaining power *through* their sons. Viewed through the lens of dis-identification, mothers are under suspicion of exerting excess power *over* their sons. In other words the Bad Mother has a new muscularity about her.

As Christiane Olivier puts it in her book *Jocasta's Children*, boys are potentially 'pinioned in the maternal love trap'.[4]

Psychoanalytic understanding of the role of the mother in the construction of gender identity has thus changed in emphasis over a comparatively short period of time. It is still evolving. As Andrew Samuels has commented, 'psychological theorising about parenting both mirrors and plays a part in hammering out cultural processes'.[5] Social and political change – in particular the upsurge of feminism in the second half of the twentieth century – has led both to an actual expansion of women's lives and to a reappraisal of maternal subjectivity. Feminist psychoanalytic theorists argue that women are no longer 'only mothers'; they bring complex and diverse unconscious identifications to their mothering.[6] Thus, for example, Ruth de Kantor argued that a part of a woman always remains outside the mother–child dyad.[7] Her history as an individual, her 'womanness' as opposed to her 'motherness', carves out the space between herself and her child, previously understood to have been created by the father, or by the son's dis-identification process. Christiane Olivier's image of boys 'pinioned in the maternal love trap' can be counterpointed by an image of women pinioned in the trap of maternity.

My argument throughout this book has been that reflecting upon ambivalence provides a key to understanding motherhood. I would suggest that all the competing or sequential theories about the role of mothering in the construction of gender identity can be redefined and understood as illustrating tensions *within* an individual mother. Motherhood is about the experience of lack *and* plenitude, about a sense of power *and* powerlessness, about the desire to hold on *and* to be rid of the children. The theories – or at least their living out – co-exist within a single mother even as the competing theorists of motherhood fail to get along.

Accompanying children in their acquisition of gender identity demands a thoughtful ambivalence on the part of a mother and can provoke unmanageable ambivalence. Recognition of the central part played by uncertainty, particularly in the construction of masculinity, is of enormous importance for any exploration of the subjective experience of mothering. Samuels has suggested that gender confusion and gender certainty are warring elements in the formation of gender identity. Gender confusion is not always 'bad' and gender certainty is not always 'good'. He revises the conventional psychodynamic formulations whereby unconscious gender confusion lies behind apparent gender certainty. He postulates instead that unconscious gender certainty lies behind apparent gender confusion, and argues that we always have to keep in mind that there will be movement between gender certainty and gender confusion.[8]

Hence we can reformulate the received wisdom that mothers are on the painful receiving end of a son's bloody struggle to separate and become masculine – a struggle they can either impede or facilitate. Instead, I would regard mothers as occupying a variety of positions in relation to their son's struggle with the shifting field of gender certainty and gender confusion. Of course, the need to separate out from his mother, denigrating her in the process, may be a feature of the son's struggle. But it is not inevitable. Whilst I have encountered mothers who do indeed experience themselves as their son's identified enemy, I know of others who find themselves more in the role of ally. Neither position can be designated good or bad, right or wrong.

In her book, *The Trouble with Boys*, Angela Phillips has explored the experience of mothers in the context of what she sees as the current cultural uncertainty over what constitutes masculinity.[9] Her overarching argument is psychoanalytic in that she sees boys as engaged in fighting to get away from their mothers in a culture that sets separation as a target but is markedly unempathic with the emotional difficulties entailed. She suggests that the culture of masculinity which provides boys with an abstract reference point outside their mothers' influence demands a painful process of desensitisation – painful for both mother and son. 'Mothers look at the world outside,' writes Phillips, 'and feel afraid of what it will do, and yet they know their sons must go out there.'[10] The mothers in her study manifest, not a refusal to separate, but fear and confusion in the face of their children's fight to find what it means to be masculine without the aid of a facilitating father. Phillips comments that 'the reality is that many fathers have no idea what it means to be a parent, and they live in a culture which gives them very little help'.[11] Psychologically and practically mothers are in charge more often than not.

The mothers Phillips interviewed do not report a smooth progress towards separation and the evolution of masculinity in their sons, but rather fluctuations: 'He wants his mother, but he wants to be male too and it may at times feel very hard to have both.'[12] A son's ambivalence magnifies a mother's conflicts. One minute he wants her and the next his very existence appears to depend on opposing her wishes and refusing her authority. She must neither acquiesce in her own destruction nor must she insist on her total omnipotence. This is as apparent in a two-year-old as in an adolescent; the tension is always there, intensifying at some periods and subsiding at others, according to the pattern of the individual child. Phillips, describing a 'late developer', commented that, 'As he takes a crash course in masculinity he may well alienate the very people he is trying to attract – and drive his poor mother mad as she wonders whatever happened to her gentle little boy.'[13]

The paradox of stereotypical masculine behaviour is that the boisterousness and wildness which marks a boy off from his mother and sisters is precisely the behaviour that is denigrated at school and in domestic settings. A mother has to cope with the aggravation of his aggression towards her in the service of differentiation, as well as the disapproval of her son that she encounters in teachers and other mothers. Some mothers do experience a covert pleasure in their son's 'subversiveness', but for others their son's disruptiveness – for him the very badge of strength in his peer group – is a source of shame and helplessness. She feels a bad mother and resents her son for it.

Of course, boisterousness and wildness as a mode of gaining approbation from peers and effecting separation from mother is not the prerogative of boys. Girls too adopt this 'masculine' way of being in order to dis-identify with their mothers and earn the awed admiration of their gang. This can provoke intense conflict in mothers. They may admire the way their daughter appears to be grasping life with both hands, while regarding her way of being female as utterly alien and unacceptable.

The sense of helplessness and guilt a mother can experience in the face of her child's struggle with gender certainty and gender confusion can determine whether ambivalence remains manageable or not. Sabrina has a four-year-old son, John. He has recently started school, where his evolving sense of gender identity has come up against insistent peer-group norms. Sabrina says,

> John used to come running to me if anything went wrong and I could usually help one way or another. And I liked that so much. It felt for the first time in my life that I was useful and effective. Now, if he hurts himself, he'll still come running but either he will almost instantly pull away before I can kiss it better, or he will be so determinedly inconsolable that I end up feeling reproached and almost hating him.

Sabrina neither rejects nor clings but, like her small son, she is plunged into doubt. She had a clear image of what mothering meant and it had given her a new sense of potency, but accompanying her son in his battle with gender confusion and gender certainty leaves her feeling unsure and resentful.

Sabrina's sense of being reproached by her child was due, in part, to her psychological investment in motherhood. At last she had felt effective and useful. Finding herself on the receiving end of a child's insistence that a mother both fail and remain omnipotent can induce a corrosive sense of reproach in any mother. It can intensify for psychological reasons, as in Sabrina's case, or if a mother is not conforming to a socially approved conventional way of mothering. A lone mother or a lesbian parent may feel her child's reproach replicates the social condemnation she fears. Women mothering in contexts other than the heterosexual couple are vulnerable to the suggestion that their circumstances impede their child's acquisition of gender identity despite the fact that an element of mystery does still surround the place of parents in its acquisition. For, as Andrew Samuels has commented, 'At the present time, we simply do not know the exact balance between differences introduced by the sex of the parent and those aspects of parenting that are the same for both sexes.'[14] Neither can we predict what the impact of the absence of a male called father has on a mother and children. According to Samuels's research with single parents, 'there are no inevitable psychological outcomes of the single-parent state'.[15]

The Role of the Father

Where maternal ambivalence is concerned, an only partially present father can at times be more problematic than a father absent through separation or divorce. Family life and work are so structured that the burden of childcare still falls primarily on mothers. Angela Phillips cites a survey carried out by Peter Moss and Julia Brannan which reveals that, in dual-career families, full-time working mothers spend nearly five times as long as their partners in sole charge of their infants.[16] Yet, at the same time, there is an increasing expectation that fathers will play a larger part in their children's upbringing.

Mothers may acquiesce in the traditional division of labour, their economic circumstances permitting, possibly abandoning a satisfactory – or less than satisfactory – job for the sake of the children, while their partners continue an uninterrupted career. Some women find this perfectly acceptable and 'retire' or go part-time with a sigh of relief. For others the resentment they feel at the sight of their partner out in the world and guilt-free is translated into deeply negative feelings towards the children.

An accusation often levelled at women is that they are in fact unwilling to relinquish the rewards that come from being first in their children's lives. On the other hand, as Angela Phillips suggests, men who have grown up without experiencing a warm, involved father often behave in ways that do not inspire mothers with confidence in their partners when it comes to childcare. Some mothers complain that when fathers do look after the children it feels as if they deliberately flout the rules and structures a mother has developed: 'When Sam takes the kids I come home and find them all slumped in front of the TV with cans of Coke in their hands.' Her antipathy embraces them *all*.

Where sons are concerned the absent or partially present father can become an exciting outsider; the representative of masculine culture which demands repudiation of Mum. Then a mother who has invested so much of herself in a child's upbringing feels bitterly marginalised.

Angela Phillips cites the separated mother of a twelve-year-old boy who confessed to feeling condemned to invisibility and silence when the boy was with his father. To underscore his allegiance to his father, her son falls silent with her except for 'sometimes late at night'. Otherwise communication is restricted to her criticisms of the state of his bedroom and the condition of his laundry. She concludes sadly, 'I think he is coming to see me as a nag.'[17]

These rather generalised scenarios of mother–son relating I have been discussing are shaped by the particular, unseen force of each mother's unconscious – specifically her internal parental objects. Her perception of a partner's relationship to her son is inevitably coloured by her own experience of being parented. But just as I emphasised that the sort of mother a woman becomes cannot be *predicted* from the kind of mothering she experienced, while undoubtedly being *affected* by it, so too a woman's response to her partner's relationship with her children cannot be read off from her own relationship with her father. A woman who enjoyed a powerful link with her own father and suffered from her mother's jealousy could be just as likely to encourage as to discourage her children's relationship with their father. A woman whose father had been signally absent may, on the one hand, feel it is fine for her children to be fatherless or, on the other, desire passionately that they experience all she felt she had lacked – only to find that she is pierced with envy at their happy relationship with their father. Thus, as well as fully acknowledging the social and political structuring of childcare, we also need to bear in mind the endless permutations provoked by each mother's specific emotional life, past as well as present.

Although fathers do often inadvertently magnify the element of hatred in maternal ambivalence, the opposite can be there as well. Seeing the love they feel for their children mirrored in another's eyes provides permission, celebration and affirmation of maternal passion, while the presence of another protective parent figure can enable a mother to feel it safe to acknowledge ambivalence. Although I am specifically discussing fathers, it is important to bear in mind that the role of the partner in confirming the lovableness of the child or rendering ambivalence bearable may equally be carried out by a female partner. In Chapter 3 I described how seeing a partner struggle with rage and hatred can enable a woman to contain her own powerfully negative emotions towards a child; so too seeing her partner – whether man or woman – experience love can deepen a woman's experience of her pride or in affection for a child.

I am aware that I have moved away from focusing specifically on mothers and the construction of masculinity, and I want to return to that theme. Earlier, I cited Samuels's theory that gender confusion and gender certainty are invisible, warring elements in the formation of gender identity, that there needs to be movement between the two, and that we should resist approving of one at the expense of the other. Nowhere is this more clearly illustrated in contemporary culture than in the relationship between a son, his mother and the unending craze for superheroes.

Little boys employ a huge battery of transformers, monsters and superheroes as signifiers of masculinity. In her 1994 Reith Lectures, Marina Warner analysed the specific components of masculinity these encompassed. The 1980s and 1990s saw a massive encouragement and exploitation of their popularity by video-makers and toy manufacturers. I asked my son Joel and his friend Baz (aged seven and ten) to name some superheroes for me. They were pleased to be asked, but suspicious. They enjoyed sharing their knowledge with me and conveying their enthusiasm. Yet they anticipated – and indeed seemed to want – my disapproval. They listed Turtles, Swamp Monsters, Ghostbusters, Thundercats, Ring Raiders, Toxic Crusaders, Mighty Morphin, Captain Scarlet, Captain Planet, Power Rangers and a further array of video-game heroes. Knowledge of their names, attributes and activities creates a generational and gender frontier. As soon as a mother learns the culture of one set of superheroes, the knowledge is rendered obsolete by an ever-changing, increasingly esoteric cast of heroes. Their implacable, unquestionable, reassuring masculinity indicates both the sense of gender confusion in the boys that gives the superheroes their value as signposts to manhood *and* their sense of unconscious gender certainty struggling to achieve social actualisation.

Mothers respond in different and quite complex ways to the superheroes. In her desire to please her son, to be loved by him and see him compete successfully in his peer group, a mother can reinforce his enthusiasm for the world of transformers, connectibles, and so on. Yet she inevitably – and indeed has to – get it wrong. A mother told me:

> My son asked me to give him models of Toxic Crusaders for his birthday, I went to Woolworth's and found racks of the hideous things. But when my son unwrapped them, he burst into tears. I had bought only goodies – no baddies.

Sports followed and played mainly by males can fulfil the same function as toys in the negotiation of the warring elements of gender confusion and gender certainty. Many mothers find it easier to fill the role of ally, rather than functioning as the opposition, when it comes to sports. They support their son's favourite team, watch matches and learn the football league tables. They describe their pleasure in gaining access through their sons to 'masculine' interests previously closed to them. Others, however, feel alienated by their sons' preoccupation, and frankly bored by their obsession.

The various ways in which mothers can view their son's involvement with the signifiers of masculinity provides a salutary reminder of the diversity of mother–son relationships. A monolithic view of engulfing feminine mothers and escaping masculine sons would belie the different unconscious identifications maintained by each individual mother and son.

Freud insisted that femininity as well as masculinity develops in both sexes. The post-Freudian recognition by psychoanalysis of the importance of the pre-Oedipal mother–son relationship has not only highlighted mother as a threat, it has also given new weight to the idea of psychological bisexuality.

Dana Breen described how Freud's insight has been reassessed in the light of the very early mother–son relationship:

> The recognition of the role and importance of feminine identification in male sexuality and masculine development both as a threat to masculinity but, more importantly, as positive for intrapsychic and interrelational balance has been a major line of development in the recent decades. This psychobisexuality is increasingly understood to be fundamental not just for sexuality but for psychic integration and structuring more generally.[18]

Winnicottians and Jungians also consider that male and female elements are present in both sexes, and Kleinian theorists believe that psychic bisexuality derives from early identificatory processes. The introjection of each parental object leads to the ability to have a differentiated image of the two parents in interaction with each other.

For mothers, the experience of encountering their sons' struggle to encompass 'the bisexual nature of mental states' within a culture confused about its own gender confusion and wedded to gender certainty can be perplexing and anxiety provoking. Accompanying her son's evolving identification with *both* internal parental objects can confuse and bemuse a mother. Take, for example, Sandra's description of a simple question posed by her son. Her husband has a large collection of contemporary music cassettes which he plays in his car and which the children enjoy. Sandra says her son asked,

> 'Mum, do you like modern music?' I had the feeling that my answer would really matter to him. If I said, 'No, I hate it, give me classical any day', I think he would have been delighted at one level – it would have meant that he and his Dad could have claimed 'modern music' and cut me out. I had an impulse to bring it about – to say, effectively, OK go off with your father. Yet I also felt in him an equally intense longing for us all to share modern music together.

Sandra acknowledges that she reacts ambivalently to her son's developing gender identity. She is aware of an impulse to throw him into his father's arms yet, *loving* him, she senses his parallel identification with her and the importance to his inner equilibrium of having his two parents there inside himself, separate yet somehow also together. Once again we see the key role of maternal ambivalence. Mothers rarely simply 'promote or hinder' their sons' identificatory processes. Rather, they endlessly negotiate and manoeuvre within a state of ambivalence that, contrary to expectations, promotes thought and reflection.

Just Like I Was

Since the upsurge of feminism in the 1960s, the relationship between mother and daughter has been a focus for fiction, fine art, poetry, autobiography and psychoanalytic theory flowing from women. Some have celebrated the sense of continuity, strength and mutual recognition in the relationship. Others have condemned the mutual suffocation and the reproduction of oppressive roles through identification.

I want to examine feminist theorising of the mother–daughter relationship with the mother's perspective always in mind. However, at the outset I need to acknowledge Adrienne Rich's warning against too marked a splitting of motherly and daughterly perspectives. She concluded a chapter on motherhood and daughterhood with the following words:

> To accept and integrate and strengthen both the mother and the daughter in ourselves is no easy matter, because patriarchal attitudes have encouraged us to split, to polarize, these images, and to project all unwanted guilt, anger, shame, power, freedom onto the 'other' woman. But any radical vision of sisterhood demands that we integrate them.[19]

Rich blames patriarchal attitudes for splitting off the mother's and the daughter's perspectives from each other. I would explain it further in terms of the conflicting impulses within a woman to identify with her mother and to separate from her. This characterises the mother–daughter relationship. Thus, there is something within this relationship, in patriarchal cultures at least, which makes subsequent integration of motherly and daughterly perspectives very difficult. The life within that relationship renders the maintenance of a perspective stemming from the relationship itself so hard. Hence the need both to valorise and to denigrate it – tendencies which Rich herself writes about. Here, more than in any other aspects of the mother–daughter relationship, creative mutual ambivalence is absolutely central. Ambivalence maintains the loving linkage whilst hatred protects against excessive identification.

Feminist object relations theorists writing in the 1970s and '80s contended that a mother's conscious and unconscious feelings about girls and boys will have a significant effect on how she relates to children of each sex. In particular, mothers and daughters are understood to maintain an unconscious fantasy of continuity with one another. This is believed to impede the necessary evolution of separation between the two.

In Britain Luise Eichenbaum and Susie Orbach elaborated how mothers and daughters remain in a state of 'merged attachment' for longer than do mothers and sons.[20] In the USA an issue of the journal *Feminist Studies* focused on motherhood. In a paper entitled 'The Conflict between Nurturance and Autonomy in Mother–Daughter Relationships and within Feminism' Jane Flax wrote that, because women tend to identify more strongly with their girl children, more internal conflict is likely to be stimulated by their role as mothers. Memories of unresolved wishes from their own infancy are more powerfully evoked: 'Women often admit that one motive for becoming a mother is to regain a sense of being mothered themselves. With girl children, the confusion over who is the child and who is mother is intensified.'[21] She believes that girls thus find it hard to take a distance from their mothers – their mothers' conflictual feelings towards them render the daughters too insecurely attached to risk separation. Flax suggests that women are less likely to have these confusions or expectations aroused with boy children because men are not seen as nurturers in our culture. Daughters, on the other hand, can occupy the role of confidante and carer from an early age, aware of their mothers' needs and vulnerabilities. The role of confidante can confer a certain status on the daughter, but later on mothers can feel depleted by the presence of the daughter's friends and partners, while the mother's unacknowledged dependence on the daughter can provoke anger and resentment on both sides.

Luise Eichenbaum and Susie Orbach have interestingly pursued the implications of women's position in society as the nurturers, not the nurtured. They write that the effect of having to curtail wants and desires for years is that many women are unaware of feeling need. Hence, in experiencing and responding to her daughter, a woman projects her own needy parts into the girl. They suggest that this leads to mothers relating inconsistently to daughters – as inconsistently as they relate to their own neediness. At times they respond selflessly, but at the same time 'a taboo on rage and neediness exists in the mother–daughter relationship'.[22]

In other words, because women as nurturers feel they must restrain their own needs for nourishment, they swing between imposing the same deprivation on their daughters and trying to compensate for it. In Eichenbaum and Orbach's words, 'there is a push–pull dynamic in mother–daughter relationships'.[23]

Given that mothers of daughters feel unable to contain and process anxiety, rage, greed and negativity in their daughters, their daughters never feel securely attached. Sheila Ernst applies the 'merged attachment theory' to Winnicott's account of the graduated, creative separation process of the mother and baby.[24] She suggests a reassessment of Winnicott's scheme in the light of the arguably longer and more intense mother–daughter pre-Oedipal bond, and points out how each state of the sequence of movements towards the separation of mother and baby would be hampered by a mother's history of having failed to achieve a proper separation from her own mother. Ernst proposed that, for example, the stage of primary maternal preoccupation, rather than being achieved and then abandoned, 'is more likely to be continuous with women's ongoing lack of psychological separation'.[25] The subsequent stage – the mirror stage – is, according to Ernst, particularly problematic for women 'who are emotionally deprived and lacking in the social mirroring of their reality'.[26] Thus they look to their daughter for the mirroring they have lacked and daughters, perhaps inevitably, are not likely to receive adequate reflection back from their mothers.

In 1989 Nini Herman suggested a reassessment of the merged attachment theory. She describes mother and daughter as replicas of each other. The sense of likeness, in Herman's view, stimulates predatory impulses, envy of all distinction and above all permeable boundaries. Mothering a replica of oneself inevitably transforms a woman: 'Any mother invested in a replica can never hope to revert to as inviolable a self as can the mother of a son.'[27]

She considers that her position differs from those feminist theorists who posit that the particular quality of the mother–daughter relationship is to be found on 'the symbiotic map'. What she sees as specific to the mother–daughter dyad is 'the range and extent, content and velocity of projective identification which is found to operate in the relationship, in the connectedness between replica and replica'.[28] She instances the words of Aurelia Plath, mother of Sylvia, to illustrate this permeability:

> Between Sylvia and myself there existed – as between my own mother and me – a sort of psychic osmosis, which at times was very wonderful and comforting; at other times an unwelcome intrusion of privacy.[29]

Perhaps the best-known feminist psychoanalytic theorist who has worked from the premiss of an unconscious sense of continuity between mother and daughter (although in her later writing she suggests that there is no *single* way in which aspects of the relationship with the mother are worked out for women in contrast to how they are worked out for men) is Nancy Chodorow.[30] In Chapter 5 I described her early theory that women's lack of separation from their own mother determines their capacity, and indeed need, to undertake the prolonged, intense style of mothering dictated by Western culture, producing daughters who will reproduce that form of mothering.

Theories which rest on the symbiotic or osmotic tendencies in the mother–daughter relationship have provided a very important way of thinking about the transmission of certain characteristics, associated with femininity, across generations; for example a tendency towards fused or merged relationships, a shaky sense of self-identity, 'restricted initiative', 'fitting in' and 'permeability'. However, in my view there are problems with the belief that biological and cultural 'sameness' provide the touchstone of identification, facilitating projective processes. It suggests an unmediated relationship between biological and psychological events, and fails to take into account the power of the unconscious.[31] For example, a daughter may be physiologically and psychologically like her mother, but a son may contain all the unconscious aspects a mother has not actualised. Separation from a son who represents aspects of herself – agency, activity, heroism or a striving for power – that she has denied in herself can be just as problematic for a mother as detaching from a daughter.

Nini Herman has also questioned whether the behaviour in mothers assumed to arise from an unconscious sense of continuity with daughters is in fact exclusive to the mother–daughter relationship. Are not sons also the recipient of inconsistent nurture? In my view it is an open question whether a mother's sense of deficit is indeed magnified by identification with a daughter. For some mothers set out to create daughters who contain all the so-called masculine qualities they believe they lack. They become involved in what is both a conscious and an unconscious process as they both project unconsciously their denied masculine attributes into their daughters and consciously urge the girls to live them out. One mother said to me, 'When I see her elbowing and shoving her way to the front of the queue for the climbing frame, I feel pretty good about it.'

On the whole, since 1970, perhaps too much has been made of mother–daughter sameness. So many factors can determine how each mother reacts to having a son or a daughter, for example the positive or negative relationship she had with her own mother and other women in her life, with her father and with significant men in her life.[32] While as Valerie Walkerdine and Cathy Urwin have argued, the world outside their relationship constantly directs the mother's attention away from her daughter.[33]

Mothers themselves cite numerous personal and sociocultural factors which mitigate the impact of gender. They may not override it but they certainly inflect the meaning a child's gender has for the mother. Take, for example, the age of the child. Some mothers find toddler girls 'easier' than boys, only to discover the dynamic reversed at the renewed process of separation initiated by adolescence. Another example is birth order. Many mothers feel that this plays a crucial though varying role in their relation to their children.

Birth order gains a particular importance in a culture where women have little direct experience of babies prior to having their own. The enormous changes brought about by motherhood – the dramatic change in identity, in responsibility and in mobility – are initiated and worked through with a first child. 'He made me a mother,' as one mother put it, with gratitude and resentment. In consequence, the first child is often the object of most intense conflict provoked by ambivalence whatever its sex, and the sequential steps of separation from a first child are often fraught, especially when subsequent children are widely spaced, or not conceived. A first child, lacking siblings to dilute the relationship, often feels particularly involved with its parents whose sole object of care it has been.

Mothers also speak of inhibitions with regard to separating from their youngest child. The last child is often 'kept a baby' whatever its sex. Many mothers acknowledge that while they needed their first child to 'grow up fast', almost to bear witness to their capacity to nurture, they are loath to relinquish the mother–infant bond with their last, knowing that they will never again regain the pleasures, even while positively anticipating the flexibility of life without dependent children.

Another factor which casts doubts on generalisations about the difficulties daughters face in separating from their mothers is that being mothered actually enables and encourages girls to 'use' other women in the process of separating out. Take, for example, the situation of black women in the USA. Johnetta B. Cole, in her preface to the anthology *Double Stitch: Black Women Write about Mothers and Daughters*, writes:

> What is of particular interest with respect to black women in America is that racism and poverty frequently bring about situations in which many black children will have surrogate mothers. These are the women who care for our young and fill in for mothers who cannot be there. This means that many African-American girls have multiple models of 'mother'.[34]

Patricia Hill Collins suggests that 'Other mothers' in the black community often play central roles in 'defusing the emotional intensity of relationships between bloodmothers and their daughters', as well as fostering conscious identification with a much wider range of models of black womanhood.[35]

Ruth de Kanter believes that a similar dynamic can operate in lesbian households: 'I suggest that children of lesbian mothers can possibly separate and differentiate more easily between mother and woman than children in heterosexual families who have only "one" mother.'[36] This is not to say that for a child to 'use' other women as poles of separation is necessarily conflict-free. Writing as an irate daughter, Nancy Friday comments on the need for and taboo against second mothers. She cites a professor of psychiatry who observes that mothers 'hate the child, they hate their role, they hate everything about it, but they can't stand that the child should be emotionally attached to someone else'.[37] Missing the significance of maternal ambivalence, the professor fails to grasp that many women, even while suffering jealousy of the woman who helps their child to independence and differentiation, also feel gratitude and relief.

And the One Doesn't Stir without the Other

I want now to turn to French psychoanalytic feminist theorising of the mother–daughter relationship. Whereas many British and American psychoanalytic feminists view the relationship in the object-relations language of projective identification and identity, French thinkers tend to celebrate the potential of the relationship and to mourn the hatred that infuses it today.

In 'Stabat Mater', Julia Kristeva points out that amongst the things left out of the myth of the Virgin Mary is the war between mother and daughter, 'a war masterfully but too quickly settled by promoting Mary as universal and particular, but never singular – as "alone of all her sex".'[38]

Luce Irigaray also elaborated the absence of linguistic, social, semiotic, structural, theoretical or mythical representations of the mother–daughter relationship. She contends that an unsymbolised mother–daughter relationship makes it difficult if not impossible for women to have an identity distinct from the maternal function.[39]

Accepting the clinical view that women have difficulties separating from their mothers, Irigaray sees this not as a result of their cultural or biological sameness but as 'a symptom or result of women's position in the symbolic order'.[40] There is only the place of the mother. She describes what this does to the relationship. It initiates interminable rivalry because there is no room for more than one at a time in the place of the mother. It means the daughter can never accomplish the work of mourning the loss of the object (separation from the mother) because she has no representation of the relationship she has lost. Following on from Freud's theory that powerfully ambivalent feelings towards the lost object hinder the work of mourning, Irigaray observed:

> Now, the relation of the daughter to her mother is not without ambivalence, and becomes even more complicated when the little girl realizes her mother is castrated, while the person to whom her love was addressed was – according to Freud – a phallic mother.[41]

According to Irigaray a little girl gains a sense of her feminine sexuality through pre-Oedipal unity and sameness with her mother. Women are, however, alienated from their innate feminine identification with the mother through the intervention of patriarchal culture which represents woman as phallic or castrated but ultimately as mother. Margaret Whitford, summarising Irigaray's essays on language, suggests she is elaborating the possibility of love of self for women, and the recognition of the debt to the mother, 'thus freeing the mother to be a sexual and desiring woman, and freeing the daughter from the icy grip of the merged undifferentiated relationship'.[42]

Speaking from the perspective of the daughter, Irigaray offers a thesis of considerable complexity. But when she adopts the voice of the mother the message is quite clear:

> We bring something other than children into the world, we engender something other than children; love, desire, language, the social, the political, the religious, for example. But this creation has been forbidden us for centuries, and we must re-appropriate *this* maternal dimension that belongs to us as women.[43]

According to Irigaray, mothers hate their children because their fertility is only validated through literal maternity – which is then culturally devalued. We could rephrase this as mothers hate their children because they are expected to love only them and not engender and love anything else. In Irigaray's prose poem, 'And the One Doesn't Stir Without the Other', she writes of the mutual destruction and dependence created by the absence of a maternal genealogy. The words come from the mouth of the daughter and depict suffocation:

> – imprisoned by your desire for a reflection, I become a statue an image of your immobility

> – And if I leave, you lose the reflection of life, your life.

> – and if I remain, am I not guarantee of your death.[44]

Irigaray believes that to actually acknowledge our intimate connection to our mothers' bodies – even in their potentially destructive and engulfing aspects – is paradoxically freeing. And this recognition, in its turn, will allow mothers a wider spectrum of being as women who love, work, suffer, create *and* mother.

Like Irigaray, Kristeva indicates that it is the denial of feelings between mother and daughter that sours and obstructs the relationship. Aligned with her analysis of the myth of the Virgin Mary are thoughts on her own experience of childbirth. The two texts gain meaning by their proximity. Here she writes of her relationship with her own mother:

> Almost no voice in her placid presence. Except perhaps, and more belatedly, the echo of quarrels: her exasperation, her being fed up, her hatred. Never straightforward, always held back, as if, although the unmanageable child deserved it, the

daughter could not accept the mother's hatred – it was not meant for her. A hatred without recipient or rather whose recipient was no 'I' and which, perturbed by such a lack of recipience, was toned down into irony or collapsed into remorse before reaching its destination.[45]

Where there is no 'I' there can be no hate, and where there is no hate there can be no live connection. Kristeva is primarily concerned to illustrate the outcome of the absence of female subjecthood in the mother–daughter relationship. But I think that her description of the mother and daughter, both bemused and unable to process maternal hatred, makes my point about the significance of unacknowledged ambivalence. Once owned, maternal passion can deepen both self-knowledge and knowledge of the other. Kristeva herself celebrates this potential. She writes that the mother–daughter relationship can enable women slowly to 'differentiate between same beings'. Motherhood, she believes, 'lifts the fixations, makes passions circulate between life and death, self and other, culture and nature . . .'[46]

Christiane Olivier, unlike Irigaray and Kristeva, holds out little hope for the mother–daughter relationship. She considers that girls can never offer mothers the affirmation they long for because they belong to the subjugated sex. Hence mothers are unable to separate not from daughters but from sons.[47] Olivier's basic thesis is that girls, lacking sexual and self-affirmation from mothers, seek it in their fathers, and later in men. The latter, in flight from their engulfing mothers, vengefully desire submission from women, who search in vain for repair of the narcissistic damage inflicted on them by maternal denigration.

Olivier contends that the girl's trouble is that her body is not like anyone's. She has neither penis, nor breasts nor pubic hair. And thus the 'mother cannot be a locus of identification for the girl'.[48] I think this ties unconscious identification far too closely to conscious apprehension of anatomy. And, moreover, it overlooks the significance of generational difference for the daughter. The daughter is able to see her future outlined on her mother's body. Helene Deutsch believed that the little girl feels anger towards her mother because the mother stands in the way of her being an adult – preventing her from being a grown-up. But surely a little girl also sees the *promise* of future potency and fertility in her mother's body? Whether the mother's body signifies subjugation or potency is to some extent militated by a mother's experienced feelings towards her own body. These feelings can, in turn, be influenced by the small daughter's intense interest and curiosity.

> My daughter aged five likes coming into the bathroom and watching me in the bath. She sits and chats and scrutinises my breasts and pubic hair. She examines her own body for signs of becoming like mine. I suspect she fears changing shape, but also she connects it to adult power and privilege. I must say, I enjoy it, the sense of shared destiny co-existing with my daughter's mysterious future.

Listening to this mother inevitably provokes questions about envy. Rivalry and envy are considered indelibly to mark the mother–daughter relationship. A mother may enjoy the companionship of shared gender, but she nevertheless recognises that her young daughter possesses the signs of youth so desired and admired by her culture, while her own loosening skin and incipient wrinkles devalue her, and associate her with death.

Melanie Klein wrote of envy as a form of infantile aggression directed towards 'the riches' of the mother's body. The small infant desires to possess itself of the contents of the mother's body and to destroy her by means of every weapon that sadism can command. Both sexes experience envious impulses in relation to the mother's body and, according to Klein, both fear the mother's retaliation. But what of the mother who is in receipt of these impulses? In my view, a mother can experience counter-envy and hostility irrespective of the sex of the child. However, there can undoubtedly be an added sting where daughters are concerned for some mothers:

> She wants to be me, and I'm resented because I'm in the way of her actually being me. I deeply feel her desire to get rid of me – and her need for me. I'm locked into it.

Where a daughter can often want to 'be' her mother is in relation to her father. And, indeed, some mothers feel enormous resentment at the favours their daughters do achieve with their male partners:

> She gets whatever she wants out of her father. She comes and sits on his knee and whispers to him and he's completely captivated. It makes me furious, partly because I've always been ashamed of using feminine wiles myself.

Nini Herman, reflecting on Winnicott's reasons why mothers hate their babies, similarly questions whether they hate their daughters more than their sons. She concludes that, though hatred may be outweighed by, for example, the pleasures of companionship, envy of daughters does magnify maternal hatred. The daughter possesses youthful beauty and sexual prospects and will soon displace the mother in our culture's sexual arena.[49]

In my view, the envy and rivalry between mother and daughter has been read predominantly from the daughter's perspective and interpreted as utterly destructive; whereas from the point of view of the mother, the aspects of the daughter that evoke envy can also promote constructive narcissistic pride and pleasure:

> She's affectionate, flirtatious and downright defiant towards her father. I was much too scared of my dad and he was much too distant from me to have behaved as she does. I do admire her for it. I watch them together and feel, well, I've got something right with her.

This mother sees all she wished for herself developing in her daughter. The daughter constitutes herself reborn perfect and she herself is the origin of the 'miracle'. She comments,

> As a girl I would spend hours drawing pictures of how I would like to look. Imagine how it feels to have in Carol a daughter with the looks I longed for. I just love watching her.

A mother's narcissistic pleasure in her daughter can counteract, or rather balance, envy. But if a daughter behaves in such a way as to wound the mother's narcissism, she receives a double dose of denigration. Her mother's self-hatred fuses with the hatred provoked in her by her daughter.

The site of battles in contemporary Western family life is almost always around appearances. A girl demarcates her difference from her mother by adopting peer group fashions that are, by definition, a foreign language to her mother. Thus a mother can experience her daughter's struggle towards independence and individuation as a deliberate attempt to spoil her own beautiful creation – indeed, to spoil her self. Deviations on the daughter's part from the mother's desire are experienced by some mothers as an almost physical wound:

When I see her wearing unflattering shapes, clashing colours
and horrid fabrics, I feel actually ill. We started fighting over
her clothes when she was about five. I remember her shouting
at me, 'It's my body, Mum.' I knew she was right but just
as I struggled to control and improve my appearance, I felt
compelled to control hers.

This mother experiences her daughter's body as if it were hers. After
all, it was once part of her body. And just as she focuses her desire
for control and self-worth on the manipulation of her bodily shape
and size, so she tries to control her daughter's appearance. In one
sense this *is* about an unconscious sense of continuity between
mother and daughter, with the mother resisting differentiation.
However, it is *also* about both mother and daughter's struggle with
the warring elements of gender certainty and gender confusion. For
the mother gender confusion is to be warded off by the daughter
'making the best of herself' as a woman. For the daughter, the
conflict is expressed by affiliation to a specific style of femininity
in opposition to her mother's. For both, gender certainty arising
from an unconscious alliance with culture's demands makes them
creatures of the process rather than creators of it.

Just as boys utilise superheroes in their battle between gender
certainty and gender confusion, so girls employ an array of Barbies,
Sindys, Susies and My Little Ponies. Their flowing pink spangled
locks, their feet forever arched in high heels, their wasp waists and
emaciated limbs signify a sexuality and femininity in opposition to
maternal femininity. As with the son's superheroes, mothers find
themselves in an ambiguous situation. They disapprove and yet they
acquiesce. They know that Sindy presents a feminine ideal bound
to bring pain in its wake yet, as my daughter Lydia told me, 'you
need them to play with friends'. Paradoxically, Sindys in all their
blatant pinkness testify to the *mutability* of femininity. It is a historically changing concept. Daughters are discovering a femininity
other than that associated with their mothers and employing Sindy's
implacable gender certitude to do it. For, even while playing with
the arch-representatives of gender certainty, the children are aware
of a spectrum of gender positions produced by the co-existence of
gender confusion and gender certainty. I remember overhearing a
conversation between my daughter and son, then aged six and seven,
in which they classified their friends according to whether they were
Boy-Boys, Boy-Girls, Girl-Girls or Girl-Boys.

As for mothers, they find themselves positioned as both friend and foe in the process by which their children forge their own gender identity through playing with impossible stereotypes. And, perhaps, confrontation with Sindy also alerts them to the existence of their own gender confusion – in other words to the still evolving and changing dynamics of their own gender identity, beyond the role of mother, beyond the heterosexual matrix itself.

Great Expectations

Empirical psychological research into the question of mothers' response to having boys or girls usually focuses on how the mother's attitude shapes gender-specific behaviour in her offspring. Different theoretical areas of psychological study draw different conclusions as to how the mother–child relationship effects the formation of gender identity – and the conclusions are often contradictory. For example, behaviourists disagree as to the extent of mothers' different behaviour with boys and girls, while research based on attachment theory demonstrates that in stressful, anxiety-provoking situations, the behaviour of girls and boys is very similar and 'only occasionally are girls reported as staying closer to their mothers'.[50]

Some studies, for example those by Dana Breen,[51] Ann Oakley,[52] Joan Raphael-Leff,[53] and Jacqueline McGuire[54] have, from different theoretical perspectives, focused specifically on mothers' *feelings* for sons and daughters.

All see as crucial a mother's particular preference for the sex of the child. Joan Raphael-Leff, however, warns against generalising with respect to sex preference, commenting that 'In Western societies we find a mixture of both social and personal conscious and unconscious preferences, which vary from woman to woman and in each woman, from pregnancy to pregnancy, often rooted in the constellation of her own family of origin.'[55] For example a woman from a family of girls may feel a sense of superiority in relation to her mother if she gives birth to a boy. The sense of triumph may be deeply gratifying or frankly threatening – or a mixture of both.

Mothers' preference can, of course, be powerfully determined by cultural attitudes. For example in a matrilineal society, such as the Buka of the Solomon Islands, it is girls who are desired to carry on the family line. Whereas, in societies where boys are expected to work the family land, or pursue the family business, sons are desired – especially first-born sons.[56]

Given that in contemporary Western society the family is no longer the major organising unit of production, the desire for a son might be expected to have lessened. Ann Oakley and Dana Breen in their studies of new mothers found that, on the contrary, sons were still preferred. Oakley discovered while interviewing mothers in London in the mid-1970s that 44 per cent admitted to being disappointed by the birth of a daughter, while only 8 per cent claimed disappointment with a son.[57] In her study of first-time mothers, Dana Breen found that women who were depressed postnatally were more likely to have had a girl than a boy.[58] Both Oakley and Breen suggest that their findings need to be placed in the context of the culture placing a higher value on sons. Oakley wonders whether Breen's findings on postnatal depression amongst the mothers of girls – which do not tally with her own findings – could be an expression of a sense of 'failure'.

She explores possible explanations for her own findings – that there is an association between a female birth and medium/poor feelings for the baby. She suggests that mothers feel a greater identification with the baby if it is a girl so they simply did not spell out the depth and complexity of their feelings, whereas the reason for describing and exploring clear-cut positive feelings for a son is the mother's sense of the boy child's difference from herself.

Raphael-Leff assumes that a mother responds differently to the birth of a boy and girl but refrains from attributing good or bad feelings to the response. Thus she suggests that daughters signify what she terms 'an umbilical lineage', a chain of successive navel strings connecting the baby backwards to her mother and through to her maternal grand- and great-grandmothers, and forward to the baby's unborn daughter. How a woman feels about the 'umbilical lineage' is dependent on how women are viewed in her family and on her attitude to her own femaleness. The latter can be dependent on conventional attitudes towards gender difference – in other words on sex stereotyping.[59]

A study by Jacqueline McGuire of forty families in an outer London borough supports the view that a mother's expectation of feminine compliance in a girl can lead to dissatisfaction with daughters who fail to display the 'easiness' and obedience associated with girls.[60] McGuire quotes mothers of daughters saying:

She's very difficult at the moment, she's vicious, punches and bites and kicks, she's a right tomboy.[61]

She's very difficult, a trying child and very bad tempered.[62]

McGuire comments of the latter mother that she went on to say that she herself was similar to her daughter – 'that's the trouble'. By contrast McGuire describes a mother expressing immense pleasure in her daughter's traditionally feminine behaviour:

She has a very nice temperament. She's lovely, and she's a pleasure to be with, a happy little girl. She's not aggressive, she's sociable and she loves people and children. She's very affectionate, gentle and loving.[63]

A mother impressed by current critiques of traditional feminine behaviour as over-compliant, masochistic and destructively passive might not be so happy with this daughter.

In McGuire's study, mothers of sons are more likely than mothers of daughters to describe their children in completely positive ways. They emphasise the boy's masculinity and often refer to mutual affection:

My beautiful son, he's loving and nice. He picks you flowers and kisses you better. He's very, very boy, manly, a boyish boy, a good boy, not really naughty, mischievous in a nice way.

A proper little pickle, he knows what he wants. He loves company, people, fun, a proper little boy really. He's quite a lovable little chap, he likes a cuddle.[64]

These mothers of sons who spoke to McGuire seem able to recognise an acceptable gender ideal in their sons. They want them to be tough but tender. It is something of an androgynous ideal, whereas such tendencies in little girls seem to be met with disapproval: 'She's very difficult at the moment . . . she's a right tomboy.'[65]

Yet amongst mothers I interviewed there were those who wanted to see a sense of agency develop in their daughters, in opposition to conventional notions of femininity. Indeed, they declared it easier to 'toughen' daughters than to foster a similarly subversive 'softness' in their sons. Fundamentally, though, they felt such 'engineering' was out of their hands.

Like Breen and Oakley, McGuire perceived a greater tendency

for mothers to become irritated with daughters. Mothers own up to feeling particularly irritated with girls' 'clingy' behaviour but, as McGuire points out, mothers' feelings are not necessarily related to what's observed. For instance, the mother of one of the least clingy girls in the study reports, 'Yes, she does go through phases, she hangs onto my skirt or legs, she's always there . . . I can only keep my sanity by saying "It's only a phase".'[66]

Overall, McGuire suggests there is less friction between mother and son than between mother and daughter. With girls, mothers manifest more need to be involved and a greater sense of responsibility but also more irritation when their daughters make demands on them. With regard to responsibility, McGuire maintains mothers expect fathers to be more involved with sons, whereas *they* expect to control and direct the daughter. McGuire concludes that this leads to greater satisfaction due to the level of commitment, but also more anxiety and doubt about their performance as mothers.

McGuire warns against drawing firm conclusions from her study, in that the sample was small and limited. Moreover, it is impossible to know whether a child's behaviour follows on from parental treatment, or vice versa. For example, the tendency she observed in girls to 'cling' may have considerable impact on a mother's behaviour, sparking irritation and the desire to push the child away, which in turn confirms and magnifies the child's need to cling. And, as with all observational studies, we are left wondering about the unconscious processes at work. Are the mothers who apparently responded with greater alacrity to their sons' demand for attention than to their daughters being, so to speak, programmed by male dominance in society, or are they trying to compensate for their ambivalence towards men? We do not know.

In my view a combination of socioeconomic change, new emphasis on the importance of maternal authority, and cultural awareness of gender stereotyping are working together to transform the meaning of the gender of the child for the mother. In Chapter 8 I discussed the interaction between a mother's experience of the environment as increasingly dangerous and the corresponding emphasis on maternal control and authority. Although girls are traditionally viewed as more 'vulnerable' they are also considered easier to control than boys. Sally explains why her anxiety on behalf of her little boy stirs up hostility towards him:

I find life with Mary so much easier than with Tommy. He and his friends spend their whole time getting into trouble. I have to watch him all the time, while Mary and her friends are quite happy to sit and draw and cut out. But Tommy, he's off, up, over, all the time. It terrifies me.

Maternal Desire

Freud recognised that a mother's response to the eroticism constellated between her and her children was determined by her own sexual life. He wrote:

> A child's intercourse with anyone responsible for his care affords him an unending source of sexual excitation and satisfaction from his erotogenic zones. This is especially so since the person in charge of him, who, after all, is as a rule mother, herself regards him with feelings that are derived from her own sexual life: she strokes him, kisses him, rocks him and quite clearly treats him as a substitute for a complete sexual object. A mother would probably be horrified if she were made aware that all the marks of affection were rousing the children's sexual instinct and preparing for its later intensity.[67]

Mothers in Freud's era may have been 'horrified' at the idea that their care of their children was 'rousing' the children's 'sexual instincts'. Mothers today are not so much horrified as uneasy at desire constellated between themselves and their children. There are many reasons for such unease. As Freud pointed out, their response is in part derived from their own sexuality, with which they may have a more or less conflictual relationship. Then, also, the impulses evoke the incest taboo and represent disturbing aspects of sexuality. Freud believed that a mother's relations with an infant offer the possibility 'of satisfying, without reproach, wishful impulses which have long been repressed and which must be called perverse'.[68] As Lisa Appignanesi and John Forrester point out, he considered that a mother's sexual desire meets her child's desire for her half-way, and that there was a continuity between maternal solicitude and perverse sexual relations between mother and child.[69] But the uncertainty and unease mothers feel at the presence of sexuality between themselves and their children are not only due to potential perversity, but also to the cultural split maintained between the mother and the sexually desiring woman. Maternity is understood to be the end-product, *not* the site of sexuality. Freud's work contains the potential to heal the split, but it has, if anything, widened since his time.

I want now to explore what it is that maintains maternal solicitude and checks the acting out of sexual impulses, but first I think it is necessary to look briefly at some voices that have broken the silence on maternal sexuality.

Freud observed that 'very surprising sexual activity of little girls in relation to their mothers is manifested chronologically in oral, sadistic and finally even in phallic trends directed towards her'.[70] Later commentators assume that mother–daughter eroticism must necessarily be a source of frustration for the girl. Bela Grunberger, for example, a French psychoanalyst and contributor to the influential collection of papers entitled *Female Sexuality* published in 1964, asserted that 'a true sexual object can only be of the opposite sex and (unless some kind of congenital homosexuality is assumed) the mother cannot be the satisfactory sexual object for the girl that she is for the boy'. He therefore proceeds to suggest that the pre-Oedipal – the very early mother–child – relationship is necessarily inadequate and frustrating for a girl 'because the maternal object is only a substitute for a *truly adequate sexual object*.'[71] The girl is thus understood to develop with a sense of deficit that she is condemned to spend the rest of her life attempting to repair.

Christiane Olivier pushes Grunberger's thesis to its obvious conclusion and assumes an absence of maternal sexual desire for daughters and an excess of incestuous sexual feeling for sons. She berates women for failing to acknowledge the strength of desire they feel for their sons:

> Did Jocasta live incestuously with her son of her own knowledge, or her own will? Are today's women aware of what they are doing when they take first place with their children? Do they know what they are giving rise to in their sons and daughters? These women who say quite casually of their sons: 'He's going through the Oedipal stage'; it never seems to occur to them to think to themselves even for a moment 'I'm going through my Jocasta stage.'[72]

Not only does Olivier's mother fail to be conscious of her desire for her son, but she seems to be entirely ignorant of her daughter's sexuality, seeing her as sweet, lovable, graceful and good – 'anything but sexually alive or tinged with desire'.[73]

Both Grunberger and Olivier view mother–child sexuality through the lens of the Oedipus complex, and assume that identification and desire inevitably exist in opposition to each other; that each individual identifies with the same-sex parent and desires the parent of the opposite sex.

Recently, however, feminist psychoanalytic theorists have challenged conventional readings of Oedipal dynamics, claiming that they fail to reflect the complexity of female desire, but construct and confirm an oppressive norm. In her reformulation of psychoanalytic theory, Jessica Benjamin points out that it conventionally echoes the limited understanding our culture has of maternal sexuality.[74] The father is seen as the parent with a monopoly on sexual agency and desire. Girls are thus left with difficulties in finding sources of identification for sexual agency. The girl can identify with her mother who is, in this reading of the inner family, a non-sexual creature. Father is a sexual creature but cannot be identified with, only desired. It is a thorny problem for the daughter. The element in this system that feminist theorists say needs most to open to psychic and social change is the image of the non-sexual mother.

In their work on lesbianism and psychoanalysis, Noreen O'Connor and Joanna Ryan urge that key aspects of Oedipal dynamics do not constitute a universal truth but are rather reflections of cultural structures that are utterly bounded by a commitment to heterosexuality.[75] Their work as therapists with lesbian patients demonstrates the diversity of lesbian psychological experience and reveals the usual account of a girl's psychosexual development with its split between desire (hetero) and identification (homo) to be profoundly inadequate. They suggest instead that

> the construction of heterosexuality and gender identity in terms of basic binarism needs to be thrown open so that desire is not held to follow from gender identity, and gender identity does not have to follow from biological sex.[76]

O'Connor and Ryan spell out how our thinking about gender identity would change, were this reformulation to be taken on board. Heterosexuality would not be tied so tightly to the development of 'appropriate' gender identities. Homosexuality would thus no longer be seen as indicating a 'disturbance' of gender identity. In sum, the ties between biological sex and the expression of masculinity and femininity would be loosened, providing for much more variation and diversity in the expression of gender identity.

In relation to the theme of this chapter, their suggestion that we cease reading infantile development in terms of strict basic binarism facilitates the acknowledgement of the diversity of mothers' response to their children's biological sex – that ambivalence can be manageable or unmanageable in relation to boys and girls, that identification *and* eroticism can be more or less independent of the biological sex of the child.

Even from within a relatively conventional psychoanalytic framework, a writer like Joyce McDougall can recognise that mothers do experience both heterosexual and homosexual desire towards their children:

> much homosexual libido is expressed in various ego activities, particularly in creative and professional work and in the activity of motherhood. Her normal homosexual demands on both parents find manifold sublimated satisfaction when she becomes a parent.[77]

We have thus reached a point where mother–daughter eroticism is accepted to exist alongside mother–son eroticism. Hence a challenge is now firmly mounted to the classical psychoanalytic position as expressed by Christiane Olivier and Bela Grunberger. Today theorists explore the pathological or non-pathological expression of eroticism in relation to both sexes. Estela Welldon, as we saw, goes into what happens when maternal desire is (disastrously) acted out: when mothers treat their children of either sex as part objects there to satisfy their own desires. Others, such as Nina Lykke, author of a number of works on feminism and psychoanalysis, indicate that mother–child eroticism need not be part of psychopathological fusion or symbiosis, but can be quite consistent with differentiation and recognition of the other.[78]

Nevertheless, an indication of how problematic this area remains is seen in the response, from feminists and others, to advances in understanding of the sensuousness that manifests between mother and child. There is still a strong tendency to generalise about mothers' reactions to their daughters' sexuality. It is assumed that women's sexual doubts and bodily self-hatred are inevitably conveyed to their daughters, that mothers pass on self-denial, self-sacrifice and self-denigration to daughters. Mothers are described reacting negatively to their daughters' developing sexuality out of fear for their daughters and envy of their future possibilities. They are reported as reacting with irritation to their daughters' autoerotic exploration, anxiously discouraging masturbation and maintaining silence in naming the female genitals. Also they are still assumed to be unable to accept their own erotic response to their daughter because of the taboo on homosexuality.

Uncertainty and Confusion

In fact, these monolithic views of mothers, as de-sexualised, sexually destructive or sexually anxious and envious, conceal the enormous diversity of responses amongst mothers towards their children. Take, for example, the following examples from two mothers reflecting on their daughters' bodies. Fay comments: 'We are all taught to see women as sex objects. I enjoy looking at photos of attractive women in magazines and I think my daughters are quite gorgeous.' For Cathy, however, the erotic appeal of her daughters bodies is obliterated. She says, 'When I look at the girls' developing breasts, I just think of the pain of it all and how they must hurt, but I just enjoy the boys' little male muscles.'

Some women describe the constant physical contact of childcare – the cuddling, kissing and holding – as a source of frank sensuous pleasure. Others experience it as an invasion, even an unwelcome annihilation, of their bodily boundaries. They feel devoured. For them, their sexuality and their bodies are indirect sources of a sense of autonomy and separateness from their children. Their children's exploration of their bodies feel like 'the last straw' – the end of that aspect of their identity which they see as outside motherhood. Talking of the interest her small daughters take in her breasts, one woman commented, 'I just don't feel the top half of my body belongs to me any more.'

Even amongst women who enjoy a sensuous relationship with their children, a basic ambivalence attends their experience of their children's sexuality. Nathalie expresses this clearly:

I do feel uncomfortable with the feelings Micky stirs in me. Recently he has really got into touching me – touching my breasts. It is nice yet there has to be a line. I find it very difficult to know where to draw the line. I don't want to seem to shove him off, or appear really rejecting, but I need to be able to say, 'This is mine'.

Nathalie's description of the confusion her small son evoked in her (he was five years old at the time) is a good example of how the management of ambivalence can assist the mother–child relationship. Although she says she does not want to 'shove him off', she does feel invaded and irritated, as much by her sense of confusion as by anything else. Yet, as she says, 'it is nice'. She does love her child and does not want to seem or to be rejecting. Love, desire, irritation, protectiveness and cultural taboo are all stirred in her and demand resolution. She appeals to the only certainty that she has. She says, 'This is mine' and thus lays down a containing boundary without constituting a rejection. The son's exploration of his mother's body could have led in another direction. The mother in her confusion could have exploited or rejected the child, while the son's desire and frustration could have been motivated by a sadistic wish to smash all boundaries. In other words, the element of sadism and aggression within the sexuality constellated between mother and child could have overwhelmed loving concern and creative ambivalence.

It is the sadistic aspect of mother–child sexuality that Estela Welldon addresses in her work with mothers who do act out their incestuous desires for sons or daughters. She emphasises that such women are usually perpetrating the seduction that they themselves experienced; previously the victim, they become perpetrators. Incestuous acts are thus prompted by the wish for power in those who have been overpowered. Welldon writes of an incestuous mother:

The mother stopped the incest when her son was no longer 'the ideal partner' or, shall I say, part object ideally designed for her perverse purposes. As soon as the boy behaved like an adult and achieved ejaculation she no longer felt in control of the situation. She was now, in her mind and body, with a man and therefore – in her fantasies – at his mercy.[79]

Welldon observes that mothers are more ready to report incestuous feelings and actions towards their daughters than towards their sons. She does not offer any explanation as to why that should be. Perhaps mother–son incest constitutes a more shocking reversal of power relations.

Revelation of maternal child sexual abuse have forced society to confront certain realities about motherhood. But such revelations have also encouraged a division in the way mothers are thought about: there are bad unnatural mothers who abuse their children, and good normal mothers who do not. Thus the always-present and always-disturbing elements in mother–child sexuality tend to be ignored and mothers are left feeling guilty and unnatural on account of the sexuality that is inevitably present to one degree or another between them and their children.

Writing of the role of incestuous sexuality in development, Andrew Samuels commented that,

> The psychological function of incestuous sexuality is to facilitate the closeness of love. Desire in a relationship guarantees the importance of that relationship to both participants. It can go tragically wrong. It can get acted out, it can possess generation after generation of a family. But incestuous desire has the function of providing fuel for the means by which we get close to other people and, hence, grow.[80]

However, as we have seen, where there is love there is also hate; where there is affection there is also aggression. And aggression constitutes an important component of sexuality, as Freud observed: 'From the very first we recognise the presence of a sadistic component in the sexual instinct' and to this he attributes 'the familiar ambivalence of love and hate in erotic life'.[81] However, it is extraordinarily hard for the element of aggressivity in female sexuality – let alone maternal sexuality – to be acknowledged. Yet we can see and hear its unmistakable presence in mothers' response to their children's sexual exploration of their bodies. Mothers describe how they feel invaded, taken over, smothered, devoured – as well as loved. They are encountering the element of aggressivity in both their children's sexuality and their own. The primitive, passionate charge is evident in the highly familiar maternal exclamation of desire: 'I could eat you up.' It is a perfect expression of the aggressive component in sexual desire. The element of sadism is there, but accompanied by love and permitted expression through play. Janine Chasseguet-Smirgel suggests that the outcome of the conflict between love and sadistic-anal components in sexuality is 'consideration for the object'. The mother does not eat the baby; instead the active, aggressive impulse in 'I could eat you up' is transformed into protective energy and concern.

The uncertainty and unease with which mothers encounter the sexuality constellated between themselves and their children now becomes a little more understandable. Unmitigated and uncontained by love and concern (lacking, that is, the boon of ambivalence), the element of aggressivity within sexuality can be a force for harm. And mothers find it – unsurprisingly – hard to acknowledge this component in their feelings for their children. Indeed, they can be shocked and horrified when they do detect it. Psychoanalysts have described difficulties in dealing with erotic feelings 'fused with aggression' constellated between patient and analyst.[82] How much harder it is for mothers who experience such feelings so deeply at odds with the maternal ideal.

The fear and denial of the element of aggression in eroticism can provoke the by now familiar cycle in which hatred ends up outweighing love. The mother feels a bad, unnatural mother, her guilt mounts and soon the child is perceived as guilt-inducing and hateful persecutor. The potential of ambivalence to foster thought and spark concern founders. Desire produces, not care and closeness but destruction.

In sum, I believe it will continue to be tempting to generalise about the impact of a child's gender on the production of maternal ambivalence. As we have seen, there is a large body of theory which suggests that the biological sameness of mother–daughter impacts decisively with the separation-individuation process and that this intensifies mutual conflict generated by ambivalence. Yet, as I have tried to indicate, biological sameness can have profoundly different unconscious meanings for different women. With both sexes, mothers have to contend with being an actor in their child's struggle to get to grips with gender confusion and gender certainty. Mothers experience themselves more or less uneasily positioned as friend or foe to the process.

It seems appropriate to have ended this exploration of maternal ambivalence with a consideration of the impact of the child's evolving gender identity on the mother. For it is an issue which vividly highlights the way social ideals and expectations, maternal psychic reality, and the contribution of the character and circumstances of the child together determine the impact of maternal ambivalence on a woman. It is at the intersection of these currents that mothers find ambivalence manageable or unmanageable. Sometimes, conflictual feelings evoked by a child's struggle with gender issues can be deeply troubling for a mother and seem entirely at odds with her desires and expectations. Torn between outrage and concern, she can dip into unmanageable ambivalence with the intense guilt that brings. At other times, thanks to more benign circumstances, mothers are prompted by their ambivalence to think about what children themselves are trying to achieve, why and how it may differ from the mother's own experiences and aspirations. Then we can speak of the creative outcome of manageable ambivalence.

Notes

1 What Is Ambivalence?

1 C. Urwin, 'Constructing motherhood: the persuasion of normal development' in C. Steedman, C. Urwin and V. Walkerdine (eds), *Language, Gender and Childhood*, Routledge & Kegan Paul, London, 1985, provides a full account of the prescription that circumscribes the maternal role. Mothers' relationships with other mothers provide the possibility of reassurance and of resistance to normative notions of motherhood.

2 A. Phoenix, A. Woollett and E. Lloyd (eds), *Motherhood: Meanings, Practices and Ideologies*, Sage Publications, London, Newbury Park and New Delhi, 1991, elaborate on this issue. See also J. Price, *Motherhood: What it does to your mind*, Pandora, London, 1988.

3 A. Pound, 'The Development of Attachment in Adult Life – the Newpin Experiment', *British Journal of Psychotherapy*, 7, 1 (1990), pp. 77–86.

4 F. Weldon, personal communication, 1994.

5 M. Klein, 'Mourning and its Relation to Manic-Depressive States' (1940), in *Love, Guilt and Reparation and Other Works 1921–1945*, Hogarth Press, London, 1985, p. 351.

6 M. Klein, 'On the Sense of Loneliness' (1963), in *Envy and Gratitude and Other Works 1946–1963*, Hogarth Press, London, 1980, pp. 301–2. 'Full and permanent integration is never possible for some polarity between the life and death instincts always persists and remains the deepest source of conflict.' For further elaboration of the link between life and death instincts, love and hate, see R. D. Hinshelwood, *A Dictionary of Kleinian Thought*, Free Association Books, London, 1989.

7 Klein, 'Mourning and its Relation to Manic-Depressive States', p. 351.

8 M. Klein, 'Psychogenesis of Manic-Depressive States', in *Love, Guilt and Reparation*, p. 288.

9 G. Christine and A. Correia, 'Maternal Ambivalence in a Group Analytic Setting', *British Journal of Psychotherapy*, 3, 3, (1987), pp. 205–15.

10 Hinshelwood, *A Dictionary of Kleinian Thought*, provides a useful summary of W. R. Bion's theories.

11 S. Ferenczi, 'The Problem of Acceptance of Unpleasant Ideas – Advances in

Knowledge of the Sense of Reality' (1926), in *Further Contributions to the Theory and Technique of Psycho-Analysis* (Maresfield Reprints), Karnac, London, 1980, p. 371.

12 M. Waddell, 'A Local Habitation and a Name: From Resemblance to Identity', unpublished paper, 1993.

13 J. Raphael-Leff, *Pregnancy: The Inside Story*, Sheldon Press, London, 1993 p. 36. Raphael-Leff employs the term 'psychic expulsion' to describe the process whereby a mother remains unaware of pregnancy.

14 S. R. Suleiman, 'Writing and Motherhood', in S. N. Garner, C. Kahane and M. Sprengnether (eds), *The (M)other Tongue*, Cornell University Press, Ithaca, NY and London, 1985, p. 356.

15 J. Benjamin, *The Bonds of Love, Psychoanalysis, Feminism, and the Problem of Domination*, Virago, London, 1990; L. Eichenbaum and S. Orbach, 'Feminine Subjectivity, Counter-transference and the Mother–Daughter Relationship', in J. van Mens-Verhulst, K. Schreurs and L. Woertman (eds), *Daughtering and Mothering: Female Subjectivity Reanalysed*, Routledge, London and New York, 1994; Raphael-Leff, *Pregnancy: The Inside Story*; M. Mahrer Kaplan, *Mothers' Images of Motherhood: Case Studies of Twelve Mothers*, Routledge, London and New York, 1992.

16 Phoenix *et al.*, *Motherhood, Meanings, Practices and Ideologies*; Raphael-Leff, *Pregnancy: The Inside Story*; E. Nakano Glenn, G. Chang and L. Rennie Forcey (eds), *Mothering: Ideology, Experience, and Agency*, Routledge, New York and London, 1994, foregrounds 'the existence of historical, cultural, class and ethnic variation in mothering, and the existence of conflict and struggle over competing conceptions and conditions under which mothering is carried out' (p. ix).

17 P. Hill Collins, 'The Meaning of Motherhood in Black Culture and Black Mother–Daughter Relationships', in P. Bell Scott, B. Guy-Sheftall, J. Jones Royster, J. Sims-Wood, H. De Costa-Willis and L. P. Fultz (eds), *Double Stitch: Black Women Write about Mothers and Daughters*, Harper Perennial, New York, 1993, pp. 43–4.

18 Phoenix *et al.*, *Motherhood, Meanings, Practices and Ideologies*, p. 25.

19 I. Menzies, 'Thoughts on the Maternal Role in Contemporary Society', *International Journal of Child Psychotherapy*, Vol 4, No. 1 1978 pp. 5–14.

20 Phoenix *et al.*, *Motherhood, Meanings, Practices and Ideologies*.

21 M. G. Boulton, *On Being a Mother: A Study of Women with Pre-School Children*, Tavistock, London, 1983.

22 Ibid., p. 178; Price, *Motherhood: What it does to your mind*, addresses in detail the role of a woman's partner in shaping her response to motherhood.

23 Historically there has been, for example, the work of Helene Deutsch and Marie Langer. Today Dana Breen, Ann Dally, Dinora Pines, Jane Price, Joan Raphael-Leff and Estela Welldon have all written key books on the psychology of motherhood.

24 J. Flax, *Thinking Fragments: Psychoanalysis, Feminism, and Postmodernism in the Contemporary West*, University of California Press, Berkeley and Los Angeles, 1990.

25 P. Caplan and I. Hall-McCorquodale, 'Mother Blaming in Major Clinical

Journals', *American Journal of Orthopsychiatry*, 55 (1985) pp. 345–53. See also J. van Mens-Verhulst, 'Daughtering and Mothering: Female Subjectivity Rethought and Reevalued' in van Mens-Verhulst *et al.*, *Daughtering and Mothering*.

26 M. Plaza, 'The Mother/The Same: Hatred of the Mother in Psychoanalysis', *Feminist Issues*, Spring 1982. pp. 75–100.

27 Ibid., p. 75.

28 See E. V. Welldon, *Mother, Madonna, Whore. The Idealization and Denigration of Motherhood*, Free Association Books, London, 1988.

29 M. Hirsh, *The Mother/Daughter Plot: Narrative, Psychoanalysis, Feminism*, Indiana University Press, Bloomington and Indianapolis, 1989, p. 169.

30 D. W. Winnicott, 'Hate in the Countertransference' (1949) in D. W. Winnicott, *The Maturational Processes and the Facilitating Environment*, Hogarth Press, London, 1979.

31 S. Freud, *The Interpretation of Dreams* (1900), in *The Standard Edition of the Complete Works of Sigmund Freud* [hereafter *SE*], 24 vols, ed. and trans. James Strachey *et al.*, London, Hogarth Press and the Institute of Psycho-Analysis, 1953–73. Vol. 5.

32 Freud, 'A Case of Obsessional Neurosis' (1909), *SE* Vol. 10, p. 240.

33 Freud, 'Instincts and their Vicissitudes' (1915), *SE* Vol. 14, pp. 89–90.

34 Freud, 'Thoughts for the Times on War and Death', (1915), *SE* Vol. 14, p. 299.

35 Freud, 'Mourning and Melancholia', (1917 [1915]), Vol. 14, p. 251.

36 Freud, 'Female Sexuality' (1931), *SE* Vol. 16, p. 235.

37 J. Bowlby, 'Psychoanalysis and Child Care' (1958), in *The Making and Breaking of Affectional Bonds*, Tavistock/Routledge, London, 1979, p. 7.

38 Klein introduced her theory of the infantile depressive position in 'A Contribution to the Psychogenesis of Manic-Depressive States' and elaborated it in 'Mourning and its Relation to Manic-Depressive States'.

Hinshelwood, *A Dictionary of Kleinian Thought*; T. Ogden, *The Matrix of the Mind: Object Relations and the Psychoanalytic Dialogue*, Jason Aronson, New York, 1986; H. Segal, *Klein*, Fontana, London, 1979: all of these books provide clear summaries of the transition from the paranoid schizoid position to the depressive position.

39 M. Klein, 'Love, Guilt and Reparation', in *Love, Guilt and Reparation*.

40 Ibid., p. 312.

41 Ibid., p. 317.

42 J. Rheingold, *The Fear of Being a Woman: A Theory of Maternal Destructiveness*, Grune & Stratton, New York and London, 1964.

43 Ibid., p. 143.

44 M. Apprey, 'Projective Identification and Maternal Misconception in Disturbed Mothers', *British Journal of Psychotherapy*, 4, 1 (1987), pp. 5–23.

45 Klein, 'Love, Guilt and Reparation', p. 317.

46 J. Raphael-Leff, *Psychological Processes of Childbearing*, Chapman and Hall, London and New York, 1991, p. 315.

47 J. Kristeva, cited in Garner *et al.*, *The (M)other Tongue*, p. 366.

48 S. Ruddick, *Maternal Thinking: Towards a Politics of Peace*, Women's Press, London, 1989, p. 70

49 J. Lazarre, *The Mother Knot* (1976), Virago, London, 1987, p. ix.
50 Ibid.
51 R. Parker, *The Subversive Stitch: Embroidery and the Making of the Feminine*, Women's Press, London, 1984.

2 *The Fantasy of Oneness*

1 J. Benjamin, *The Bonds of Love, Psychoanalysis, Feminism, and the Problem of Domination*, Virago, London. 1990, p. 211.
2 S. de Beauvoir, *The Second Sex*, (1949), Penguin Books, Harmondsworth, 1972, p. 527.
3 S. Freud, 'On Narcissism: an Introduction', in *The Standard Edition of the Complete Works of Sigmund Freud*, 24 vols, ed. and trans. James Strachey *et al.*, London, Hogarth Press and the Institute of Psycho-Analysis, 1953–73, Vol. 14, pp. 89–90.
4 Ibid., p. 91.
5 R. Parker and G. Pollock, New Introduction to *The Journals of Marie Bashkirtseff*, Virago, London, 1985.
6 M. Likierman, 'Maternal Love and Positive Projective Identification', *Journal of Child Psychotherapy*, 14, 2 (1988) p. 31.
7 W. R. Fairbairn, cited in J. R. Greenberg and S. A. Mitchell, *Object Relations in Psychoanalytic Theory*, Harvard University Press, Cambridge, Mass. and London, 1983, p. 159.
8 V. Woolf, *To the Lighthouse* (1927) Grafton Books, London, 1977.
9 V. Woolf, *A Sketch of the Past* (1939), cited in E. Abel, *Virginia Woolf and the Fictions of Psychoanalysis*, University of Chicago Press, Chicago, 1989, p. 45.
10 Ibid.
11 M. Hirsh, *The Mother/Daughter Plot: Narrative, Psychoanalysis, Feminism*, Indiana University Press, Bloomington and Indianapolis, 1989.
12 Woolf, *To the Lighthouse*, p. 20.
13 Ibid., p. 98.
14 Ibid., p. 58.
15 Ibid.
16 M. Sprengnether, *The Spectral Mother. Freud, Feminism and Psychoanalysis*, Cornell University Press, Ithaca, NY, 1990.
17 C. G. Jung, *Psychology of the Unconscious* (1912), ed. W. McGuire (Bollingen series xx), Princeton University Press, Princeton, New Jersey, 1991, p. 334.
18 K. Silverman, *The Acoustic Mirror*, Indiana University Press, Bloomington and Indianapolis, 1988, p. 73.
19 Abel, *Virginia Woolf and the Fictions of Psychoanalysis*, p. 68.
20 Hirsh, *The Mother/Daughter Plot*.
21 V. Woolf, 'Moments of Being. Unpublished Autobiographical Writings', cited ibid., p. 109.
22 Woolf, *To the Lighthouse*, p. 49.
23 Ibid., p. 66.

24 Ibid., p. 69.

25 Ibid., p. 89.

26 J. Uglow, 'Medea and Marmite Sandwiches', in K. Gieve (ed.), *Balancing Acts: On Being a Mother*, Virago, London, 1989, p. 149.

27 Ibid.

28 J. Kristeva, 'Stabat Mater', in T. Moi (ed.), *The Kristeva Reader*, Basil Blackwell, Oxford, 1986, p. 161.

29 E. Erikson, *Young Man Luther*, Norton, New York, 1968, cited in L. H. Silverman, F. M. Lachmann and R. H. Milich, *The Search for Oneness*, International Universities Press, New York, 1982, p. 237.

30 E. S. Person, *Dreams of Love and Fateful Encounters*, Norton, New York, 1988; Penguin, Harmondsworth, 1989, p. 120.

31 V. Hamilton, *Narcissus and Oedipus: The Children of Psycho-Analysis*, Routledge & Kegan Paul, London, 1982. See also M. Balint, *The Basic Fault: Therapeutic Aspects of Regression*, Tavistock, London and New York, 1968.

32 J. Mitchell-Rossdale, Review of J. Kristeva, *Black Sun, International Review of Psycho-Analysis*, 18, 4 (1991) p. 559.

33 Silverman *et al.*, *The Search for Oneness*.

34 Ibid., p. 84.

35 Ibid., p. 85.

36 Ibid., p. 56.

37 B. Bettelheim, *A Good Enough Parent*, Thames & Hudson, London, 1987.

38 Ibid., p. 25.

39 B. Bettelheim, *Dialogues with Mothers*, The Free Press, New York, 1962, p. 66, cited in *m/f*, 8 (1983), p. 30: 'Two Psychoanalysts and a Pacifier', by Marie-Hélène Brousse Delanoe.

40 P. Hill Collins, 'The Meaning of Motherhood in Black Culture and Black Mother–Daughter Relationships', in P. Bell Scott *et al.* (eds), *Double Stitch Black Women Write about Mothers and Daughters*, Harper Perennial, New York, 1993, p. 55.

41 R. Coward, *Our Treacherous Hearts: Why Women Let Men Get Their Way*, Faber & Faber, London, 1992.

42 Ibid., p. 80.

43 Ibid., p. 87.

44 Ibid., p. 77.

45 M. Elliott, 'The Ten Worst – and Best – Things You Can Say to Your Kids', *Family Circle*, 28 (1991), pp. 16–46.

46 K. Watkins, 'You Can Damage Your Children in So Many Ways – I Feared I Would Harm Mine', ibid., pp. 48–50.

47 D. Lloyd, 'School for Scandal!', ibid., pp. 46–8.

48 'Treasure', *Guardian*, 21 September 1993.

49 A. Rich, *Of Woman Born. Motherhood as Experience and Institution* (1976), Virago, London, 1977, p. 21.

50 S. Freud, 'On Narcissism: An Introduction', p. 98.

51 E. Nakano Glenn, G. Chang and L. Rennie Forcey (eds), *Mothering: Ideology, Experience, and Agency* (Routledge, New York, and London, 1994) explores the existence of diverse constructions of mothering alongside the dominant model.

3 *The Unacceptable Face of Ambivalence*

1 C. Campbell, 'I Wish We'd Never Had Our Child', *Marie Claire*, August 1992.
2 E. Badinter, *The Myth of Motherhood: An Historical View of the Maternal Instinct*, Flammarion, 1980; English translation, Souvenir Press, London, 1981.
3 Ibid., p. xix.
4 L. Jordanova, 'Children and Reproduction: Historical Perspectives', paper prepared for symposium on 'The Politics of Reproduction', Wenner-Gren Foundation for Anthropological Research, Brazil, 1991.
5 V. Fildes (ed.), *Woman as Mothers in Pre-Industrial England*, Routledge, London, 1990.
6 Ibid., p. 29.
7 J. Boswell, *The Kindness of Strangers: The Abandonment of Children in Western Europe from Antiquity to the Renaissance*, Pantheon Books, New York, 1988.
8 P. M. Brinich, review in *International Review of Psycho-Analysis*, 17, 3 (1990), p. 374.
9 M. G. Boulton, *On Being a Mother: A Study of Women with Pre-School Children*, Tavistock, London, 1983.
10 Ibid., p. 19.
11 Ibid., p. 45.
12 L. Comer, *Wedlocked Women*, Feminist Books, Leeds, 1974, p. 180.
13 A. Oakley, cited in Boulton, *On Being a Mother*, p. 26.
14 Ibid., p. 35.
15 R. Rapoport, R. Rapoport and S. Streilitz, *Fathers, Mothers and Others: Towards New Alliances*, Basic Books, New York, 1977.
16 Ibid., p. 19.
17 Ibid., p. 87.
18 Ibid., p. 86.
19 A. Hochschild with A. Machung, *The Second Shift: Working Parents and the Revolution at Home*, Piatkus, London, 1989.
20 Ibid., p. 10.
21 D. W. Winnicott, 'Hate in the Countertransference' (1949), in D. W. Winnicott, *The Maturational Processes and the Facilitating Environment*, Hogarth Press, London, 1979.
22 A. Phoenix, A. Woollett and E. Lloyd (eds), *Motherhood: Meanings, Practices and Ideologies*, Sage Publications, London, Newbury Park and New Delhi, 1991.
23 D. Riley, *War in the Nursery: Theories of the Child and Mother*, Virago, London, 1983.
24 D. W. Winnicott, 'The Theory of the Parent–Infant Relationship' (1960), in *The Maturational Processes*, p. 54.
25 D. W. Winnicott, 'The Ordinary Devoted Mother and her Baby', in *Babies and their Mothers*, Free Association Books, London, 1988, p. 12.
26 N. Farhi, 'Winnicott and Narcissism: A Theoretical Perspective', unpublished paper, 1994.

27 Winnicott, 'The Theory of the Parent–Infant Relationship', p. 49.

28 M. Mears, cited in V. Jones (ed.), *Women in the 18th Century: Constructions of Femininity*, Routledge, London, 1990, p. 57.

29 Winnicott, 'The Ordinary Devoted Mother and her Baby', p. 13.

30 K. Horney, 'The Distrust Between the Sexes' (1930), in *Feminine Psychology*, Norton, New York, 1967, p. 107.

31 D. W. Winnicott, 'The Child in Health and Crisis' (1962), in *The Maturational Processes*, p. 70.

32 D. W. Winnicott, *The Child, the Family and the Outside World*, Penguin Books, Harmondsworth, 1964, p. 10.

33 Winnicott, 'Hate in the Counter-Transference', p. 201.

34 Ibid.

35 Ibid.

36 Ibid., p. 195.

37 Ibid., p. 199.

38 Ibid., p. 200.

39 Ibid.

40 Ibid., p. 202.

41 Ibid.

42 J. Vellacott, 'Motherhood in the Imagination', in K. Gieve (ed.), *Balancing Acts: On Being a Mother*, Virago, London, 1989, p. 177. J. Doane and D. Hodges, *From Klein to Kristeva: Psychoanalytic Feminism and the Search for the 'Good Enough' Mother*, University of Michegan Press, Ann Arbor, 1992.

43 P. Adams, 'Mothering', *m/f*, 8 (1983), pp. 40–52.

44 Ibid., p. 46.

45 Ibid., p. 44.

46 M. Khan 'On Symbiotic Omnipotence: Phenomenology of Symbiotic Omnipotence in the Transference Relationship (1969), in *The Privacy of the Self*, Hogarth Press, London, 1986, p. 88.

47 Ibid.

48 Ibid., p. 91.

49 Ibid.

50 Ibid., p. 88.

51 J. Bowlby, 'Psychoanalysis and Child Care' (1958), in *The Making and Breaking of Affectional Bonds*, Tavistock/Routledge, London, 1979, p. 17.

52 J. Raphael-Leff, *Psychological Processes of Childbearing* (Chapman and Hall, London and New York, 1991) discusses the mechanics of mother–infant projection.

53 L. Purves in *She*, October 1992.

54 D. Pines, *A Woman's Unconscious Use of Her Body: A Psychoanalytic Perspective*, Virago, London, 1993; Raphael-Leff, *Psychological Processes of Childbearing*.

55 M. Waddell, 'Infantile Development: Kleinian and Post-Kleinian Theory, Infant Observational Practice', *British Journal of Psychotherapy*, 4, 3 (1988), pp. 313–28.

56 A. Freud, 'The Concept of the Rejecting Mother', in E. J. Benedek and

T. Anthony (eds), *Parenthood, Its Psychology and Psychopathology*, Little, Brown, Boston, 1970, p. 385.

57 C. G. Jung, 'The Psychological Aspects of the Mother Archetype' (1939/1954), in *Collected Works*, Vol. 9, Part I, ed. Herbert Read *et al.*, Routledge and Kegan Paul, London, 1959, p. 92.

58 A. Samuels, *The Political Psyche*, Routledge, London and New York, 1993, p. 129.

59 G. Brown and T. Harris, *The Social Origins of Depression*, Tavistock, London, 1978.

60 Raphael-Leff, *Psychological Processes of Childbearing*, p. 484.

61 Pines, *A Woman's Unconscious Use of Her Body*.

62 Raphael-Leff, *Psyschological Processes of Childbearing*, p. 74. J. Price, *Motherhood: What it does to your mind*, Pandora, London 1988 usefully explores mother-daughter relating through pregnancy and the child's early life.

63 S. Freud, 'Femininity' (1932), in *The Standard Edition of the Complete Works of Sigmund Freud*, 24 vols, ed. and trans. James Strachey *et al.*, London, Hogarth Press and the Institute of Psycho-Analysis, 1953–73, Vol. 22, p. 133.

64 D. Stern, 'How Can We Now Understand Mother–Infant Interaction: Implications for Parenting', Annual Sigmund Freud Lecture, London, 1994. Psychoanalytical researchers in Britain and the USA suggest that a woman's capacity to mother is determined, not so much by the actual mothering she received, but by whether she maintains a clear, reflective thoughtful picture of childhood experience. For implications of this 'reflective self' see P. Fonagy, G. S. Moran and M. Target, 'Agression and the Psychological Self', *International Journal of Psycho-Analysis*, 74, 3 (1993), pp. 471–85.

65 M. Klein, 'Envy and Gratitude' (1957), in *Envy and Gratitude and Other Works 1946–1963*, Hogarth Press, London, 1980, p. 183.

66 M. Klein, 'Love, Guilt and Reparation' (1937), in *Love, Guilt and Reparation and Other Works 1921–1945*, Hogarth Press, London, 1985, p. 318.

67 Ibid., p. 341.

68 Ibid.

4 Beyond Endurance

1 A. Dally, *Mothers, Their Power and Influence*, Weidenfeld & Nicolson, London, 1976.

2 Ibid., p. 182.

3 Ibid., p. 186.

4 Ibid., p. 187.

5 M. Klein 'Love, Guilt and Reparation' (1937), in *Love, Guilt and Reparation and Other Works (1921–1945)*, Hogarth Press, London, 1985, p. 309.

6 M. Klein, 'Our Adult World and its Roots in Infancy' (1959), in *Envy and Gratitude and Other Works*, Hogarth Press, London, 1980, p. 257.

7 D. H. Lawrence, *Sons and Lovers* (1913), Penguin Books, Harmondsworth, 1989, p. 74.

8 J. Raphael-Leff, *Psychological Processes of Childbearing*, Chapman and Hall, London and New York, 1991, p. 315.

9 M. Klein 'On the Theory of Anxiety and Guilt' (1937), in *Envy and Gratitude*, p. 37.
10 M. Langer, *Motherhood and Sexuality*, Guildford Press, New York and London, 1992, p. 60.
11 M. Klein, 'Mourning and its Relation to Manic-Depressive States', in *Love, Guilt and Reparation*, p. 350.
12 Ibid., p. 353.
13 Klein, 'Love, Guilt and Reparation', p. 311.
14 D. W. Winnicott, 'Aggression in Relation to Emotional Development' (1950–55), in *Through Pediatrics to Psychoanalysis*, Hogarth Press, London, 1982, p. 206.
15 D. W. Winnicott, 'Reparation in Respect of Mother's Organized Defence against Depression', ibid. p. 92.
16 Raphael-Leff, *Psychological Processes of Childbearing*. See also J. Price, *Motherhood: What It Does to Your Mind*, Pandora, London, Sydney and Wellington, 1988.
17 Winnicott, 'Aggression in Relation to Emotional Development', p. 206.
18 W. R. Bion, 'A Theory of Thinking' (1962), in *Second Thoughts*, Maresfield Reprints, London, 1984, p. 114.
19 Bion, *Second Thoughts*, p. 116, cited in A. Phillips, *On Kissing, Tickling and Being Bored: Psychological Essays on the Unexamined Life*, Faber & Faber, London and Boston, 1993, p. 113.
20 R. Britton, 'The Oedipus Situation and the Depressive Position', in R. Anderson (ed.), *Clinical Lectures on Klein and Bion*, Tavistock/Routledge, London and New York, 1992, p. 41.

5 *Separation: Both Loss and Release*

1 D. Daws, *Through the Night: Helping Parents and Sleepless Infants*, Free Association Books, London, 1989.
2 C. Gilligan, 'Reflections on the Psychology of Love', *Daedalus*, 113, 3 (1984), pp. 75–93.
3 J. Benjamin, *The Bonds of Love, Psychoanalysis, Feminism, and the Problem of Domination*, Virago, London, 1990.
4 J. Surrey, 'The Mother–Daughter Relationship: Themes in Psychotherapy', in J. van Mens-Verhulst, K. Schreurs and L. Woertman (eds), *Daughtering and Mothering: Female Subjectivity Reanalysed*, Routledge, London and New York, 1994, pp. 114–24.
5 M. S. Mahler, F. Pine and A. Bergman, *The Psychological Birth of the Human Infant: Symbiosis and Individuation*, Hutchinson, London, 1975.
6 A. Balint, 'Love for the Mother and Mother Love', in M. Balint, *Primary Love and Psycho-Analytic Technique*, (1952), Maresfield, London, 1985.
7 Ibid., p. 116.
8 Ibid., p. 122.
9 E. Rayner, *The Independent Mind in British Psychoanalysis*, Free Association Books, London, 1990.
10 R. D. Hinshelwood, *A Dictionary of Kleinian Thought*, Free Association Books, London, 1989, p. 142.

11 M. Wandor, 'The Conditions of Illusion', in S. Allen, L. Sanders and J. Wallis (eds), *Conditions of Illusion*, Feminist Books, Leeds, 1974, p. 204.

12 M. Balint, 'On Love and Hate', in *Primary Love and Psycho-Analytic Technique*.

13 Ibid., p. 154.

14 Ibid., p. 149.

15 Ibid.

16 Daws, *Through the Night*, p. 130.

17 B. D'Silva, 'The Growing Pains of Separation', *The Independent on Sunday*, 23 August 1992, p. 38.

18 T. Brennan, *The Interpretation of the Flesh: Freud and Femininity*, Routledge, London and New York, 1992, p. 196.

19 D. W. Winnicott, *Psychoanalytic Explorations*, ed. C. Winnicott, R. Shepherd and M. Davis, Karnac Books, London, 1989, p. 146.

20 Ibid.

21 D. W. Winnicott, *Playing and Reality* (1971), Penguin, Harmondsworth, 1980, p. 106.

22 Ibid., p. 110.

23 A. Samuels, *The Plural Psyche: Personality, Morality and the Father*, Routledge, London and New York, 1989, p. 208.

24 H. F. Searles, 'Violence in Schizophrenia', in *Countertransference and Related Subjects*, Hogarth Press, London, 1979, p. 325.

25 Benjamin, *The Bonds of Love*, p. 24.

26 Ibid., p. 82.

27 J. van Mens-Verhulst, 'Daughtering and Mothering: Female Subjectivity Rethought and Reevalued', in van Mens-Verhulst *et al.*, *Daughtering and Mothering*.

28 Daws, *Through the Night*, p. 128.

29 A. Shuttleworth, 'Being a Parent', *Free Associations* Vol. 1, No. 1, 1985, p. 12.

30 H. F. Searles, *Collected Works on Schizophrenia and Related Subjects* (Hogarth Press, London, 1965), Karnac Press, London, 1986.

31 Ibid., p. 46.

32 L. Appignanesi and J. Forrester, *Freud's Women*, Weidenfeld & Nicolson, London, 1992.

33 Ibid., p. 460.

34 J. Silverman van Buren, *The Modernist Madonna: Semiotics of the Maternal Metaphor*, Indiana University Press, Bloomington; Karnac, London, 1989, p. 23.

35 S. Moore, 'Home Alone Home Alone Mum', *Guardian*, 19 February 1993, p. 11.

36 A. Hochschild with A. Machung, *The Second Shift: Working Parents and the Revolution at Home*, Piatkus, London, 1989, p. 12.

37 A. Phoenix, A. Woollett and E. Lloyd (eds), *Motherhood: Meanings, Practices and Ideologies*, Sage Publications, London, Newbury Park and New Dehli, 1991; see pp. 34–6, 184 and 199 for a discussion of J. Belsky's work.

38 M. Benn, J. Hurst and M. McFadyean in the *Guardian*, 26 February 1992.

39 Ibid.

40 *Sunday Times*, 26 January 1992.

41 *The Times*, 13 November 1991.

42 *New Woman*, November 1991.

43 H. Franks, *Mummy Doesn't Live Here Anymore: Why Women Leave their Children*, Doubleday, London and New York, 1992. Since the completion of my book another study of women who leave their children has been published: R. Jackson, *Mothers Who Leave: Behind the Myth of Women Without their Children*, Pandora, London, 1994.

44 Franks, *Mummy Doesn't Live Here Anymore*, p. 26.

45 Ibid.

46 W. R. D. Fairbairn's ideas are usefully summarised in J. R. Greenberg and S. A. Mitchell, *Object Relations in Psychoanalytic Theory*, Harvard University Press, Cambridge, Mass., 1983.

47 Ibid., p. 171.

48 See J. Holmes, *John Bowlby and Attachment Theory*, Routledge, London and New York, 1993 and B. Tizard, 'Employed Mothers and the Care of Young Children' in *Motherhood: Meanings, Practices and Ideologies*, p. 179.

49 Ibid.

50 J. Bowlby, 'Psychoanalysis and Child Care' (1958), in *The Making and Breaking of Affectional Bonds*, Tavistock/Routledge, London, 1979, p. 8.

51 E. J. Benedek and T. Anthony, *Parenthood, Its Psychology and Psychopathology*, Little, Brown, Boston, 1970 p. 385.

52 Bowlby, *The Making and Breaking of Affectional Bonds*, p. 8.

53 Ibid., p. 14.

54 Ibid., p. 17.

55 Ibid., p. 15.

56 D. E. Eyer, *Mother–Infant Bonding: A Scientific Fiction*, Yale University Press, New Haven, Conn., 1992.

57 A. Karpf, review in *New Statesman and Society*, 5 February 1993.

58 A. Samuels, *The Political Psyche*, Routledge, London and New York, 1993, p. 141.

59 D. W. Winnicott, 'Development of the Theme of the Mother's Unconscious as Discovered in Psycho-Analytic Practice' (1969), in *Psycho-Analytic Explorations*, p. 250.

60 Daws, *Through the Night*, p. 104.

61 See Benjamin, *The Bonds of Love*, for an elaboration of this theme.

6 *Unravelling Femininity and Maternity*

1 J.-J. Rousseau, *Emile*, trans. W. H. Payne, Edward Arnold, London, 1902, Book 1.

2 W. Buchan, *Domestic Medicine, or a Treatise on the Prevention and Care of Diseases by Regimen and Simple Medicines*, 1769.

3 Ibid.

4 M. Wollstonecraft, *A Vindication of the Rights of Woman* (1792) Penguin, Harmondsworth, 1978, p. 266 .

5 Mrs Ellis, *Mothers of England: Their Influence and Responsibility*, Fisher, London, 1843, p. 11.

6 Ibid., p. 52.

7 Ibid., p. 2.
8 D. Russell, *Hypatia or Woman and Knowledge*, Kegan Paul, Trench, Trubner, New York, 1925, p. 42.
9 Ibid., p. 47.
10 B. Friedan, *The Feminine Mystique* (1963) Penguin, Harmondsworth, 1965, p. 251.
11 J. Lampl de Groot, 'Problems of Femininity', *Psychoanalytic Quarterly*, 2 (1933). pp. 489–518.
12 L. Appignanesi and J. Forrester, *Freud's Women*, Weidenfeld and Nicholson, London, 1992, p. 397.
13 Appignanesi and Forrester provide a useful summary of the development of Freud's thinking on the castration theory. See *Freud's Women*, p. 411.
14 J. Mitchell, 'Psychoanalysis: Child Development and Femininity' (1977), in *Women: The Longest Revolution*, Virago, London, 1984, p. 256.
15 Ibid., p. 313.
16 Ibid., p. 308.
17 M. Sprengnether, *The Spectral Mother: Freud, Feminism and Psychoanalysis*, Cornell University Press, Ithaca, NY and London, 1990.
18 S. Freud, 'Femininity' (1932), in *The Standard Edition of the Complete Works of Sigmund Freud* [hereafter *SE*], 24 vols, ed. and trans. J. Strachey *et al.*, London, Hogarth Press and the Institute of Psycho-Analysis, 1953–73, Vol. 22, p. 119.
19 Ibid., p. 115.
20 Ibid.
21 S. Freud, 'Female Sexuality' (1931) *SE*, Vol. 16, p. 231.
22 Freud, 'Femininity', p. 122.
23 Freud, 'Female Sexuality', p. 237.
24 D. Levy, 'The Concept of Overprotection', in E. J. Benedek and T. Anthony (eds), *Parenthood, Its Psychology and Psychopathology*, Little, Brown, Boston, 1970, p. 405.
25 A. Freud, 'The Concept of the Rejecting Mother' (1954) ibid., p. 376.
26 O. Kernberg, 'Further Contributions to the Treatment of Narcissistic Personalities', *International Journal of Psycho-Analysis*, 55, cited in V. Hamilton, *Narcissus and Oedipus, The Children of Psycho-Analysis*, Routledge & Kegan Paul, London, 1982, p. 69.
27 D. Breen (ed.), *The Gender Conundrum: Contemporary Perspectives of Femininity and Masculinity*, Routledge, London and New York, 1993.
28 Mitchell, 'Psychoanalysis: Child Development and Femininity', p. 271.
29 L. Appignanesi and J. Forrester, *Freud's Women*, Weidenfeld & Nicolson, London, 1992, p. 433.
30 J. Chasseguet-Smirgel, *Female Sexuality* (1964), Virago, London, 1981, p. 26.
31 Lampl de Groot, 'Problems of Femininity', p. 513.
32 H. Deutsch, *The Psychology of Women*, Vol. 2, Grune & Stratton, New York, 1944, p. 18.
33 Appignanesi and Forrester, *Freud's Women*, p. 440.
34 J. Sayers, *Mothering Psychoanalysis*, Hamish Hamilton, London, 1991.
35 Deutsch, *The Psychology of Women*, Vol. 2, p. 22.

36 T. Brennan, *The Interpretation of the Flesh, Freud and Femininity*, Routledge, London and New York, 1992, p. 36.
37 Deutsch, *The Psychology of Women*, Vol. 2, p. 52.
38 Brennan, *The Interpretation of the Flesh*.
39 Deutsch, *The Psychology of Women*, pp. 18–19.
40 Ibid.
41 Ibid., p. 311.
42 Ibid., p. 306.
43 Ibid., p. 330.
44 Ibid., p. 306.
45 K. Horney, 'The Flight from Womanhood' (1926), in *Feminine Psychology*, W. W. Norton, New York and London, 1973, p. 61.
46 Ibid., p. 60.
47 K. Horney, (1930), 'The Distrust between the Sexes', in *Feminine Psychology*, p. 107.
48 K. Horney, 'Maternal Conflicts' (1933), ibid., p. 180.
49 Ibid., p. 178.
50 J. Sayers, *Mothering Psychoanalysis*.
51 Horney, 'Maternal Conflicts', p. 181.
52 Deutsch, *The Psychology of Women*, Vol. 2, p. 293.
53 A. Freud, 'The Concept of the Rejecting Mother', p. 378.
54 R. Spitz, 'Effect of the Mother's Personality Disturbances on her Infant' (1965), in Benedek and Anthony, *Parenthood: Its Psychology and Psychopathology*, p. 504.
55 Ibid.
56 A. Oakley, *Women Confined: Towards a Sociology of Childbirth*, Martin Robertson, Oxford, 1980.
57 Ibid., p. 57.
58 Ibid., p. 284.
59 D. Breen, *Talking with Mothers*, Free Association Books, London, 1989, p. 150.
60 L. Comer, *Wedlocked Women*, Feminist Books, Leeds, 1974, p. 187.
61 M. Wandor, 'The Conditions of Illusion', in S. Allen, L. Sanders and J. Wallis (eds), *Conditions of Illusion*, Feminist Books, Leeds, 1974, p. 201.
62 J. Mitchell, *Psychoanalysis and Feminism*, Penguin Books, Harmondsworth, 1974, p. 363.
63 Brennan, *The Interpretation of the Flesh*.
64 Ibid., p. 217.
65 H. Cixous, cited in J. Silverman van Buren, *The Modernist Madonna: Semiotics of the Maternal Metaphor*, Indiana University Press, Bloomington; Karnac, London p. 17.
66 N. Chodorow, *The Reproduction of Mothering: Psychoanalysis and the Sociology of Gender*, University of California Press, Berkeley and Los Angeles, 1978.
67 N. Chodorow, *Feminism and Psychoanalytic Theory*, Yale University Press, New Haven, Conn.; Polity Press, Cambridge, 1989.
68 Brennan, *The Interpretation of the Flesh*, p. 68.

69 Chodorow herself offers a corrective view in *Femininities, Masculinities, Sexualities. Freud and Beyond* (Free Association Books, London, 1994), where she warns against generalisation and emphasises that 'passivity or activity, aggression and submission' may enter into the mother–child relationship (p. 85).

70 J. Flax, *Thinking Fragments: Psychoanalysis, Feminism, and Postmodernism in the Contemporary West*, University of California Press, Berkeley and Los Angeles, 1990.

71 A. Samuels, *The Plural Psyche*, Routledge, London and New York, 1989.

72 S. R. Suleiman, *Subversive Intent: Gender, Politics and the Avant-Garde*, Harvard University Press, Cambridge, Mass. and London, 1990, p. 166.

73 H. Cixous, cited in Silverman van Buren, *The Modernist Madonna*, p. 18.

74 J. Rose cited in T. Moi (ed.),*The Kristeva Reader*, Basil Blackwell, Oxford, 1986, p.11.

75 D. C. Stanton, 'Difference on Trial: A Critique of the Maternal Metaphor in Cixous, Irigaray and Kristeva' in *The Poetics of Gender* (ed.) N. K. Miller, Columbia University Press, New York, 1986, p. 172.

76 M. Montrelay, 'Inquiry into Femininity' (1970), in D. Breen (ed.), *The Gender Conundrum*, pp. 20–23, for Breen's discussion of Montrelay's theories.

77 J. Kristeva, 'Stabat Mater' (1977), in Moi, *The Kristeva Reader*. See also S. R. Sullivan, 'Writing and Motherhood' in S. N. Garner *et al* (eds.), *The (M)other Tongue*, Cornell University Press, Ithaca NY and London, 1985.

78 Ibid., p. 179.

79 J. Doane and D. Hodges, *From Klein to Kristeva: Psychoanalytic Feminism and the Search for the 'Good Enough' Mother*, University of Michigan Press, Ann Arbor, 1992.

80 J. Kristeva, *Black Sun: Depression and Melancholia*, trans. L. S. Roudiez, Columbia Press, New York, 1989. K. Silverman, *The Acoustic Mirror*, Indiana University Press, 1988, traces the development of Kristeva's thinking on motherhood across a number of texts. See also Doane and Hodges, *From Klein to Kristeva*, in *Black Sun*.

81 J. Kristeva, 'Women's Time' (1979) in Moi, *The Kristeva Reader*, p. 205.

82 J. Kristeva, *Black Sun*, p. 28.

83 M. Whitford, *Luce Irigaray: Philosophy in the Feminine*, Routledge, London and New York, 1991, p. 89.

84 Breen, *The Gender Conundrum*.

7 Like a Child

1 J. Hillman, 'The Bad Mother, An Archetypal Approach', in P. Berry (ed.), *Fathers and Mothers*, Spring Publications, Dallas, 1990.

2 Ibid., p. 107.

3 Ibid., p. 111.

4 Ibid., p. 114.

5 Ibid., p. 115.

6 A. Rich, *Of Woman Born: Motherhood as Experience and Institution* Virago, London, 1983, p. 194.

7 J. Lazarre, *The Mother Knot,*Virago, London, 1987, p. 160.
8 L. Irigaray, 'The Bodily Encounter with the Mother' (1981), in M. Whitford (ed.), *The Iriqaray Reader*, Basil Blackwell, Oxford, 1991, p. 37.
9 Ibid., p. 43.
10 Whitford, *The Irigaray Reader*, p. 25.
11 Irigaray, 'The Bodily Encounter with the Mother', in *The Irigaray Reader*, p. 43.
12 Irigaray, 'Women – Mothers, the Silent Substratum of the Social Order', in *The Irigaray Reader*, p. 50.
13 Ibid.
14 M. Wandor 'The Conditions of Illusion', in S. Allen, L. Sanders and J. Wallis (eds), *Conditions of Illusion*, Feminist Books, Leeds, 1974, p. 200.
15 A. Samuels, *The Plural Psyche*, Routledge, London and New York, 1989, p. 274.
16 H. F. Searles, *Collected Papers on Schizophrenia and Related Subjects*, Hogarth Press, London, 1965; repr. Karnac, London, 1986, p. 278.
17 Ibid., p. 256.
18 C. Urwin, 'Constructing Motherhood: The Persuasion of Normal Development', in C. Steedman, C. Urwin and V. Walkerdine (eds), *Language, Gender and Childhood*, Routledge and Kegan Paul, London, 1985, p. 166.
19 D. W. Winnicott, *The Child, the Family and the Outside World*, Penguin Books, Harmondsworth, 1964, p. 26.
20 Ibid., p. 27.
21 P. Leach, *Baby and Child: From Birth to Age Five* (1977), Penguin, Harmondsworth, 1985, p. 16.
22 M. Stoppard, *Baby Care Book: A Practical Guide to the First Three Years* (1983), Dorling Kindersley, London, 1986, Preface.
23 C. Jabs, 'How to Raise a Happy Child', *She*, March 1992.
24 Urwin, 'Constructing Motherhood'.
25 J. S. Bruner, 'Learning to do Things with Words', cited ibid., p. 184.
26 Leach, *Baby and Child*, p. 23.
27 M. G. Boulton, *On Being a Mother: A Study of Women with Pre-School Children*, Tavistock, London, 1983, p. 77.
28 R. Coward, *Our Treacherous Hearts: Why Women Let Men Get Their Way*, Faber & Faber, London, 1992, p. 77.
29 Ibid., p. 79.
30 Ibid., p. 81.
31 D. E. Eyer, *Mother–Infant Bonding: A Scientific Fiction*, Yale University Press, New Haven, Conn., 1992.
32 I. Suttie, *The Origins of Love and Hate* (1935), Free Association Books, London, 1988, p. 6.
33 Ibid., p. 23.
34 Ibid., p. 104.
35 Eyer, *Mother–Infant Bonding*, p. 56.
36 Ibid., p. 69.
37 Cited in J. Doane and D. Hodges, *From Klein to Kristeva: Psychoanalytic Feminism and the Search for the 'Good Enough' Mother*, University of Michigan Press, Ann Arbor, 1992, p. 21.

38 D. W. Winnicott, 'Postscript: D. W. W. on D. W. W.' (1967), in C. Winnicott, R. Shepherd and M. Davis (eds), *Psychoanalytic Explorations*, Karnac, London, 1989, p. 569.
39 A. Phillips, *On Kissing, Tickling and Being Bored*. Faber & Faber, London and Boston, 1993, p. 199.
40 S. Freud, 'Studies on Hysteria, with J. Breuer', (1893–5) in *The Standard Edition of the Complete Works of Sigmund Freud*, 24 vols, ed. and trans. James Strachey *et al.*, London, Hogarth Press and the Institute of Psycho-Analysis, 1953–73, Vol. 2, p. 305, cited ibid., p. xiii.
41 D. W. Winnicott, 'Primary Maternal Preoccupation' (1956), in *Through Pediatrics to Psycho-Analysis*, Hogarth Press, London, 1979, p. 302.
42 Ibid.
43 Ibid.
44 D. W. Winnicott, *Playing and Reality*, Penguin Books, Harmondsworth, 1980, p. 131.
45 Ibid.
46 Ibid., p. 137.
47 Ibid., p. 131.
48 Ibid., p. 55.
49 Ibid., p. 48.
50 Ibid., p. 55.
51 Ibid.
52 Ibid., p. 63.
53 Ibid., p. 56.
54 Phillips, *On Kissing, Tickling and Being Bored*, p. 109.
55 Winnicott, 'Primary Maternal Preoccupation', p. 303.
56 Winnicott, *Playing and Reality*, p. 55.
57 Winnicott, *The Child, the Family and the Outside World*, p. 16.
58 Phillips, *On Kissing, Tickling and Being Bored*, p. 113.
59 A. Samuels, *The Political Psyche*, Routledge, London and New York, 1993, pp. 272–4.
60 Phillips, *On Kissing, Tickling and Being Bored*, p. 111.
61 M. Mahler, F. Pine and A. Bergman, *The Psychological Birth of the Human Infant: Symbiosis and Individuation*, Hutchinson, London, 1975, p. 138.
62 D. N. Stern, *The Interpersonal World of the Infant: A View from Psycho-analysis and Developmental Psychology*, Basic Books, New York, 1985.
63 Ibid., p. 202.
64 Ibid., p. 208.
65 P. Cushman, 'Ideology Obscured: Political Uses of the Self in Daniel Stern's Infant', *American Psychologist*, March, 1991, pp. 206–19.
66 A. Woollett and A. Phoenix, 'Psychological Views of Mothering' in A. Phoenix, A. Woollett and E. Lloyd, (eds) *Motherhood: Meanings, Practices and Ideologies*, Sage Publications, London, Newbury Park and New Delhi, 1991.
67 T. Berry Brazelton and B. G. Cramer, *The Earliest Relationship: Parents, Infants and the Drama of Early Attachment* (1990), Karnac, London, 1991.
68 Ibid., p. 219.

69 A. Cooper, 'Psychic Change: Development in the Theory of Psychoanalytic Change', *International Journal of Psycho-Analysis*, 73, 2 (1992), p. 248.

70 L. Miller, M. Rustin, M. Rustin, J. Shuttleworth, *Closely Observed Infants*, Duckworth, London, 1989.

71 J. Shuttleworth, in *Journal of Analytical Psychology*, 38, 1 (1993), p. 116.

72 Ibid.

73 Ibid.

74 T. Berry Brazelton, cited in Eyer, *Mother–Infant Bonding*, p. 155.

75 Phillips, *On Kissing, Tickling and Being Bored*, p. 111.

76 An example of such research is A. Pound, C. Puckering, T. Cox and M. Mills, 'The Impact of Maternal Depression on Young Children', *British Journal of Psychotherapy*, 4, 3 (1988), pp. 240–62.

77 Samuels, *The Plural Psyche*. pp. 143–74.

78 R. Coward, in the *Observer*, 28 March 1993.

8 *Powerlessly Powerful*

1 T. Morrison, *Beloved*, Knopf, New York, 1986, p. 23, cited in L. P. Fulte, 'Images and Motherhood in Toni Morrison's Beloved', in P. Bell-Scott *et al.* (eds), *Double Stitch: Black Women Write about Mothers and Daughters*, Harper Perennial, New York, 1993.

2 Morrison, *Beloved*, p. 234.

3 For full discussions of the dialectics of oppression and resistance of mothers in situations of colonial and racial domination see E. Nakano Glenn, G. Chang and L. Rennie Forcey (eds), *Mothering: Ideology, Experience and Agency*, Routledge, New York and London, 1994.

4 J. Chasseguet-Smirgel, 'Feminine Guilt and the Oedipus Complex', in *Female Sexuality*, Virago, London, 1981.

5 Ibid., p. 132.

6 S. Freud, 'Femininity' (1932) in *The Standard Edition of the Complete Works of Sigmund Freud*, 24 vols, ed. and trans. James Strachey *et al.*, London, Hogarth Press and the Institute of Psycho-Analysis, 1953–73, Vol. 22.

7 T. Brennan, *The Interpretation of the Flesh: Freud and Femininity* Routledge, London and New York, 1992, p. 232. D. Dinnerstein, *The Mermaid and the Minotaur: Sexual Arrangements and Human Malaise* (Harper and Row, New York and London, 1976) explores the implications of maternal power and powerlessness.

8 J. Raphael-Leff, *Psychological Processes of Childbearing*, Chapman and Hall, London and New York, 1991. D. Pines, *A Woman's Unconscious Use of her Body*, Virago, London, 1993.

9 S. de Beauvoir, *The Second Sex* (1949), Penguin Books, Harmondsworth, 1972.

10 J. Kristeva, 'Stabat Mater', in T. Moi (ed.), *The Kristeva Reader*, Basil Blackwell, Oxford, 1986, p. 168.

11 For discussions of antenatal unconscious phantasies see: M. Langer, *Motherhood and Sexuality* Guildford Press, New York and London, 1992; Pines, *A Woman's Unconscious Use of her Body*; Raphael-Leff, *Psychological Processes of Childbearing*.

12 Raphael-Leff, *Psychological Processes of Childbearing*.

13 K. Payne (ed.), *Between Ourselves: Letters Between Mothers and Daughters* (1983), Virago, London, 1994, p. 282.

14 Raphael-Leff, *Psychological Processes of Childbearing*.

15 K. Gieve (ed.), *Balancing Acts: On Being a Mother*, Virago, London, 1989, p. 43.

16 Ibid., p. ix.

17 Raphael-Leff, *Psychological Processes of Childbearing*.

18 J. Raphael-Leff, *Pregnancy: The Inside Story*, Sheldon Press, London, 1993, p. 138.

19 Payne, *Between Ourselves*, p. 282.

20 B. Ehrenreich and D. English, *For Her Own Good: 150 Years of Experts' Advice to Women*, Pluto Press, London, 1979, p. 192.

21 Gieve, *Balancing Acts*, p. 45.

22 Payne, *Between Ourselves*, p. 281.

23 M. Klein, 'The Emotional Life of the Infant' (1952), in *Envy and Gratitude and Other Works (1946–1963)*, Hogarth, London, 1980, p. 166.

24 M. Klein, 'Mourning and its Relation to Manic-Depressive States' (1940), in *Love, Guilt and Reparation and Other Works (1921–1945)*, Hogarth, London, 1985, p. 349.

25 M. Klein, 'A Contribution to the Psychogenesis of Manic Depressive States', (1933), ibid., p. 288.

26 Klein, 'The Emotional Life of the Infant', p. 74.

27 Klein, 'Mourning', p. 368.

28 Klein, 'The Emotional Life of the Infant', p. 73.

29 R. Mack Brunswick, 'The Pre-Oedipal Phase of the Libido Development' (1940), cited in Chasseguet-Smirgel, *Female Sexuality*, p. 25.

30 Ibid., p. 112.

31 Ibid.

32 Ibid., p. 113.

33 I. Menzies, 'Thoughts on the Maternal Role in Contemporary Society', *International Journal of Child Psychotherapy*, Vol. 4, No. 1, (1978) pp. 5–14.

34 J. and E. Newson, *Patterns of Infant Care in an Urban Community*, Pelican Books, London, 1965, p. 244.

35 H. Gavron, *The Captive Wife: Conflicts of Housebound Mothers*, Pelican Books, London, 1966, p. 38.

36 C. Lasch, *Haven in a Heartless World*, Basic Books, New York, 1977.

37 M. Barrett and M. McIntosh, *The Anti-social Family*, Verso, London, 1982.

38 *Guardian*, 16 September 1991.

39 P. Lilley, cited by O. James in 'Vicious Outcome of the Poverty Trap', *Observer*, 23 May 1993.

40 N. Dennis, *Families without Fathers*, Institute of Economic Affairs, London, 1992.

41 E. Crellin *et al.*, *Born Illegitimate*, National Foundation for Educational Research, London, 1971.

42 I. Kolvin *et al.*, *Continuities of Deprivation*, Avebury, Aldershot, 1990.

43 O. James, 'Vicious Outcome of the Poverty Trap', *Observer*, 23 May 1993.

44 J. Benjamin, *The Bonds of Love, Psychoanalysis, Feminism, and the Problem of Domination*, Virago, London, 1990, p. 21.
45 S. de Beauvoir, *The Second Sex* (1949), Penguin Books, Harmondsworth, 1972, p. 527.
46 Ibid., p. 529.
47 A. Rich, *Of Woman Born: Motherhood as Experience and Institution*, Virago, London, 1977, p. 38.
48 L. Kaplan, *Female Perversions*, Doubleday, New York and London, 1991. E. V. Welldon, *Mother, Madonna, Whore: The Idealization and Denigration of Motherhood*, Free Association Books, London, 1988.
49 Welldon, *Mother, Madonna, Whore*, p. 37.
50 Ibid., p. 8.
51 Ibid., p. 9.
52 Ibid., p. 83.
53 Ibid., p. 105.
54 Ibid., p. 75.
55 S. Fraiberg (ed.), *Clinical Studies in Infant Mental Health: The First Year of Life*, Tavistock, London, 1980.
56 Kaplan, *Female Perversions*, p. 174.
57 Ibid., p. 451.
58 Cited in R. Storm, 'Would God Use the Rod?', *Guardian*, 11 May 1993.
59 Ibid.
60 Ibid.
61 Ibid.
62 S. Lonsdale, 'Smacking Children May Be Made Illegal', *Observer*, 2 May 1992.
63 Ibid.
64 *The Times*, 17 March 1994.
65 A. Tyler, *Dinner at the Homesick Restaurant* (1982), Vintage, London, 1992.
66 Ibid., p. 2.
67 Ibid., p. 54.
68 Ibid., p. 65.
69 Ibid., p. 191.
70 E. Rayner, *The Independent Mind in British Psychoanalysis*, Free Association Books, London, 1990, p. 98.
71 D. W. Winnicott, 'The Ordinary Devoted Mother and her Baby', in *Babies and their Mothers*, Free Association Books, London, 1988, p. 9.
72 A. Alvarez, *Live Company*, Tavistock/Routledge, London and New York, 1992, p. 9.
73 R. Windle, 'External/Internal Reality: The Subject as Parental Object and the Problem of Personal Responsibility', unpublished paper, 1989.
74 J. Sandler, 'Reflections on Developments in the Theory of Psychoanalytic Technique', *International Journal of Psycho-Analysis*, 73, 2 (1992), p. 197.
75 A. Samuels, *The Plural Psyche*, Routledge, London and New York, 1989, pp. 15–47.
76 Alvarez, *Live Company*, p. 72.
77 Ibid.

78 H. Segal interviewed by J. Rose in *Women: A Cultural Review*, 1, 2 (Summer 1990).
79 *International Journal of Psycho-Analysis*, 72, 3, (1991).

9 Does Gender Make a Difference?

1 D. Breen (ed.), *The Gender Conundrum: Contemporary Psychoanalytic Perspectives on Femininity and Masculinity*, Routledge, London and New York, 1993, p. 2.
2 R. Greenson, 'Disindentifying from the Mother: Its Special Importance for the Boy', in D. Breen (ed.), *The Gender Conundrum*, p. 258.
3 Ibid.
4 C. Olivier, *Jocasta's Children: The Imprint of the Mother* (1980), trans. George Craig, Routledge, London, 1989, p. 40.
5 A. Samuels, *The Political Psyche*, Routledge, London and New York, 1993, p. 135.
6 See, for example, J. Benjamin, *The Bonds of Love: Psychoanalysis, Feminism and the Problem of Domination*, Virago, London 1990; and L. Eichenbaum and S. Orbach, 'Feminine Subjectivity Counter-transference and the Mother', in J. van Mens-Verhulst, K. Schreurs and L. Woertman (eds), *Daughtering and Mothering: Female Subjectivity Reanalysed*, Routledge, London and New York, 1994.
7 R. de Kantor, 'Becoming a Situated Daughter: "Later, When I Am Big, I Will Be Daddy, So Then We Will Have a Father in Our House" – Hannah, Four Years Old', in van Mens-Verhulst *et al. Daughtering and Mothering*.
8 Samuels, *The Political Psyche*, pp. 130–1.
9 A. Phillips, *The Trouble with Boys: Parenting the Men of the Future*, Pandora, London, 1993.
10 Ibid., p. 10.
11 Ibid., p. 158.
12 Ibid., p. 112.
13 Ibid., p. 113.
14 Samuels, *The Political Psyche*, p. 135.
15 Ibid., p. 133.
16 Phillips, *The Trouble with Boys*, p. 147.
17 Ibid., p. 127.
18 Breen, *The Gender Conundrum*, p. 35.
19 A. Rich, *Of Woman Born*, Virago, London 1977, p. 253.
20 L. Eichenbaum and S. Orbach, *Outside In . . . Inside Out*, Penguin Books, Harmondsworth, 1983.
21 J. Flax, 'The Conflict between Nurturance and Autonomy in Mother–Daughter Relationships and within Feminism', *Feminist Studies*, 2 (1978), p. 174.
22 L. Eichenbaum and S. Orbach, *Understanding Women*, Penguin Books, Harmondsworth, 1985, p. 40.
23 Ibid., p. 49.
24 S. Ernst, 'Can a Daughter be a Woman? Women's Identity and Psychological

Separation', in S. Ernst and M. Maguire (eds), *Living with the Sphinx*, Women's Press, London, 1987.

25 Ibid., p. 84.

26 Ibid., p. 85.

27 N. Herman, *Too Long a Child: The Mother–Daughter Dyad*, Free Association Books, London, 1989, p. 234.

28 Ibid., p. 329.

29 Ibid., p. 236.

30 N. Chodorow, *The Reproduction of Mothering: Psychoanalysis and the Sociology of Gender*, University of California Press, Berkeley and Los Angeles, 1978. See also N. Chodorow, *Femininities, Masculinities, Sexualities. Freud and Beyond*, (Free Association Books, London, 1994), in which she argues that the sense of gendered self is *individually* created out of a *unique* fusion of cultural meaning with a personal emotional meaning.

31 Breen, *The Gender Conundrum*.

32 J. Raphael-Leff, *Psychological Processes of Childbearing*, Chapman and Hall, London and New York, 1991.

33 V. Walkerdine and C. Urwin, *Language, Gender and Childhood*, Routledge & Kegan Paul, London, 1985.

34 J. B. Cole, 'Preface' in Patricia Bell-Scott et al, *Double Stitch: Black Women Write about Mothers and Daughters*, Harper Perennial, New York, 1993, p. xv.

35 P. Hill Collins, 'The Meaning of Motherhood in Black Culture and Black Mother–Daughter Relationships', ibid., pp. 54–6.

36 R. de Kantor, 'Becoming a Situated Daughter', in van Mens-Verhulst *et al.*, *Daughtering and Mothering*, p. 32.

37 N. Friday, *My Mother My Self*, Delacorte Press, New York, 1977, p. 256.

38 J. Kristeva, 'Stabat Mater', in T. Moi (ed.), *The Kristeva Reader*, Basil Blackwell, Oxford, 1986, p. 183.

39 M. Whitford, *Luce Irigaray: Philosophy in the Feminine*, Routledge, London, 1991, pp. 76–7.

40 Ibid., p. 80.

41 Ibid., p. 87.

42 M. Whitford (ed.), *The Irigaray Reader*, Basil Blackwell, Oxford, 1991, p. 77

43 Irigaray, 'The Bodily Encounter with the Mother', ibid., p. 43.

44 L. Irigaray, 'And the One Doesn't Stir without the Other', trans. H. V. Wenzel, *Signs*, 7, 1, (1981), pp. 60–67.

45 Kristeva, 'Stabat Mater', p. 180.

46 J. Kristeva, 'Nouveau Type d'intellectuel: Le dissident', *Tel Quel*, 74 (Winter 1977), p. 6, cited by S. Suleiman in 'Writing and Motherhood', in S. N. Garner *et al.* (eds) *The (M)other Tongue*, Cornell University Press, Ithaca, NY and London, 1985, p. 366.

47 Olivier, *Jocasta's Children: The Imprint of the Mother*.

48 Ibid., p. 46.

49 Herman, *Too Long a Child*, p. 333.

50 J. McGuire, 'Sons and Daughters', in A. Phoenix, A. Woollett and E. Lloyd (eds), *Motherhood: Meanings, Practices and Ideologies*, Sage Publications, London, Newbury Park and New Delhi, 1991, p. 144.

51 D. Breen, *Talking with Mothers*, Free Association Books, London, 1989.
52 A. Oakley, *Women Confined: Towards a Sociology of Childbirth*, Martin Robertson, Oxford, 1980.
53 Raphael-Leff, *Psychological Processes of Childbearing*.
54 J. McGuire, 'Sons and Daughters' in Phoenix *et al.*, *Motherhood: Meanings, Practices and Ideologies*.
55 Raphael-Leff, *Psychological Processes of Childbearing*, p. 120.
56 Ibid., p. 119.
57 Oakley, *Women Confined*.
58 Breen, *Talking with Mothers*.
59 Raphael-Leff, *Psychological Processes of Childbearing*.
60 McGuire, 'Sons and Daughters'.
61 Ibid., p. 148.
62 Ibid.
63 Ibid., p. 149.
64 Ibid., p. 151.
65 Ibid.
66 Ibid., p. 154.
67 S. Freud, 'Three Essays on the Theory of Sexuality' (1905), in *Standard Edition of the Complete Works of Sigmund Freud* [hereafter *SE*], 24 vols, ed. and trans. James Strachey *et al.*, London, Hogarth Press and the Institute of Psycho-Analysis, 1953–73, Vol. 7, p. 223.
68 S. Freud, 'Leonardo da Vinci and a Memory of Childhood' (1910), in *SE*, Vol. 11, p. 117.
69 L. Appignanesi and J. Forrester, *Freud's Women*, Weidenfeld & Nicolson, London, 1992.
70 S. Freud, 'Female Sexuality' (1931), in *SE*, Vol. 16, p. 237.
71 B. Grunberger, 'Outline for a Study of Narcissism in Female Sexuality', in J. Chasseguet-Smirgel (ed.), *Female Sexuality: New Psychoanalytic Views*, Virago, London, 1978, p. 72.
72 Olivier, *Jocasta's Children*, p. 2.
73 Ibid., p. 44
74 Benjamin, *The Bonds of Love*.
75 N. O'Connor and J. Ryan, *Wild Desires and Mistaken Identities: Lesbianism and Psychoanalysis*, Virago, London, 1993.
76 Ibid., p. 245.
77 J. McDougall, 'Homosexuality in Women', in Chasseguet-Smirgel, *Female Sexuality*, p. 173.
78 N. Lykke, 'Questing Daughters: Little Red Ridinghood, Antigone and the Oedipus Complex', in van Mens-Verhulst *et al.*, *Daughtering and Mothering*.
79 E. V. Welldon, *Mother, Madonna, Whore: The Idealization and Denigration of Motherhood*, Free Association Books, London 1988, p. 93.
80 A. Samuels, *The Plural Psyche*, Routledge, London and New York, 1989, p. 69.
81 S. Freud, 'Beyond the Pleasure Principle' (1920), in *SE* Vol. 18, pp. 53–4.
82 J. K. Welles and H. Kimble Wyre, 'The Maternal Erotic Countertransference', *International Journal of Psycho-Analysis*, 72, 1 (1991), p. 93.

Index

Rozsika Parker is a psychoanalytic psychotherapist in practice in London. She is author of *The Subversive Stitch: Embroidery and the Making of the Feminine*, co-author of *Old Mistresses: Women, Art and Ideology* and co-editor of *Framing Feminism: Art and the Women's Movement 1970–1985* (both with Griselda Pollock).